"McDonald's book is strong, original, and thoughtful. He has the daring to challenge directly the traditional, indeed entrenched, scholarly view of Jonson and Shakespeare: namely, that their artistic temperaments and goals were strikingly different, if not diametrically opposed. He will provoke his readers to reexamine their assumptions, and they will gain from his genuine critical insights."—Robert Ornstein, Case Western Reserve University.

Comparisons of William Shakespeare and Ben Jonson have usually been at the expense of Jonson and rarely to the benefit of both. Shakespeare is seen as genial, romantic, spontaneous, and versatile; Jonson, as acerbic, classical, drudging, and narrow. These characterizations have discouraged comparative study of their works. Their dramatic styles have been thought to mirror the oppositions of their legendary personae.

Russ McDonald contests this orthodox view in *Shakespeare and Jonson/Jonson and Shakespeare*. He surveys the plays of both dramatists and, in Jonson's case, the critical remarks, in order to identify their many points of contact and divergence. Topics he reconsiders include the problem of influence, the adequacy of the traditional comic categories, and Shakespeare's complex relation to satire and Jonson's to romance. In particular, his comparative study brings into focus a series of unexpected thematic and formal parallels in Shakespeare's major tragedies and Jonson's comic masterpieces. *Shakespeare and Jonson* does not dismiss the familiar antitheses of form and idea, but rather attempts to put more precisely the distinctions that do exist, to modify those that have been overstated, and to suggest that, for all the differences between the two playwrights, there is something of the other in each.

SHAKESPEARE AND JONSON / JONSON AND SHAKESPEARE

Shakespeare & Jonson
Jonson & Shakespeare

Russ McDonald

University of Nebraska Press: Lincoln and London

Copyright © 1988 by the University of Nebraska Press
All rights reserved
Manufactured in the United States of America

The paper in this book meets the minimum require-
ments of American National Standard for Information
Sciences – Permanence of Paper for Printed Library
Materials, ANSI Z39.48-1984.

Library of Congress Cataloging in Publication Data
McDonald, Russ, 1949-
Shakespeare and Jonson/Jonson and Shakespeare.
Bibliography: p.
Includes index.
1. Shakespeare, William, 1564-1616 –
Contemporaries. 2. Jonson, Ben, 1573?-1637 –
Contemporaries. 3. Shakespeare, William,
1564-1616 – Criticism and interpretation. 4. Jonson,
Ben, 1573?-1637 – Criticism and interpretation.
5. Dramatists, English – Early modern, 1500-1700 –
Biography. 1. Title.
PR2958.J6M25   1988   822'.3'09   87-19158
ISBN 0-8032-3116-4 (alk. paper)

FOR GAIL

Contents

Acknowledgments

I have worked profitably and happily in three major libraries—Rush Rhees Library of the University of Rochester, the Folger Shakespeare Library, and the Furness Library of the University of Pennsylvania—and wish to thank the members of the staff at each, especially Phyllis Andrews, Shirley Ricker, Betsy Walsh, and Georgianna Ziegler. The National Endowment for the Humanities and the University of Rochester College of Arts and Science Research Fund provided financial assistance, for which I am grateful. At various points I received help with the manuscript from Cindy Warner, Kay Strassner, Hanna Richardson, and Rebecca Sumner. An early version of Chapter 4, then entitled "Sceptical Visions: Jonson's Comedies and Shakespeare's Tragedies," appeared in *Shakespeare Survey*, vol. 34, and I wish to thank the editor and publisher of that journal for permission to reprint.

The following friends and colleagues are among those who have provided help, criticism, and encouragement: Anne Barton, Thomas Berger, Avis Hartley, Jarold Ramsey, David Richman, Jeanne Addison Roberts, Joseph Summers, Robert Y. Turner, and George Walton Williams. I am especially grateful to Cyrus Hoy.

Thanks are due to my parents for their patience and support. Jack McDonald tried unwittingly to keep me from finishing the manuscript. I am indebted above all to the dedicatee.

A NOTE ON TEXTS

I quote throughout from individual editions in *The New Arden Shakespeare*, gen. eds. Harold F. Brooks, Harold Jenkins, and Brian Morris (London: Methuen, 1951–), except for one passage, noted within; and from *Ben Jonson*, ed. C. H. Herford and Percy and Evelyn Simpson, 11 vols. (Oxford: Clarendon Press, 1925–52). Jonson's spelling of *i/j* and *u/v* has been modernized, and citations from *Every Man in His Humour* refer to the Quarto edition of 1601.

Introduction

Literary history has separated William Shakespeare and Ben Jonson, created two distinct personae, taught us what to think about each in relation to the other, and established a simplified construction of each dramatic style in relation to its antithesis. Although the division has probably increased in our time, increased even in the past few decades, it is by no means a recent phenomenon. "In the seventeenth century it was fashionable, and profitable, to compare them, as Dryden did, to set them side by side as the two giants of the English theater, to discuss their respective virtues and evaluate their respective merits. By the time the century was over criticism had rendered its verdict: Shakespeare's preeminence would henceforth pass unchallenged. But by this time the luckless Jonson was yoked to Shakespeare in an odious tandem from which two centuries of subsequent comment would scarcely suffice to extricate him."[1] Thus Jonas A. Barish summarizes the process which has dissociated Shakespeare and Jonson from each other or, rather, joined them in a familiar and invariable relation. This book attempts to challenge the segregation of the two playwrights' work.

Personal mythology has helped to shape critical response. Barish goes on to point out that eighteenth-century editors of Shakespeare "discovered early that a convenient and safe way to praise 'their' poet was to abuse Jonson. The well-authenticated tradition of Jonson's conviviality gave way to a fraudulent countermyth: that Jonson, throughout his life, harbored an envenomed dislike of Shakespeare, whom he lost no opportunity of reviling and ridiculing, despite the fact—so ran the tale—that it was Shakespeare to whom he owed his start in the theater."[2] These myths were nourished, one suspects, by the differences in the two dramatists' origins: Shakespeare's Warwickshire boyhood distinguishes him from the urban Jonson, and the warm country heart has been preferred to the sharp urban eye. Such legends of personality might be passed over with a word or two about outdated prejudice did they not still influence our thinking about the men and their achievements. Shakespeare as the genial natural who composed romantic comedies, Jonson as the crabbed classicist who spat forth bilious satires— these myths die hard, and even critics who consciously reject them still describe the works in terms that reflect such assumptions.

Neither in critical studies nor in lecture halls are the two most important playwrights of the English Renaissance normally brought together. Robert Ornstein's suggestion that they may be seen "either as the twin pillars of Elizabethan comedy or as its opposite poles" illustrates the space usually assumed to exist between them, and rarely has this critical structure been challenged.[3] Jonson has for many years been a whipping boy for Shakespeare, and most students of the period either whip him or seek to protect him. Many of Shakespeare's partisans are offended by the suggestion that Jonson might have been considered the more significant figure in the seventeenth century and insulted by the idea that the two playwrights should be compared at all.[4] On the other side are those sympathetic critics of Jonson's work who, leery of the power of traditional prejudice, find it advisable to remove their subject from the shadow cast by the colossus of Shakespeare.[5] The boundaries probably became even more rigid during the period of the New Criticism, when the preference for discrete units of art and organic literary careers fostered the treatment of each dramatist's work in isolation. From time to time voices have been raised against these ironclad categories, but only recently have critics in any number begun to reconsider the contemporaneity of the two playwrights and thus tentatively to explore the artistic connections between them and their work.[6] If the poststructuralist subversion of canons and literary authority has loosened the prevailing division somewhat, there is still much to be said.[7]

Jonson himself must bear partial responsibility for his critical estrangement from Shakespeare, for he seems to have wanted it that way.

Passages from the inductions, prologues, poems, and reported commentary indicate that Jonson conceived of himself, and offered himself to the public, as one who wore the ancient, honorific mantle of Poet, a persona that required him to elevate his Works above the entertainments of mere playwrights. As he became more successful and well-known, he also became increasingly candid in his attacks on Shakespeare's dramatic predilections. Yet these celebrated pronouncements are only part of the story. The more we study Jonson the more we recognize discrepancies between his dogma and practice,[8] and it strikes me that his dealings with his colleagues—notably John Marston—are among the most revealing of these inconsistencies.[9] The Olympian declarations about his fellows must be considered in the larger context of a professional connection that included personal acquaintance, suspicion, certain common assumptions, theoretical disagreement, professional association, artistic borrowing, and in some cases even collaboration. In short, we should not allow ourselves to be hoodwinked by Jonson's claims to uniqueness, nor should we accept as gospel his shrill insistence upon the great distance between his work and Shakespeare's. It is highly ironic that literary critics have used Jonson's self-proclaimed singularity against him and perpetuated the opinion that he and his rival have nothing in common, but in the sense opposite to that intended. The artistic distinctions that Jonson established have become canonical, but now it is Shakespeare who is beyond compare.

Shakespeare contributed to the traditional separation, perhaps unwittingly, perhaps not, by saying nothing at all, or very little. He refused, so far as we can tell, to participate wholeheartedly in the imbroglio known as the War of the Theaters, and he mostly eschewed prologues, inductions, and theoretical asseverations. By remaining aloof from public controversy, Shakespeare allowed future generations to imagine him as the private, diligent artist, untainted by the personal and literary squabbles of the time. This image may be accurate, but it is almost surely an oversimplification promoted by scant evidence, and it has had far-reaching consequences. Two similar biographical passages, written over two hundred years apart, illustrate the tenacity and power of fable. As late as 1970 Ivor Brown, in an essay tellingly entitled "Not So Big Ben," could write:

The two men met and matched their wits amid the canakin's clink of the inns, but Will kept sober while nimbly outwitting the heavier and more learned man. He remained a countryman at heart and went home to Warwickshire as a man of property. Jonson, of Scottish origin on his father's side, was essentially a Londoner, with no idea of becoming a landowner. He said that in all his life he made only two hundred pounds in the theatre. The masques were his prop.

Will was a friendly and agreeable person; there is no sign of his dominating in company. Ben became, from the City to Westminster, increasingly a public figure and a Personage. If Will had died in London would he have been buried in the Abbey? Ben was. One feels that he had to be.[10]

Are the prejudices here much different from those contained in the following forged sentence which Robert Shields added to Drummond of Hawthornden's recollections in 1753?

[Jonson] was in his personal character the very reverse of Shakespear, as surly, ill-natured, proud, and disagreeable, as Shakespear with ten times his merit was gentle, good-natured, easy, and amiable.[11]

Jonson as public, bellicose, and censorious, Shakespeare as private, affable, and above dispute—these characterizations have proved to be durable. Rarely is it profitable to contest such familiar legends, which are usually fairly harmless, but in the cases of Shakespeare and Jonson, the personae have unjustly limited critical response to their work, particularly their comedies; and our conception of their dramatic styles, in turn, has reinforced the outlines of their portraits. Surmounting the obstacles erected by biographical mythology may afford a fresh and expansive view of territory traditionally separated and may reveal that Shakespeare's and Jonson's artistic concerns and achievements are not as distinct as the supposed personalities of their creators might imply.

No one denies that Shakespeare and Jonson were personally acquainted, but the critical segregation of their work has brought with it a tendency to minimize evidence of professional interchange or even to exaggerate suggestions of rivalry into acrimony and dislike. Jonson's complaints about romantic comedy are often interpreted personally, for example, or his association with the children's companies is sometimes assigned more importance than it warrants, and these distortions have created the impression that Shakespeare and Jonson were leaders of warring camps who attacked each other from across the Thames. In fact there is little proof of enmity and considerable evidence of artistic cooperation. In the first place, the two playwrights often wrote for the same actors.[12] Shakespeare's commitment to the Lord Chamberlain's–King's Men was official and constant, in that he was a shareholder who composed all except perhaps his earliest works for these players; Jonson, on the other hand, was a sometime contributor of scripts. Still, while Shakespeare was actively associated with it the company produced six of Jonson's most significant plays (*Every Man in His Humour, Every Man out of His Humour, Sejanus, Volpone, The Alchemist,* and *Catiline*); Shakespeare participated in the staging of at least two of these. The list of actors in the 1616 Folio version of *Every Man In* places Shakespeare's name at its head, and even disallowing Rowe's claim that Shakespeare sponsored the production,[13] he was still a party to Jonson's first hit on the London stage. Although the newcomer withdrew from the company after the failure of *Every Man Out* in 1599, giving his next two comical satires to the children (and sniping at some of his former colleagues), he returned in 1603 with *Sejanus,* and again Shakespeare took a role, perhaps acting Tiberius. This evidence of professional contact reminds us that Shakespeare was not oblivious to Jonson's work, that he could not have escaped familiarity with the younger playwright's dramatic tastes, prejudices, methods, and accomplishments. He knew at least parts of two of Jonson's plays, a comedy and a tragedy, by heart. Although proof that Jonson was similarly associated with the performance of any of Shakespeare's plays is wanting, it is superfluous in light of Jonson's repeatedly declared objections to them. Recognition of personal and professional fraternity is the first step in judiciously defining the relationship between the two dramatists and properly comparing their theatrical styles.

Jonson's gibes at Shakespeare begin early, in *Every Man Out* (pub. 1600), and continue long after Shakespeare's death, in the "Ode to Himselfe" (1629).[14] Scrutiny of some of these discloses a primary source of modern thinking about the relationship. Occasionally Jonson permits himself a personal jab, as when he mocks Shakespeare's recently acquired coat of arms, with its motto *Non sanz droict:* Puntarvolo recommends that the parvenu Sogliardo make the motto for his crest *"Not without mustard."* And there is resentment at the public favor that came easily to Shakespeare and often eluded Jonson, as in the contention that the audience that had disliked *The New Inn* would have preferred "no doubt a mouldy tale, / Like *Pericles*."[15] But the personal allusions matter less than the complaints about Shakespeare's dramaturgic choices, and such criticism is directed chiefly at the means of theatrical mimesis and the moral function of drama.

Shakespeare's liberal approach to verisimilitude offended Jonson's classically derived view of how truth can be most effectively represented on the stage. Thus, most of the familiar reflections on Shakespeare's lapses, the body of proof "That Shaksperr wanted Arte," are devoted to sins against credibility. (It is worth remembering that Jonson abandoned an adaptation of one of Plautus' comedies because he could not cast it with actual twins.) The notorious Prologue to *Every Man In,* possibly written as Jonson was preparing text for the Folio, is a representative statement of the aesthetic objections that Jonson regularly lodged against his most famous rival. The speaker laments that other playwrights—the principal offender, though unnamed, is obvious—are willing

> To make a child, now swadled, to proceede
> Man, and then shoote up, in one beard, and weede,
> Past threescore yeeres: or, with three rustie swords,
> And helpe of some few foot-and-halfe-foote words,
> Fight over *Yorke,* and *Lancasters* long jarres:
> And in the tyring-house bring wounds, to scarres.
> He rather prayes, you will be pleas'd to see
> One such, to day, as other playes should be.
> Where neither *Chorus* wafts you ore the seas;
> Nor creaking throne comes downe, the boyes to please;
> Nor nimble squibbe is seene, to make afear'd
> The gentlewomen; no roul'd bullet heard
> To say, it thunders; nor tempestuous drumme
> Rumbles, to tell you when the storme doth come;
> But deedes, and language, such as men doe use:
> And persons, such as *Comoedie* would chuse,
> When she would shew an Image of the times,
> And sport with humane follies, not with crimes.
> (lines 7–24, Folio text)

Alluding unmistakably to the *Henry* plays and perhaps glancing at *Pericles, The Winter's Tale,* and *The Tempest,*[16] this anatomy of abuses backhandedly commends "realism," local specificity, recognizable persons, and morally significant situations. It is the same antiromantic conviction that gives rise to the tart critique of improbable fictions in the Induction to *Bartholomew Fair:* "If there bee never a *Servant-monster* i' the *Fayre;* who can helpe it? he [the author] sayes; nor a nest of *Antiques?* Hee is loth to make Nature afraid in his *Playes,* like those that beget *Tales, Tempests,* and such like *Drolleries*" (lines 127–30). Shakespeare's imaginative genius is never at issue; it is the use of that gift that disturbs Jonson. He protests especially Shakespeare's neglect of the didactic opportunities provided by the stage. Mitis's desire to see a romantic comedy instead of something "thus neere, and familiarly allied to the time" is met by Cordatus with the pseudo-Ciceronian definition recorded by Donatus: proper comedy is an "*Imitatio vitae, Speculum consuetudinis, Imago veritatis;* a thing throughout pleasant, and ridiculous, and accommodated to the correction of manners" (*EMOH,* III.vi.200–201, 206–9). Virtually all of Jonson's comments, personal and theoretical, must be interpreted in light of such assumptions.[17] Finally, there is the problem of the Folio poem, which I take to be a document of genuine, if reserved, respect. Most of the comments cited are familiar and amusing. Their acerbity should not be dismissed, but the artistic assumptions from which they proceed and the specific contexts in which they appear must be kept in mind.

Knowledge that Shakespeare acted in two of Jonson's plays does not tell us what he thought of his younger colleague's work. There is little to go on except for some oblique remarks on the War of the Theaters. Rosencrantz's gossip about the "eyrie of children, little eyases" who are "now the fashion" (*Hamlet,* II.ii.337, 339) reveals little beyond possible resentment at the faddish popularity of the recently revived children's companies and perhaps some implied censure of Jonson's encouraging such pointless competition.[18] In the Prologue to *Troilus and Cressida,* Shakespeare's armed speaker is apparently an imitation of the identical device in *Poetaster,* which probably preceded *Troilus* by a season. Whereas Jonson's presenter announces that he is prepared for attack in the theatrical wars, Shakespeare's disclaims local associations and explains his costume as appropriate to the dramatic subject ("suited / In like conditions as our argument" [lines 24–25]). This is probably a witty defense of drama against topical commentary—a private joke attacking private misuse of the stage—and thus one of the rare instances in which Shakespeare glances disapprovingly at Jonson's work.

The search for portraits of Jonson in certain Shakespearean characters, a sport that flourished in the nineteenth century, produced some ridiculous conclusions, and modern suggestions of this kind, while more judicious, have won little support. For instance, few critics accept that Jaques himself represents Jonson, although his satiric credo may fairly be called Jonsonian. The most nearly convincing work in this line has been done by William Elton, who makes a forceful case for identifying Ajax in *Troilus* with Jonson.[19] He believes, on the strength of the biographical parallels and the nasty pun on Ajax's name ("A-jakes" or "privy"), that *Troilus* is the "purge" that Shakespeare is said to have administered to Jonson as revenge for the attack on the Chamberlain's Men in *Poetaster*.[20] Such personal comment is inconsistent with almost everything we know about Shakespeare's usual practice,[21] and yet *Troilus* itself is similarly anomalous. Whatever the truth may be, to conclude that Shakespeare rarely remarked publicly on Jonson's (or other dramatists') work is not to claim that he was ignorant of or uninterested in it.

Jonson's theoretical prolixity and Shakespeare's reticence make for a basic difference that is consistent with other important distinctions, most of them unexceptionable and familiar. First is the issue of professional orientation. Shakespeare apparently considered himself a commercial playwright who from the beginning to the end of his professional life was concerned chiefly with the attraction and satisfaction of paying customers, whereas Jonson thought of himself as a Poet, a historically distinguished vocation that included the activity of writing for the stage. Shakespeare retired from the theatrical and urban scene while still creative, while Jonson remained until his death a central fixture in the London literary milieu. Shakespeare seems to have shown no interest in publishing his plays, and the fact that his was the usual practice made Jonson's presentation of his *Works* in 1616 all the more egregious. Jonson's exalted view of the poet's role is responsible for his well-known insistence on the moral and social functions of dramatic writing. In dedicating *Volpone* to the two universities, Jonson differentiates between his own and others' views of "dramatick, *or (as they terme it) stage*-poetrie" (lines 36–37), an analysis that Shakespeare probably would not have disputed. Shakespeare evidently conceived of the theater as an end in itself, not as a vehicle for instruction or revelation. This is not to say that he rejected the Horatian dicta of *utile et dulcere*, but doubtless his interpretation of the utility of drama was considerably less specific than his colleague's. Jonson's didactic impulses have sometimes been overstated or misconstrued: the morality of *The Alchemist* is vastly more subtle and sophisticated than that of *Poetaster,* for example. But Jonson and Shakespeare would have certainly disagreed on whether a poem should mean or be.

Jonson's famous left-handed compliment, that Shakespeare ranked with the ancient masters despite inadequate classical learning, points to the celebrated difference in their response to classical literature. Jonson advertises his allegiance to the ancient poets repeatedly, in his extra-dramatic commentary, such as Cordatus's coaching of Mitis; in depicting himself as Horace in *Poetaster;* in his scrupulous citation of Latin sources in the quarto text of *Sejanus;* in the philosophical assumptions that govern the dedicatory letter to *Volpone;* in his frequent dependence on Lucian; in his attraction to the epigram; in his portrait of Cicero in *Catiline;* and in his occasional remarks on Shakespeare's betrayal of classical rule. Jonson's reverence for antiquity constitutes one of his trademarks, and Shakespeare did not share this passion, at least not in the same way. Shakespeare seems generally to have preferred contemporary authors, from whom he took most of his plots. Despite the Plautine sources of *The Comedy of Errors* and the ancient settings of many of the tragedies, Shakespeare's classical plays have a modern stamp upon them: he reached Rome by North. The pen-and-ink sketch (attributed to Peacham) of an early performance of *Titus Andronicus* with the actors in Elizabethan interpretations of Roman costume captures the essential relation between Shakespeare and the ancient masters. The classics were useful to him, but no more than any other kind of literature.

These distinct responses to classical example account for the disagreement over the unities. Jonson subscribed to the ancient doctrine because he believed that it helped to sustain dramatic illusion, to bridge the gap between nature and art, to present "things (like truths) well fain'ed" (Second Prologue to *Epicoene,* line 10). For instance, the unity of time demarcates and comments on the action of *Volpone:* the opening speech is an aubade, the Fox is in the full heat of passion at noon, and his gold is confiscated and his scheme exploded as darkness descends. In *The Alchemist* the unities of time and place contribute an invaluable sense of claustrophobia and potential comic calamity.[22] That his commitment to the unities was not absolute is revealed by the time sequence in *The Case Is Altered* or *Sejanus,* but Jonson claims that the principles are fundamental to his strict conception of dramatic mimesis.[23] Shakespeare's celebrated flouting of the unities reflects not only his relative indifference to classical stipulations but also his more flexible attitude toward dramatic representation in general. At times Shakespeare seems to have been willing, as in the choral admonitions from *Henry V,* to credit the spectator's imagination with greater power than Jonson was. At other times, however, he seems to have doubted the possibility of bridging the gap between life and art, believing with Dr. Johnson that the audience is always conscious that "the stage is only a stage, and that the players are only players."[24] Even when he strives to create an illusionistic fiction, he does so with other means than the unities.

Contrary ideas on the functions of drama led Shakespeare and Jonson to select different kinds of stories to dramatize. The plays that make Shakespearean romantic comedy what it is, those from *Dream* to *Twelfth Night,* derive from narratives of love and courtship, tales that Shakespeare found in fiction (in both poetry and prose) by Ariosto, Lodge, Barnabe Rich, and Spenser. A similar predilection is apparent in virtually all the other comedies, which originate in stories by Montemayor, Giovanni Fiorentino, Painter, Golding's Ovid, Cinthio, and the *Gesta Romanorum.* Shakespeare could invent actions when he wished to but was mostly content to adapt the narratives of his contemporaries and of comparatively modern English and Continental authors. If Jonson read such tales he did not dramatize them; in fact, the search for Jonson's sources is almost pointless because he invented most of his comic actions. With notable exceptions, such as Coleridge's commending the plot of *The Alchemist,* criticism has tended to underrate the contribution of action to Jonsonian comedy, but still it is a fact that story was less important to Jonson than to Shakespeare. He concocted the fable to suit his thematic and heuristic purposes. For tragedy, Jonson went directly to classical sources, at least for the two tragedies by which he wanted to be remembered, *Sejanus* and *Catiline:* from the mine of ancient history he chose two careers offering unmistakable moral patterns.[25] Shakespeare, again, preferred modern sources for tragedy, adapting the stories of Belleforest or Cinthio or plays with proven appeal, and when he did select an ancient subject, he relied upon Elizabethan intermediaries such as North or Chapman. Shakespeare's choice of sources, unlike Jonson's, does not bespeak an informing dramatic theory or predetermined aim.

Jonson's suspicion of narrative for its own sake is accompanied by a commitment to and a gift for satiric portraiture. Nevill Coghill, in an influential discussion of the two dramatists' different styles, remarks upon the primacy of character in Jonsonian comedy:

Like Chaucer, [Shakespeare] never troubled to invent a plot if he could find one invented by somebody else. A good story was the first necessity in imagining his plays.

Ben Jonson worked differently. Satire was his object and he therefore had to begin with *character* (or a group of characters) fitted to his lash. He then placed them in a certain situation calculated to show them at their worst, and by a prodigious intellectual mastery contrived the complete series of their logical development into successive scenes, working from his data to his Q.E.D. with the stunning ingenuity of a master in algebra. By doing so he almost in some cases achieved a story.[26]

Overlooking the manifest preference in this summary (indeed, it is usually necessary to ignore the evaluative tone of such formulations) we find a clear statement of the orthodox view. Evidence of this difference in emphasis is that it is often difficult to recall the events in Jonson's comedies but easy to remember the persons who perform them. Jonson's corrective bent, especially his interest in manners, prompted him to imagine characters guilty of outlandish moral and social faults. Shakespeare, of course, began with no such agenda, and their difference on this point results in two styles of characterization. "It is a truism that [Shakespeare's] characters are 'round' where Jonson's are 'flat,' that they have changes of mood and motive, that they develop and surprise us. . . . his people seem 'natural' to us, like people that we know, like ourselves. This is never so in Jonson."[27] Coghill's last pejorative phrases reflect the taste, stimulated by influences such as the Victorian novel and the criticism of A. C. Bradley, for "real people." But the central article in the analysis is indisputable: Shakespeare took a greater interest in character for its own sake, as he did in story, than did Jonson. For the most part, Jonson seems to have regarded his characters as means to an end; Shakespeare rarely did so. These technical biases naturally produce two very different kinds of comedy.[28] Shakespeare's geniality toward his persons and their actions is consistent with his fundamental interest in narrative, especially tales of love and courtship; and Jonson's satiric asperities proceed naturally from his primary concern with eccentric figures whose interactions constitute a dramatic action.

These several oppositions of technique and taste signify two distinct attitudes toward experience, two visions that may fairly be described in antithetical terms: tolerant versus critical, optimistic versus pessimistic, positive versus negative, progressive versus conservative. Shakespeare offers a version of life that admits the opportunity for happiness, for improvement, for second chances. Oliver repents his tyranny over Orlando and mends his behavior; Don "John is ta'en in flight, / And brought with armed men back to Messina." Even when the agents of folly and evil are allowed to escape or remain uncorrected, there is the suggestion that they may be entreated to a peace, as Orsino urges for Malvolio. If humans are not perfect, they are at least corrigible, and it is on this possibility that Shakespeare throws the dramatic pressure. His characters are assisted by luck, by good fortune, by chance, by Providence, and such happy coincidence is the manifestation of benevolent natural forces. Shakespeare uses all his dramatic expertise to attract his audience and encourage participation in the theatrical transformation, a strategy altogether appropriate to a vision that urges us to accept people for what they can become. Jonson's depiction of humans in society disturbs us, for he is pessimistic about the penalties of Adam. His characters are rarely better off at the end than at the beginning of his comedies, and those who accidentally profit do so only financially. The Jonsonian world is static and confined, hardly subject even to change, much less amendment. Shakespeare's benevolent Providence, which links effects to causes and ironically converts mischance into fruitful possibility, is here replaced by a universe that is random and perilous. When Fortune does intrude, it is usually in the form of hard luck for everyone concerned. There is a logic to experience, but it is a scheme tied to human will and fallibility. Shakespeare observes and smiles at humanity and its ways; Jonson mocks and fulminates.

It would be pointless to dispute these antitheses, for they are generally valid, their familiarity being a result of their utility. There is some point, however, in attempting to modify them, to state them more precisely, and we may begin by recognizing that the accepted oppositions derive from the juxtaposition of certain typical plays—say *Dream, Much Ado, As You Like It,* and *Twelfth Night* against *Every Man Out, Volpone, The Alchemist,* and *Bartholomew Fair*—and that it is risky to generalize about either comic style on the basis of a few works, however important and representative. Too often each category is stretched to encompass virtually all the comedies of each dramatist, so that Jonson's "satiric realism" is invoked in discussions of plays to which it scarcely pertains, such as the unrevised *Every Man In* or *The New Inn*. Or a play may be wedged into a category, a process that often requires distortion or peculiar emphasis. Occasionally the familiar labels attach themselves even to noncomic texts, so that Shakespeare's romantic idealism is extended even to his tragedies. Most readers of Renaissance drama are capable, when studying the work of either dramatist alone, of making fine discriminations, of noticing the darker shades in *Twelfth Night* or of appreciating the boisterous mirth of *Volpone*, for example. Yet once Shakespeare and Jonson are placed next to each other, the well-known differences assert themselves and some of our most sensitive readers are satisfied with clichés. Criticism has been restricted by a monolithic conception of each style, an assumption evident in Ornstein's metaphor of "the twin pillars." If each canon is regarded as homogeneous and fixed, then we can do little more than look upon this picture and on this.

In fact, however, each canon is various and irregular, containing experiments and false starts and atypical plays, and such variations arise from conceptions of experience that are dynamic and complicated. Every text of each dramatist embodies a vision of life marked by tensions and competing impressions: in any of Shakespeare's comedies, for instance, faith in human resiliency and providential aid is subverted by doubts about universal weakness and inevitable limitation. Similarly, in each of Jonson's comic masterpieces, the critique of self-interest and baseness coexists with awareness of and respect for man's extraordinary powers of imaginative invention. When all these particular responses and conclusions are collected into the abstraction that we call Shakespeare's or Jonson's artistic vision, we have a very capacious and sophisticated thing indeed. Even though the two visions are distinct from each other, it is also true that they contain similar subjects, parallel shapes, related colors, and that they blend together at the edges. A similar relationship obtains among the dramatic means employed to mediate these visions. Shakespeare's exploitation of romantic conventions depends upon ironic and even satiric tactics that serve to qualify and, paradoxically, to amplify the effect of romance, while Jonson's assault on human failings is sometimes supported by romantic possibilities that must be denied or displaced. In short, the complexity of the two visions makes them appropriate for comparison: their contents and the strategies that convey them are more closely related than most criticism has been willing to allow.

The traditional polarization of Shakespearean and Jonsonian comedy has tended to obscure the two dramatists' attraction to similar themes. *Twelfth Night* and *Every Man Out*, plays from roughly the same period, are usually (and rightly) held to represent the two types of Elizabethan comedy, romantic and satiric, New and Old. Yet the source of conflict, the focus of attention in both works is the human penchant for affectation and self-absorption. The fantasies and self-delusions that Jonson derides in Puntarvolo, Fastidious Briske, and Sordido also afflict Orsino, Olivia, and particularly Malvolio. This simple instance of likeness within difference attests to a pervasive thematic consistency. Both dramatists were concerned with what Sidney called "the common errors of our life," and even though Jonson's response to the ubiquitous evidence of humanity's fallen state is usually more contemptuous than Shakespeare's, both devote their attention to the irresistible pressures of the flesh, the inevitable defeat of innocence, the familiar desire to take advantage, the lamentable effects of inconstancy. In play after play audiences are invited to contemplate that weakness that comprehends and fosters many others—human pride. Exploration of its power and influence is not confined to the comedies, however. Numerous characters suffer from self-love and from exaggerated conceptions of themselves, and the actions devised to puncture such inflated ideas may be comic, tragic, or satiric. Both dramatists also seem vitally interested in the natural impulse to transcend natural limitations. The lawyer's clerk in *The Alchemist*, the young nun in *Measure for Measure*, the aging lovers in *Antony and Cleopatra*, the Stoic Germanicans in *Sejanus*—all these very different figures exhibit a will to overcome mortal restrictions of one kind or another, and the vastly different nature of their actions or of the responses they provoke ought not to obscure the similarity of their desires. One token of the significance of this effort at transcendence is the two playwrights' similar fascination with the uses of language. This subject may be of greater obvious importance to Jonson—indeed it is the mainspring of *Poetaster*—but throughout both canons (and in the nondramatic works as well) we find an abiding interest in the power of words.

Words are the medium of the imagination, and virtually all of Shakespeare's and Jonson's dramas address themselves directly to the problem of the imaginative faculty. The human imagination is presented as a gift and a curse, and both dramatists show especial concern for its misapplication or perversion. The connection between words and imaginative ability is clearly discernible in any number of their comedies and comical satires, in figures such as Master Ford, Thorello, Giuliano (Downright), Mistress Quickly, Puntarvolo, Beatrice and Benedick, Dogberry, Captain Tucca, Don Armado, and many others. In most of the romantic comedies Shakespeare addresses himself to the creative value of fancy, and in the comical satires Jonson is concerned to show the products of the disciplined imagination in Crites and Horace. But many of their greatest plays, notably Shakespeare's major tragedies and Jonson's middle comedies, are based upon the experience of imaginative idealists who seek to impose subjective visions of experience upon an intractable world. The result of these imaginative efforts is failure. And yet the very works that generate such doubts about the imagination imply that its greatest fulfillment is to be found in the dramatic artifact itself. It is therefore appropriate that late in their careers both playwrights take what we might call a romantic turn: pessimism and failure are supplanted by a new perspective and confidence in the compensatory and even redemptive powers of the imagination.

My attempt to define more precisely the relationship between Shakespearean and Jonsonian drama does not fall into a neat scheme: I look at some major and some minor works, scrutinize certain texts at very close range and look at others from a great distance, examine a few dramas in one context and then return to them in another, and practically ignore many important plays.[29]

In the first chapter I argue that *The Case Is Altered* is un-Jonsonian and artistically unsuccessful because Jonson was laboring under the consciousness of Shakespeare's success: the apprentice playwright attempted to reproduce the structure of an Elizabethan romantic comedy without endorsing the meanings implicit in the form. Chapter 2 compares *The Merry Wives of Windsor* and *Every Man in His Humour*, plays for which the traditional categories of romantic and satiric comedy are inadequate. Shakespeare and Jonson address themselves to the same topics—imagination, fancy, fantasy, madness, language—and do so in some unexpectedly similar ways. The focus widens considerably in Chapter 3, devoted to several plays written between 1599 and 1604. For both dramatists this was a transitional phase: Shakespeare gave up comedy for tragedy, but not without a struggle, and Jonson devised and then abandoned the mixed mode of comical satire. The formal tensions resulting from these experiments and shifts in direction suggest artistic growth and changing visions. In Chapter 4, I set Jonson's comic master-pieces against Shakespeare's mature tragedies: in these two different modes the experience of disillusionment is used to establish the gap between imaginative possibility and actual necessity. And, finally, Chapter 5 takes up Shakespeare's romances and Jonson's masques, plays in which affirmative visions are conveyed by similarly artificial and sophis-ticated theatrical means.

This method of comparison has its perils, for in looking at two sets of texts in a certain way, we are prohibited from seeing them in other ways, at least at the same time. The critical tendency thus far has been to concentrate on differences in comic tone, which are mostly a function of Shakespeare's and Jonson's respective attention to narrative and char-acter. The patent differences that come to light in such an investigation naturally overshadow other potentially meaningful resemblances. When the focus of attention is shifted to form and theme, however, parallels emerge which suggest that Shakespeare and Jonson were ad-dressing themselves to similar issues and sometimes doing so in analo-gous ways. When we stand back from the two dramatists' *oeuvres*, some lines and details are bound to be blurred, but such a vantage point also exposes shapes and tones that do not appear with such clarity when we adhere to the conventional ways of looking. The comparative approach I employ is, at times, bound to appear tendentious. In suggesting parallels between authors as different as these I may appear to be ignorant of, or to have suppressed for my own purposes, the fundamental distinctions between them. It is true that there are formidable differences in style and purpose, little proof of direct influence, and, above all, some irrefutable differences in quality between the two playwrights' work. I risk appear-ing to elevate Jonson at the expense of Shakespeare. Certain data, some of it important and well known, must be neglected. Some readers will think that I am finding salmons in dissimilar rivers. Fluellen, with his peculiar method of comparison, comes up frequently in criticism these days and has suffered a good deal of ridicule. Perhaps it is worth point-ing out that, notwithstanding his bizarre logic, the Welshman's com-parison of Henry and Alexander was not entirely without merit.

CHAPTER I

A Pleasant Comedy

The Case Is Altered in Context

When Jonson told Drummond in 1619 that half his comedies were not in print, he seems not to have mentioned that this was so probably because he wanted it that way.[1] The famous public figure allowed nothing to compromise the apodictic persona that he had scrupulously created for himself. His dramatic practice and especially his theoretical pronouncements in the early years of the seventeenth century helped to produce an artistic self-portrait that represents the mature Jonson. There are enough cracks in the surface, however, to disclose a more various and less polished picture underneath, and one of the most telling features of this covered portrait is that the subject looks much less distinctive than in the finished, approved version: some of his early work unmistakably resembles the contemporary efforts of other dramatists. *The Case Is Altered* is one of the plays, composed before he had found his own distinctive style, that Jonson wished to suppress. Most of it was apparently written in 1597, with some of the topical, satiric references to Anthony Munday instated around 1599 or 1600; it was printed, apparently without authorial assistance, in quarto in 1609. Jonson declined to include it in the Folio. Modern critics, following their author in regarding the play as an artistic stepchild, either attempt to make it more like Jonson's other dramatic progeny or, more commonly, neglect it altogether.[2] The second title page of the Quarto promises "A Pleasant

Comedy," a description that explains much of the critical discomfort with the play: except for the satiric portraits in the subplot, *The Case Is Altered* seems un-Jonsonian. And yet, as the only certain example we possess of Jonson's comedy before *Every Man in His Humour* (1598), it is an uncommonly instructive text because it reveals what Jonson attempted to conceal: that his early work was not as assured and original as his later, that at one time the great man himself was an apprentice, and that Shakespeare was one of the masters in whose school he learned.

Shakespeare dominated the theatrical scene by the middle of the 1590s: the great crop of playwrights who had flourished at the beginning of the decade—Marlowe, Kyd, Lyly, Peele, Greene, and Lodge—were dead or had given up drama by 1593. It is inconceivable that in 1597 Jonson had not noticed (and not coveted) Shakespeare's unmatched success. Jonson was always alert to the theatrical fashions of his day, not only quick to notice and to remark on the work of others, but also willing, supercilious comments notwithstanding, to borrow. (The indisputable relation between *Every Man In* and Chapman's *An Humorous Day's Mirth* of the previous year should call attention to the discrepancy between Jonsonian pronouncement and practice.) Jonson must have been acquainted with several of the five or six Shakespearean comedies that had been staged when he turned his hand to the form, and these would have been likely models for a young playwright seeking to make his way. Or so it would naturally seem, but in this case the traditional segregation of Shakespeare and Jonson has had a damaging effect.

The Case Is Altered resembles one of Jonson's mature plays much less than it does a late Elizabethan romantic comedy, specifically a Shakespearean comedy.[3] It is a tale of adventure, military captivity, divided families, buried treasure, threatened love, and miraculous reunions. Jonson sought to win public favor and to make a name for himself in the London theater by devising the kind of comedy with which Shakespeare had made his professional fortune. But *The Case Is Altered* lacks the charm of its models because it was composed by one with little sympathy for the ideas implicit in such a story. It would be helpful to know more about Jonson's beginnings, particularly what the other lost comedies were like; this play is only one piece of a puzzle that can never be fully reconstructed.[4] But we do have an exceptionally rich text to examine, and to study *The Case Is Altered* in context is to revise the orthodox view of Jonson's artistic apprenticeship. I shall argue that

Jonson, in seeking to establish himself professionally, appropriated a Shakespearean dramatic form but could not commit himself whole-heartedly to the positive spirit of that mode; thus, the weaknesses of the play derive largely from the novice's uncertain attitude toward his borrowed structure. In other words, this comedy furnishes a rare glimpse at a twenty-five-year-old playwright's effort to make his way in a field dominated by a comic style for which he had little feeling.

§ I

After his first flush of success at the turn of the century, Jonson could boast that his "works" were intended for "understanders," playgoers and readers capable of appreciating his distaste for the popular style and his fidelity to classical example. But when he composed *The Case Is Altered,* either he had not developed or he was able to suppress his celebrated disdain for those playwrights who amused their audiences with clowns and complicated tales. Indeed, he selected the kind of stories that had been attracting spectators of all varieties to the public theaters, the kind that he would soon ridicule in his prologues and lampoon in the actions of his comedies, the kind that had made Shakespeare the most successful comic dramatist working at the time. When T. S. Eliot remarked that Jonson's "immense dramatic-constructive skill" was "not so much skill in plot as skill in doing without a plot"—a conclusion that has had a great effect on our conception of Jonsonian drama—he was not referring to *The Case Is Altered.*[5] Intricate action is the primary source of this play's appeal, a fact that gives an unintended ironic point to the foolish Balladino's claim that, in his own plays, "no matter for the pen, the plot shall carry it" (1.ii.76–77). Jonson's well-known demand for faithful imitation of the present, his contempt for romantic story, and his refusal to "serve th'ill customes of the age," as he says in the Prologue to the revised *Every Man In,* had yet to manifest themselves. The young playwright's choices of what to adapt and how to develop it seem to contradict the famous Jonsonian principles; in fact, they appear popular and Elizabethan.

That Jonson adapted someone else's material at all makes this play somewhat unusual, and that he elected to consolidate two plays of Plautus is even more surprising. Plautus was not Jonson's kind of Roman.[6] (The most that can be said is that the *Casina* and the *Mostellaria* seem to have exerted a very general kind of situational influence on *Epicoene* and *The Alchemist*.) Although Jonson's attraction to *Aulularia*, a satiric assault on a miserly fool, is understandable, *I Captivi* seems an unlikely candidate for adaptation. The latter is an identity play, a comic thriller in which survival, not money or power, is the principal issue. The plot depends upon the device of the lost infant; themes of loyalty and friendship predominate; and the audience is expected to react finally with emotional gratitude and mirthful joy, not with laughter of scorn. As Herford points out, Plautus uses the confusion over identity to draw upon "the springs of generous emotion and tragic pathos."[7] The mature Jonson, it need hardly be said, did not dip into such springs. But in 1597 the novice was seeking to please a public in whom Shakespeare had instilled a taste for neo-Plautine delights, and in choosing *I Captivi* and *Aulularia* Jonson may have sought to do so by deliberately emulating Shakespeare's earliest comic work. There is some reason to think Shakespeare himself responsible for having made Plautus a popular literary figure at the end of the century, some evidence that his selection of *Menaechmi* and *Amphitruo* was perhaps an original stroke.[8] By 1597 Shakespeare had moved beyond adaptation to a new level of synthesis and transformation, but Jonson was looking for his first success, and it may be that he decided to go directly to the quarry that had proved so profitable, artistically and otherwise, to his senior colleague.

If Jonson's choice of stories for *The Case Is Altered* implies that his disdain for romantic drama developed gradually, his elaboration of those two stories confirms it. The dramatist's major technical problems were to expand two skeletal texts into a full-bodied work and to fuse two very dissimilar actions into a coherent whole, and at every turn Jonson makes the choices of an Elizabethan popular playwright. His first tactic is to augment two small but crucial Plautine parts, the returning son from *I Captivi* and the miser's daughter from *Aulularia*, developing the nonentities Philopolemus and Phaedria into Paulo Ferneze and Rachel de Prie.[9] By inventing a love story centered on these two figures, Jonson not only welds the actions firmly and escapes what might have been a merely mechanical alternation between plots; he also seems to court popular favor by offering the audience a suspenseful tale of endangered love. The creation of the perfidious friend Angelo, another step in the direction of amplitude, maintains that unity established between plots. Angelo serves as a bridge between households, exemplifies betrayal in a play concerned with friendship and faith, and contributes yet another scheme to an already intricate story. Such inventions and developments suggest that, uncharacteristic though such a method may seem, Jonson is devoted to the gratifications of narrative for its own sake.

Comparison of *The Case Is Altered* with its originals shows that again and again the young playwright has complicated the action to promote suspense and irony and thus to enhance the audience's pleasure in the dramatic commotion. Each of these narrative strategies furnishes a distinct pleasure: we enjoy being teased with a problem and then being gratified or surprised by its solution, and yet we also relish the privileged state of awareness that irony affords.[10] Plautus depends almost entirely upon irony: both *I Captivi* and *Aulularia* begin with prologues that, in summarizing the action to follow, provide the audience with a superior point of view. Jonson in most of his plays subordinates the pleasures of suspense to the heuristic benefits of irony, particularly in the more didactic plays like the comical satires. In this early effort, on the other hand, he exploits the effects of both. Shakespeare was by this time adept at such combined effects: according to Bertrand Evans, Shakespeare's growing technical proficiency may be measured in his increasingly ingenious management of "discrepant awareness," a phrase that includes the interlocking effects of suspense and irony.[11] Jonson must have been affected to some degree by the Elizabethan taste for a mixture of ignorance and knowledge, for a piquant blend of suspenseful tension and ironic pleasure. Although he uses irony liberally in *The Case Is Altered*, he appears to favor *dulce* over *utile* and uncharacteristically places the higher value on suspense. He eliminates the preliminary explanations essential to the effect of the Plautine originals; stimulates his audience to feel hope and anxiety for the captured Paulo and to fret for the safety of the beleaguered Rachel; introduces the two captives already in disguise, so that the audience is ignorant of the exchanged identities until the truth is revealed at the end of the scene (IV.i); and in disclosing the secret of Gasper-Camillo's parentage, allows the audience to piece it out through hints and clues that the characters unwittingly supply.[12] Surprise virtually disappears from Jonson's drama until the middle comedies, where it is employed rarely but effectively (Bonario's rescue of Celia, the revelation of Epicoene's gender); significantly, however, it reappears in the very late plays, where Jonson seems bent on recapturing the flavor of the period in which he began.[13]

Jonson's determination to compose in the popular Elizabethan style further manifests itself in certain technical choices. An interest in symmetry, for instance, accounts for the pair of brothers, Paulo and Camillo; the pair of prisoners, Chamont and Gasper-Camillo; the pair of sisters, Aurelia and Phoenixella; the pair of lost infants, Camillo-Gasper and Isabel-Rachel; the matching sets of servants from the Milanese and French camps; the contrasting friendships of Angelo with Paulo and Chamont with Camillo; the two fathers, Melun-Jaques and Ferneze; and the string of would-be lovers—Paulo, Angelo, Onion, Christophero, Ferneze—who hanker after Rachel and irk Jaques. This pleasure in design is further suggested by the contrasts and colors with which the dramatist fills the parallel lines and shapes he has sketched. In other words, his attempts at complementarity soften and variegate the numerous sets of pairs and series: Aurelia is witty and insouciant, Phoenixella somber and reserved; Chamont is faithful to his friend, Angelo perfidious; Ferneze works himself into fits over his child, Jaques over his gold; Angelo's ruthless passion for Rachel is balanced by Onion's laughable amorous pretensions, and between these come Christophero's apparently genuine affection and Ferneze's shamefaced attraction.

Such efforts at balance and contrast are repeated in Jonson's management of tone and his adumbration of theme. Obviously the inherent contrast between the source plays, an adventure narrative and a satiric portrait, satisfied the well-known Elizabethan love of variety. So the young dramatist built upon this opposition, alternating between sentiment and tumult, romance and satire, sympathy and scorn. The verbal outrages perpetrated by Juniper—

> *Juni.* *Valentine*, I prithee ruminate thy selfe welcome. What *fortuna de la Guerra?* (I.iv.16–17)

contrast implicitly with the quiet beauty of Rachel's speech:

> *Rach.* No? is your presence nothing? I shall want that, and wanting that, want all:For that is all to me. (I.x.17–19)

Each style gains in effectiveness from the contrast with its opposite. Such a technique also assists Jonson in developing his major themes, such as the ethical problem of loyalty and betrayal. In the competition for Rachel, Angelo betrays first Paulo and then Christophero, who betrays Onion and is himself betrayed by Ferneze. Angelo lies to Rachel in telling her that he is accompanying her to meet Paulo (ironically, his false promise comes true when Paulo intercepts them). Years before, Jaques had broken faith with Chamont Senior in his theft of the gold and abduction of Rachel; now Onion and Juniper steal the money from him. Gasper-Camillo demonstrates his affection for Chamont by exchanging identities and taking the risk of remaining behind in Milan; likewise, Chamont keeps his promise by returning with Paulo to redeem his friend Gasper. Phoenixella is loyal to the memory of her mother and constant in her vow of chastity. Aurelia develops an attraction to Chamont before he departs and remains true to it until she is rewarded with marriage to him in the final scene. Even Juniper defends Onion when Ferneze threatens to fire him, and Onion (after a moment of doubt) shares the windfall of the hidden gold with Juniper. Such care for balance and such devotion to amplitude and multiplicity, as well as the exuberance with which these ends are pursued, indicate the unmistakably Elizabethan origins of the comedy.

So does Jonson's uncharacteristic treatment of a love story and his range of female characters.[14] It is a commonplace that Jonson was not much interested in portraying women and not especially good at it, but he seems not to have discovered that yet. Instead of presenting whores, harridans, or weaklings, Jonson here gamely seeks to depict women who embody positive modes of behavior. Aurelia and Phoenixella represent two contrasting but legitimate kinds of womanhood. Since his Roman plots lack such figures, Jonson is forced to invent them to supplement and enrich the moral picture suggested by the action. Rachel de Prie is a rarity, both a representative of fidelity and virtue and a crucial figure in the action. Her love affair with Paulo not only commands sympathetic attention but also forms an essential part of Jonson's dramatic and moral plan.[15] *The Case Is Altered* is not mainly a love story in the way that *As You Like It* may be considered one, and Jonson does not exploit the affair for an abundance of sentiment. He usually prefers to consider the follies and mischief that love can generate (as he does with Angelo), and he is never engaged by the idea of love as Shakespeare is. Nevertheless, this love story is indispensable to the design and meaning of the comedy.

The felicitous ending of *The Case Is Altered* resembles that of any number of contemporary Shakespearean comedies, but without the penetrating ironies. Not only are losses restored and loose ends tied up, just as the exposition promises, but gains are made, pardons issued, punishment is forgone, and happiness assured. Jonson never ends his comedies with such undivided harmony. Well, as Captain Corcoran says in *Pinafore*, hardly ever. It is not as if Jonson had no choice but to follow his sources to a tidy and favorable conclusion, for he has softened the brittle endings of the Roman originals and made the final movement harmonious and positive.[16] The boy gets the girl. When the identity of the lost son is discovered, one family is reunited; another is brought together when the beggar's daughter is restored to her aristocratic brother; and those two houses are united with the pair of marriages. The faithful general, disappointed in love, declares his intention to "subdue [his] passions," and the serious sister is granted her wish for privacy and celibacy. The wicked friend sues briefly for pardon and receives it forthwith and unconditionally, the miser is not only forgiven for kidnapping but is allowed to keep the stolen treasure, the comeuppance of the thieving servants mainly creates mirth, two nations are peacefully allied, and grace is extended to all. Who wrote this? The answer, of course, is that Jonson wrote this play before he found his voice.[17] He composed it under peculiar circumstances, in response to a comic vision and method with which he was not entirely in sympathy. A modern reader familiar with the whole of Jonson's career senses a tension between the Elizabethan structure of the play and the Jonsonian reluctance to inhabit that structure. Although Jonson seems to have tried, he could not bring himself to write a Shakespearean comedy.

§ I I

The Case Is Altered looks very much like a play composed by someone familiar not only with Shakespeare's style but with specific texts. Virtually all of Shakespeare's comedies before 1597 contain situations, characters, themes, phrases, and dramatic effects that have found their way somehow into Jonson's first effort.[18] The play offering the fewest resemblances, as one might expect, is *A Midsummer Night's Dream:* although Jonson had not yet developed his strict understanding of mimesis, there were limits to his flexibility and willingness to experiment, even at this early stage. Other comedies, however, abound with possible parallels. In *Love's Labor's Lost*, for instance, broken vows provide the central conflict, most memorably in the serial capitulation of Berowne, King Ferdinand, Longaville, and Dumaine to the urgings of Cupid. Jonson contrives just this kind of symmetrical structure (although with only one object of affection) as Onion, Christophero, Ferneze, and Angelo follow Paulo in declaring their love for the beggar's daughter. The wit and good sense of the Princess of France and her ladies offer a pointed contrast to the frivolity and inconstancy of the gentlemen; so do the virtues of Aurelia and Phoenixella in *The Case Is Altered*. Shakespeare's concern throughout *Labor's* with the abuse of language—in the empty words of the young men's vows, the heroic and amorous rhetoric of Don Armado, the scurrilous jokes of Boyet, the pompously declaimed errors of Holofernes, and the dullness of Dull—offered a model for treating the topic comprehensively, and Jonson is almost equally thorough. Angelo's promises to Paulo prove meaningless; Ferneze's blessing on Christophero's desire for Rachel is immediately contradicted by the count's own attempts on her; and the French pages who speak impossible English are less ridiculous than Juniper with his preposterous diction and literary pretensions. In building the dramatic tension that will be released with the return of Chamont and Paulo, Jonson arranges a kind of fugue in which the analogous stories and cognate themes are assembled and exhibited:

> Count.   O my sonne, my sonne.
> Chris.   My deerest *Rachel.*
> Jaq.   My most hony gold.
> Count.   Heare me *Christophero.*
> Chris.   Nay heare me *Jaques.*
> Jaq.   Heare me most honor'd Lord.
> Max.   What rule is here?
> Count.   O God that we should let *Chamount* escape.
> Chris.   I and that *Rachel,* such a vertuous mayd,
>   Should be thus stolne away.
> Jaq.   And that my gold,
>   Being so hid in earth, should bee found out.
> Max.   O confusion of languages, & yet no tower of *Babel!*
>   (v.xi.18–26)

Jonson's feast of languages may not be as bountiful as Shakespeare's, but his topic is identical and his dramatic address to the problem similar. The Lord Chamberlain's Men seem to have revived *Labor's* in 1597, and it is difficult to imagine that Jonson did not know it.

The relationship between *The Case Is Altered* and *The Two Gentlemen of Verona* is even more arresting. The first major conflict to arise in Jonson's comedy, Angelo's treachery to Paulo, calls to mind the main action of Shakespeare's first romantic comedy, Proteus's betrayal of Valentine. This set of resemblances is so striking that it has received a good deal of attention; Anne Barton, for instance, thinks that Jonson was directly alluding to *Two Gentlemen,* using the reference to Shakespeare's amorous entanglements as a kind of shorthand for the love story he did not want to write.[19] Both Angelo and Proteus are entrusted with the secret of their friends' love for Rachel and Silvia; both determine to disregard friendship and to woo the ladies for themselves; both enlist the aid of yet another suitor (the hapless Christophero and Thurio); both deceivers are caught by the original lovers in the act of attempted seduction; and both Angelo and Proteus repent and receive pardon.[20] To be sure, the differences in the two actions cannot be dismissed: Rachel is a "beggar's daughter," Silvia a lady; Silvia sets out to find her lover, whereas Rachel is hoodwinked. There is nothing in *The Case Is Altered* to match the famous crux in *Two Gentlemen* where Valentine after the discovery seems to offer Silvia to Proteus, causing Julia to faint. Indeed, there is no Julia in Jonson's play. Another major distinction is that Proteus in two soliloquies struggles with the moral dilemma of duty versus passion, while Angelo spends his one soliloquy justifying his easily formed intentions:

> True to my friend in cases of affection?
> In womens cases? what a jest it is?
> How silly he is, that imagines it!
> (III.i.6–8)

Although this passage may echo Proteus's "In love, / Who respects friend?" (v.iv.53–54), Proteus is morally a more sensitive figure, at least at first.[21] Yet these two tales, despite particular differences, are remarkably alike in general shape, and even in some important details.[22]

The story of Paulo, Angelo, and Rachel is, as I have suggested, the most important feature of *The Case Is Altered* for which Jonson's Roman sources do not supply a precedent. *I Captivi* offers the positive instance of Chamont's fidelity to Camillo, and it may be that Jonson, requiring a contrary example to fit his pattern of balances and oppositions, found a ready-made story of infidelity in Shakespeare's early comedy. The main subject of *Two Gentlemen* is the power of love: Julia's selflessness, Silvia's constancy, Valentine's friendship, and Proteus's wild passion represent some of its forms. The central issue in *The Case Is Altered,* on the other hand, is fidelity. Thus, whereas Proteus deceives his friend and his betrothed, Angelo has no lover to betray (although we hear of his reputation as a womanizer). Shakespeare uses his four lovers to explore the nature of love, and in his depiction of the mischief it can generate, Proteus is the central figure. Jonson alters the emphasis and broadens the scope, inventing various examples of constancy and infirmity. Already Jonson has begun to reshape borrowed material to his own distinctive purposes, but there can be little doubt that, in this case at least, the material is borrowed, and borrowed from a distinguished if unlikely source. Finally, could Garlique, Jaques's unseen but dreaded mastiff, have been suggested by Crab?

Shakespeare casts his shadow over *The Case Is Altered* in other ways, general and specific. Jonson was interested always in the kinds of foolishness with which Shakespeare had made his comic fortunes. The two Dromios in *Errors,* Tranio, Gremio, and Grumio in *Shrew,* the mechanicals in *Dream*—all these servants may have served as models for Onion and Juniper. Of course, comic fun at the expense of servants is hardly an Elizabethan innovation, but Shakespeare and his contemporaries apparently found themselves with a lively market for these types, and Jonson obliges. The double plot in *Shrew* is much more carefully unified in subject and theme than is Jonson's, in that it presents two views of courtship, with two different suitors and two very different ladies; but it may have taught Jonson about amplitude and thematic elaboration. More specifically, the union of two Roman plays with which Shakespeare began his comic career in *Errors* was almost surely a spur to the novice in search of a story. The case of a father fretting over his daughter and his ducats is familiar to us, and *The Merchant of Venice* may have been in the repertory of the Lord Chamberlain's Men when Jonson was preparing *The Case Is Altered.* With this comparison we arrive at a gray area concerning specific works that Jonson might have known. But my aim has not been to document specific echoes; rather, it has been to describe Jonson's comedy in context. Dating aside, *The Case Is Altered* would not be out of place in a discussion of *Much Ado, As You Like It*, or *Twelfth Night.*

§ III

Still, for all its romantic conventions, its Elizabethan amplitude, its love story, and its harmonious ending, *The Case Is Altered* cannot be mistaken for a Shakespearean comedy: it lacks the comic spirit which imbues such plays as *Love's Labor's Lost* and *Much Ado About Nothing*. In other words, Jonson has apparently employed the forms of New Comedy without subscribing to the conception of experience appropriate to those forms, and I would suggest that this reserve accounts for the perfunctory quality, what we might even call the lifelessness, of *The Case Is Altered*. It is easy to appreciate the tendency of commentators to focus on the satiric vignettes in the subplot. There, one hears Jonson speaking *in propria persona*, or at least with the tones that would soon make his work instantly recognizable. But in much of the play Jonson is imitating the voice of another. We may consider, for example, the significant role of accident, which is at least as important here as it is in most of Shakespeare's romantic comedies. Jonson seems unsure of what to think: he does not deny the importance of luck in the outcome of events, but neither does he emphasize it. A pertinent counterexample might be the end of *Twelfth Night*: there, a dramatist committed to the meaning of his story—that "tempests are kind"—asks us to accept the incredible, mocks us for doing so, and thereby makes us believe all the more surely. In other words, whereas Shakespeare calls attention to the benevolent dexterity of Providence, Jonson seems a little embarrassed at the whole idea.[23]

Even more revealing is Jonson's hesitant approach to the matter of disguise in the captive plot. The fundamental issue here is identity: Chamont plays Gasper, Gasper plays Chamont, and Gasper without knowing it plays Gasper, since he is really Camillo. Yet Jonson's treatment of this fruitful theme is almost entirely literal. His characters make very little of the metaphysical implications of their false personae; soliloquies offer information, not introspection; assumed identities are hardly more than convenient devices for amusing the audience. The pedestrian quality of the role-playing here becomes all the more obvious when we compare the practice of an author who really means it: when we re-member the psychological confusion suggested by Antipholus of Syr-acuse's first soliloquy about the search for family and the loss of self; or think of the symbolic range and wealth of meaning associated with Rosalind's costume in the forest of Arden; or consider the way that deception becomes a synecdoche for imaginative creativity in the likes of Petruchio or Portia or Viola. Although Jonson manages to explore the thematic connection between linguistic indecorum and social or finan-cial overreaching, his vehicles are Onion and Juniper and his means negative and satiric. With the women of *The Case Is Altered,* one senses again that the playwright is fulfilling an obligation without endorsing the meaning of his choices. In the final moments he arranges the two marriages with hardly a hint of lyricism. (The ending also leaves us with one woman and a crew of men who do not get married.) The reunions do not provoke the wonder that they might be expected to. When "Jaques" confesses that he is the faithless steward Melun and "Rachel" the kidnapped Isabel, the first three responses are not from predictable sources:

> *Max.*   Stay *Jaques* stay! the case still alters?
> *Count.*   Faire *Rachel* sister to the Lord *Chamount?*
> *Ang.*   Steward your cake is dow, as well as mine.
> (v.xii.100–102)

Finally Paulo speaks, but Chamont's expected rejoinder is never deliv-ered, for Onion and Juniper immediately enter as gallants, and the possibilities for a joyful tone are dissipated. The conclusion exhibits a structural assurance: Jonson has effectively arranged the discoveries and cleverly juxtaposed the endings of the various stories. But he refuses to dwell upon the possibility of rebirth or hope for the future or of follies discarded and illusions dispelled. He will not allow the audience to share in the emotions—indeed, he refuses to express the emotions—that these denouements ought naturally to inspire.

This tension between letter and spirit reveals itself even in the title of *The Case Is Altered.* The repetition of the phrase produces considerable merriment as it is applied to different situations, passing from character to character as if through the sections of an orchestra; and such witty play with word and theme constitutes an early version of Jonson's skill at unifying his actions with an idea or image.[24] But does he mean it? Anne

Barton thinks not: "Only in terms of plot can the final episode of *The Case Is Altered* be said to crown the play as a whole. It provides no fewer than five opportunities for characters to remark pointedly that 'the case is altered,' as discovery crowds upon discovery. But it is in no sense a Shakespearean vantage point, a place from which the various betrayals and the suffering of five long acts can be reinterpreted and understood."[25] The alteration of external cases does not make for fundamental changes in human character or behavior, and we notice here the conservative skepticism that will become one of the informing principles of Jonson's mature works, such as *Sejanus* and *Epicoene*. Alteration, change, amendment, progress—these are the ideas implicit in the plots and endings of New Comedy. Shakespeare, in choosing and developing the stories of the Greek romancers and Plautus and their Renaissance adapters, commits himself to a progressive, favorable view of human relations: the actions of his plays are arranged so as to alter the case to suit the wishes of his characters. The world is tractable; confusion is temporary; obstacles can be overcome. But the positive developments at the end of Jonson's first comedy lack emotional force. If we try to think seriously about what we have seen, we find little reason to hope that Ferneze will become less irrational, that Angelo will become an honorable man, that Juniper and Onion will be cured of their follies. Even at the beginning of his career, Jonson does not buy such a positive assessment of experience. Only the case is altered; nature remains the same.

CHAPTER 2

Fie on Sinful Fantasy

The Merry Wives of Windsor and Every Man in His Humour

In turning from *The Case Is Altered* to *Every Man in His Humour*, Jonson undertook to write not only for Shakespeare's audience but also for Shakespeare's company and, in a practical sense, for Shakespeare himself. The Lord Chamberlain's Men presented *Every Man In* in 1598, probably in the autumn, and Shakespeare acted in the original performances.[1] This first of the humour comedies is noticeably more "Jonsonian" than its predecessor: there is less emphasis on story, more on peculiarities of character; the tone has become more assured and more nearly satiric; the young playwright is beginning to recognize the theatrical as well as the moral value of deviance. And yet in this last respect *Every Man In* is noticeably less Jonsonian than its successors: its point of view is not so ironic; its fools and follies are less alarming; its ending is more conventional than those of the masterpieces to come. Although he escaped the tyranny of unsuitable form that had troubled him in *The Case Is Altered*, Jonson was still laboring under the influence of contemporary comic formulae; he had yet to reconcile the discrepancy between the implications of his imagined actions and the meaning of his normative resolution. This undeveloped state of his artistic vision imparts to *Every Man In* a rare geniality and places it on the margins of what we call Jonsonian comedy. In such an anomalous position it invites comparison with *The Merry Wives of Windsor*, a play that exhibits a similarly marginal relation to the mode known as Shakespearean comedy. The comparison is especially pertinent because at the thematic center of both dramas is the transformational power of the human mind. Imagination can convert faithful wives into whores, servants into spies, honest suitors into thieves, cowards into heroes, buffoons into Romeos, earnest sons into delinquents, men into beasts, words into poetry, incident into art, Mistress Quickly into the Fairy Queen, bushes into bears. Each text depicts a range of imaginative activity, from the delusory to the creative; scrutinizes and evaluates virtually every character on the basis of imaginative gifts and their management; presents major and minor actions explicitly as products of the imaginative faculty; and establishes as absolute the correspondence between command of imagination and command of speech. The memorable figures in the two casts (Falstaff, Ford, Thorello, and Bobadilla) are those whose fancies possess them, but in both plays certain ingenious figures (Mrs. Ford and Lorenzo Junior) put their talents to constructive use. Moreover, parallel themes have, in this case at least, generated comparable dramatic strategies. Both dramatists devote most of their energy to portraiture; although there is much scheming and intricate action, the plots are little more than showcases for the display of imaginative talents and inadequacies, particularly verbal ones.

Above all, the dramatic tone cultivated by each dramatist seems unusual. *The Merry Wives* lacks a Rosalind or any central charismatic figure with whom the audience is encouraged to sympathize or identify; the severely abbreviated love story is eclipsed by intrigue and buffoonery; variety of incident is neglected in favor of repetition (the threefold humiliation of Falstaff); and the audience remains mostly detached, responding with the scornful laughter that Aristotle and Sidney had prescribed for comedy but to which Shakespeare rarely confined himself. If the tone of *The Merry Wives* is unusually monochromatic and ironic for Shakespeare, that of *Every Man In* is surprisingly balanced for Jonson. This comedy smiles at most human failings, presents a poet-hero with whom viewers are expected to sympathize (and usually can), concludes with his marriage feast, and stimulates an uncommonly tolerant appraisal of these actions and actors. Jonson works for once in the normative mode: although his satiric bent makes its presence felt from time to time, he creates a fiction in which virtue and wit are not only

extant but even triumphant.[2] And Shakespeare, having become engaged
by folly of an especially vivid and pervasive kind, departs temporarily
from his development of the romantic mode. Thus, *The Merry Wives*
and *Every Man In* stand close to the center of a comic scale, near each
other and at one remove from their makers' characteristic forms.

Notwithstanding the various similarities and unusual emphases I
shall propose, there is still a vast difference between Florence and Windsor, and in juxtaposing these texts I hope not to deform either. From title
to final scene, each play reveals the unmistakable hand of its creator.
Shakespeare's English comedy may not be as romantic as some of those
that surround it, but it is not virulently satiric either. Having developed
and ridiculed the delusions, vanities, and errors of his *dramatis personae*, Shakespeare still holds to his characteristic comic ending in which
recognition and a hopeful tone combine to affirm man's capacity for
amendment and happiness. We laugh at the characters' foibles without
taking them very seriously. Similarly, *Every Man In* may not be as
critical as the comical satires and great middle comedies, but it is not
romantic either. Although Jonson ends with reconciliation and a marriage feast, he cannot suppress completely the early manifestations of
that moral outrage that will shortly make him famous. For all his evident pleasure in the idiocies of his characters, he finally loses patience
with them, punishing the worst offenders and doubting the ability of the
lesser fools to make good on their enlightenment.[3] Although Jonson is
less pessimistic than he will become and Shakespeare rather less san-
guine than usual in comedy, each dramatist is recognizably himself.
Having confessed these fundamental distinctions, however, we must
also allow that *The Merry Wives* and *Every Man In* share a dominant
theme and ask their audiences to take a similar point of view toward it.

Recent scholarship, moreover, suggests a tantalizing chronological
proximity. The most careful students of *The Merry Wives*—William
Green, H. J. Oliver, and Jeanne Addison Roberts—all believe that
Shakespeare composed it for performance at court on April 23, 1597,
perhaps at the request of the queen but in any case to honor the company's patron, George Carey, Lord Hunsdon and recently lord chamberlain, upon his election to the Order of the Garter.[4] If the proposed
new date is accurate—and the evidence for the hypothesis does seem
persuasive—then the impulse to connect *The Merry Wives* with Jonson's early work in comedy becomes practically irresistible. We are

33

ignorant of the circumstances that led Jonson to write for the company, but the novice would have been familiar with his sponsors' recent productions. Perhaps he tailored his first venture for them to suit the comic style of the house dramatist, and possibly he composed with one eye on *The Merry Wives*, one of the last comedies staged by the company before he set to work on *Every Man In*. Critics who believed, perhaps still believe, that *The Merry Wives* was written later, around 1600, often concluded that Shakespeare was mocking Jonsonian practice.[5] It now appears that the notice may have worked the other way around and that Jonson's interest in *The Merry Wives* was not parodic but straightforward. In other words, although the terms of the connection must remain uncertain, it is possible that the characters and actions of *Every Man In* are the way they are because Jonson observed Shakespeare's practice in *The Merry Wives*.[6] What seems indisputable, however, is the host of technical resemblances and shared ideas, and an account of these indicates that Shakespeare's and Jonson's comic styles are not invariably worlds apart.

§ I

In the second part of *The Advancement of Learning*, Sir Francis Bacon develops a political metaphor to describe the operation of the human imagination, figuring it as an "ambassador" between "the judicial and the ministerial" offices of the mind.[7] In other words, our will presents to our reason images of its desires for the purpose of probation, and these are either approved or dismissed according to the dictates of judgment. Thus, the imagination may be an independent and unscrupulous agent that bullies the reasonable judge into endorsing the outrageous claims of the will, or it may be a reliable and witty officer that mediates fairly and helpfully in the contest between desire and judgment. Bacon's metaphor provides a useful introduction to the treatment of imagination in *The Merry Wives* and *Every Man In*, as well as to the two playwrights' concern with the topic in all phases of their careers. Although Jonson peoples his mature comedies with victims of imaginative perversion, Shakespeare normally balances delusion with ingenuity, a Viola for a Malvolio. Here both dramatists investigate a broad range of imaginative activity, both positive and negative, but their triumphs are the portraits of fancy run amok.

The jealousy that leads Ford and Thorello into absurd error is the product of "a strange and vaine imagination" (*EMIH*, iv.iii.34–35), and both playwrights reiterate such explicit descriptions so often and so emphatically that their thematic centrality quickly emerges. "This is fery fantastical humours and jealousies" (*Merry Wives*, iii.iii.158); "Why, this is lunatics; this is mad as a mad dog" (iv.ii.115); "Master Ford, you must pray, and not follow the imaginations of your own heart: this is jealousies" (iv.ii.143–45)—notwithstanding Parson Evans's Welsh accent, his diction is typical of that by which the various dramatic commentators identify and ridicule the mental disorder afflicting both husbands: "imagination," "fancy," "fantasy," "lunacy," "madness." The most detailed is Thorello's own analysis of how jealousy "doth infect / The houses of the braine" (i.iv.207-17), corrupting "the fantasie," "the judgement," "the memorie," and "every sensive part." The Renaissance conception of mental physiology in which this discussion is grounded and which used to dominate discussion of Jonsonian psychology is less important than Thorello's emphasis on the susceptibility of the imagination to abuse.[8] Once infected, the husbands see what they wish to see and persuade themselves that they are obeying the dictates of reason.

The inventive faculty sustains itself by giving its possessor unbounded confidence in his powers of penetration. He becomes adept at wordplay, at perceiving hidden meanings, and at reading texts so as to support his interpretation of the facts. When Thorello's wife and sister compliment Lorenzo Junior, he overreads their words with absolute assurance:

> Fayre disposition? excellent good partes?
> S'hart, these phrases are intollerable,
> Good partes? How should she know his partes? well, well:
> It is too playne, too cleare.
> (iii.iv.194–97)

Thorello's rampant imagination "sees" a concrete noun ("partes") where an abstract one is intended. This emphasis on special sight, on the clarity of the evidence, is one way in which both dramatists call ironic attention to the visionary propensities of their dreamers. The images passing through these overheated brains are uncommonly strong. Ford, plagued by nightmares, ridicules the insensitivity of the reasonable Page.

The slightest word is apt to trigger his visual and aural senses, as when he detains the servant with the "buck-basket" and makes much of the suggestive sounds: "Buck? I would I could wash myself of the buck! Buck, buck, buck! Ay, buck; I warrant you, buck; and of the season too, it shall appear" (III.iii.145–47).

The imaginative hypersensitivity on which the dramatists concentrate gives to their characters an eidetic quality, a gift for visualizing scenes reported or only suggested. When Cob dutifully announces that some five or six gallants have arrived at the house, Thorello reacts with "A swarme, a swarme, / Spight of the Devill, how they sting my heart" (III.iii.8–9). When Cob objects that he "heard not a word of welcome," Thorello invents a lurid scene:

> No, their lips were seal'd with kisses, and the voice
> Drown'd in a flood of joy at their arrivall,
> Had lost her motion, state and facultie.
> (III.iii.27–29)

Jonson's most pointed reference to the pictorial power of the unhealthy mind occurs in Thorello's response to a conversation between Biancha and Prospero. When she chastises Thorello for quarrelling with Giuliano, pleading that "harme might have come of it," Prospero ridicules her concern with ludicrous suggestions of what "might" happen (that her husband's clothes or dinner wine might be poisoned), sarcastic postulates that carry the weight of fact with the suggestible Thorello:

> Now God forbid: O me? now I remember,
> My wife drunke to me last; and changd the cuppe,
> And bad me ware this cursed sute to day.
> (IV.iii.19–21)

After this outburst, which continues for several lines, Hesperida seeks to calm her brother: "The strength of these extreame conceits will kill you" (IV.iii.30). And Prospero identifies precisely the fantastic nature of Thorello's and Ford's malady when he asks incredulously, "Will he be poisoned with a similie?" (lines 33–34). Their minds are so sensitive to visual stimuli that they can be slain with words.

It is appropriate that those whose imagination creates their misery should devise imaginative schemes to escape the snares they imagine to have been set for them.[9] In effect, these unconscious makers of fictions consciously turn themselves into playwrights and actors. Shakespeare's development of this histrionic bent is more complete than Jonson's, for Ford's stratagems are more extravagantly theatrical, especially his charade as Master Brook. He imagines and impersonates a disappointed suitor of the chaste Mrs. Ford, a fully developed character whose nature is antithetical to his own: poetic in love, verbally expansive, generous with bribes ("There is money; spend it, spend it, spend more; spend all I have" [II.ii.223–24]), and patient in hearing Falstaff's tirade against the obtuse Master Ford. Once persuaded of his wife's treachery, Ford assumes a role requiring no costumes or props, the meaty part of the wronged husband, with an emotional range that moves from self-pity to knowing sarcasm to commanding rage. His impersonation of the counterplotting cuckold builds to a climax in his extended fantasy of a lavish, public self-vindication (III.ii.34–44). Lying behind the imagined retribution are the imagined wrongs he has suffered, and the theatrical argot ("plots," "cue," "praised") and the sense of a performance before spectators expose his imaginative turn of mind.

Jonson develops this metaphor less exhaustively than Shakespeare, but clearly he has conceived the character as performer. Thorello from his first entrance thinks of himself and presents himself to the audience as a clever deceiver. With windlasses and assays of bias, he devises rational arguments calculated to hide his irrational fears, but the fact of his jealousy eventually emerges from the many subordinate clauses and the tortuous syntax. Throughout the comedy Thorello feels compelled to "set a face on't to the world" (I.iv.158), and he does so most ingeniously in the great scene with Piso (II.i), when he craftily tries to enlist his servant as a spy without telling him too much.[10] Throughout the interview Jonson conveys the sense that Thorello acts the part of a character known from the stage, the shrewd intriguer, a role subsumed in the part of the betrayed husband, for which Thorello, like Ford, knows the dialogue and the blocking. He reaches his histrionic peak before the crowd assembled at Cob's house as he becomes increasingly knowing, sarcastic, and self-righteous. These connections between Thorello and Ford are given a bizarre twist when we recall that Lorenzo Senior, whom Thorello attacks as "this hoary-headed letcher, this olde goate," may have been acted originally by William Shakespeare himself.

Extremists such as Thorello and Ford are especially useful to the comic playwright because they lack faith in humanity. It is not accidental that they keep themselves apart from the rest of the cast and speak frequently in asides and soliloquies: structure creates meaning in that dramatic separation signifies personal and social isolation.[11] Self-absorbed, lost in a world of figures, literally out of touch, these egoists threaten the spirit of mutuality and interdependence that comedy, even critical comedy, seeks to promote. The corollary to their sense of their own acumen and solitary rectitude is doubt about everyone else's intelligence and morality. By definition wives are slippery, servants are untrustworthy, and husbands—all but one—are wittols. Such a cynical, mechanistic conception of all human affairs is a comic version of the creed espoused by Iago and Edmund: the simple act of touching hands is to Thorello "a monstrous thing," marriage is "hell," "opportunitie" the only prerequisite for female wickedness, and human nature merely a congeries of bestial instincts. Another way of putting it is to say that Ford and Thorello see the world through the eyes of the most critical comic or satiric dramatist. They have no faith in our positive impulses.

Shakespeare at this point does retain such faith, and his depiction of Ford's awakening leads us to believe that the imagination has been cleansed and that the husband has reestablished his trust in his wife and his species: "Now doth thy honour stand / In him that was of late an heretic, / As firm as faith" (IV.iv.8–10). Nevertheless, there is room for doubt about the endurance of Ford's conversion, for vanity and self-delusion are shown to be potent forces, and the main action establishes and depends upon Falstaff's pattern of recidivism. Just a few lines after Ford's apology, Evans doubts that Falstaff can be duped a third time: "Methinks his flesh is punished, he shall have no desires" (IV.iv.23–24). This is wishful thinking; Shakespeare encourages measured faith in man's nature, not idolatry. Jonson's treatment of Thorello in the last act suggests a willingness to believe in man's power to know and to right himself: the foolish husband apologizes to Biancha and professes to "have the faithfulst wife in *Italie*." But his manner of confession, the poem concluding that "*Hornes in the minde, are worse then on the head*," implies a continuing obsession with cuckoldry and stimulates doubt about his imaginative health. Anne Barton surveys the ambiguities of this recantation and concludes that while the shape of events in the last scene would appear to endorse Thorello's alteration, "Jonson . . . cannot really bring himself to do the few things which would make such a movement of mind seem convincing."[12] The difference between Ford's and Thorello's reformations reflects the difference between the endings of the two plays generally and between the dramatists' different conceptions of the relation between folly and corrigibility. Shakespeare, although critical, is hopeful; Jonson, although he would like to hope, is dubious.

§II

Master Ford is so memorable—he seems to have engaged Shakespeare more thoroughly than any other figure—because his wild fantasies and the verve with which he declares them help to establish the leading themes of The Merry Wives: the comic dangers of imagination, its susceptibility to misuse, and the connection between linguistic and imaginative ability. The familiar view of this comedy as a slight entertainment offering rollicking action and some lovable characters has been eloquently challenged by William Carroll:

We must recognize that one of the major subjects of The Merry Wives is the use and abuse of the imagination. In its relation of Ford to Falstaff, in its inventive verbal style, and in its metaphors of playacting, the play first qualifies and then vindicates the power of the imagination to shape, even to transform "reality," and then identifies this power with the more obvious power that every dramatist wields. I believe these subjects of interest link the play with the mainstream of Shakespeare's work, and that the play's consignment to the backwaters of criticism has been unjust.[13]

To admit Shakespeare's emphasis on the "equivocal, subversive power of the imagination"[14] and to appreciate his linguistic exploration of the idea are to give The Merry Wives a chance at artistic respectability.

The play's main action, the triple gulling of Falstaff, is generated by the old fool's inflated conception of his own gifts, particularly physical attractiveness and superior wit. Vanity moves him to imagine that others see him as he sees himself: "Briefly, I do mean to make love to Ford's wife. I spy entertainment in her" (1.iii.40–41). Falstaff is adept at creative misreading of his text, and his linguistic metaphor ("I can construe the action of her familiar style") is a signal that speech and imagination are part of the same process. But he translates tendentiously, as Mistress Page declares when she reads his letter: "What an unweighed behaviour hath this Flemish drunkard picked—with the devil's name—out of my conversation, that he dares in this manner assay me?" (II.i.22–25). Recognizing that Falstaff's self-love, a product of his unregulated imagination, has provoked his attempt at seduction, the wives draw upon their own ingenuity to dupe him with a series of theatrical schemes. They cast themselves in conventional parts, Mrs. Page as the frustrated housewife unable to escape the watchful eye of her tyrannical husband, Mrs. Ford as the "sweet woman" who, in Quickly's words, "leads a very frampold life with" a "jealousy" spouse. The imaginative nature of their "plot" is apparent in the language with which they prepare for Falstaff's first visit:

> Mrs. Ford. Mistress Page, remember you your cue.
> Mrs. Page. I warrant thee; if I do not act it, hiss me.
> (III.iii.33–34)

The second visit concludes with their costuming Falstaff as "the witch of Brentford," transforming him into a familiar Elizabethan character; and the wives must summon up their improvisational skills to integrate their unexpectedly returning husbands into the skit. Their final device is a theatrical extravaganza, a full-scale play-within-the-play complete with legendary characters, a magical setting, and a large cast including children dressed as fairies. Imagination here works constructively, as illusion is used to dispel Falstaff's illusory sense of himself.

Ford's imaginative, histrionic nature is responsible for the first subplot, his intrigue to entrap his wife and Falstaff, and Shakespeare links it to the main story by deliberately connecting Ford's and Falstaff's imaginary conceptions of themselves. As Carroll puts it, "Ford and Falstaff have parallel but reversed expectations. In his delusion, each entertains a sexual dream,"[15] Ford a nightmare of adultery and Falstaff a vain hope of gratification. The parallelism is most illuminating in their scenes together, where they reinforce each other's roles. Ford encourages Falstaff in the part of roué, and Falstaff makes Ford into a wittol:

> Ford.   I am blest in your acquaintance. Do you know Ford, sir?
> Falst.   Hang him, poor cuckoldy knave, I know him not.
> (II.ii.257–59)

The second subplot, the marriage of Fenton and Anne Page, is likewise a product of its protagonist's imagination, and it too involves a secret plot, careful timing, and theatrical costume. The lovers reject the two scripts devised independently by Master and Mistress Page and substitute their own, transforming Fenton into the romantic lead and the competing suitors into buffoons. And thus Shakespeare knots together by means of theme the three major strands of action.[16]

The language spoken in *The Merry Wives*—perhaps "languages" would be the better term—is treated specifically as a branch or function of the imagination. Effective speech becomes a synecdoche for controlled imagination, and thus the verbal confusions of the minor figures reinforce and supplement the imaginative disorders of the major players. Almost everyone in the comedy talks often *about* language, and this emphasis attests to Shakespeare's interest in something more than farcical action. Even so astute a critic as Leo G. Salingar depreciates the importance of the words: "For the most part, the dialogue has very little of the inner richness and significance of Shakespeare's mature comedies; it simply adds zest to the intrigue."[17] I am persuaded, on the contrary, that the variety of dialects, the abundance of linguistic invention, and the constant chatter about words make language one of the play's chief concerns. The Latin lesson Parson Evans gives young William, occupying an entire scene (IV.i) and contributing nothing to the action, amplifies the central theme of language and its imaginative sources.[18] The jokes arising from Parson Hugh's tutelage, William's recitation, and Quickly's misprision are calculated to show that speech is a slippery instrument, that language measures imaginative balance, and that words, like wives, may be easily misunderstood. Thus, the tutorial is analogous to the interview between Prince Hal and Francis in *1 Henry IV*: linguistic poverty is a sign of imaginative destitution.[19] Here, however, Mistress Quickly adds an additional layer in seeing more than she should in the words she hears, and precisely the same kind of error leads to Ford's humiliation.

Shakespeare's most useful vehicle for linking language and imagination is Falstaff. The relation of words to wit is vital to *1 Henry IV*, where a prodigious imagination permits Falstaff both to create fictions (the men in buckram suits) and to stage them (his impersonation of the king), with words as his only medium. Falstaff in the comedy may not be as invariably amusing, but even here his verbal skills are impressively displayed under the stimulus of pride or the pressure of distress. Shakespeare calls attention to Falstaff's powers of invention at his first entrance, when in response to Shallow's charges, Falstaff retorts with a terse and rare confession: "I will answer it straight: I have done all this. That is now answered" (1.i.107–8). This startling tack, in which the self-justification is reduced to a short sentence, reverses the expansive and hyperbolic strategy used against Prince Hal in the tavern: in both cases, however, the "trick," the "device," the "starting hole," is unlooked-for, and his ingenuity at disarming opponents is one of Falstaff's greatest gifts. Falstaff is the consummate performer, and Shakespeare establishes the imaginative quality of his talent by underscoring his self-consciousness. He revels in puns, amusing turns of phrase, and outlandish images: "Such Brooks are welcome to me, that o'erflows such liquor" (II.ii.145–46); "Well, if I be served such another trick, I'll have my brains ta'en out and buttered, and give them to a dog for a New Year's gift" (III.v.6–8). Both these jests, located in soliloquies, arise from Falstaff's direct communication with the audience. His self-consciousness heightens the comedy of the second interview with Master Brook, when Falstaff narrates the watery climax of his assignation with Mrs. Ford (III.iv.85–108). Falstaff has found himself in the Thames because he has trusted the dictates of his own unruly imagination and thus fallen prey to the superior wits of Mrs. Ford and Mrs. Page. Yet that same imagination is able to transmute with mere words and images an actual calamity into a triumphantly comic narrative.[20] Which is what Shakespeare himself has done, converted the antics of the merry wives into *The Merry Wives*.

To Shakespeare's treatment of the possibilities of language—its value as a creative instrument and its vulnerability to abuse—his minor players are indispensable.[21] They do little to drive the plot; instead, they augment Shakespeare's critical survey of the consequences of abused fancy by commenting on the vain excesses of Falstaff and the rampages of Ford. And their commentary itself becomes a subject of comment. In the final scene, Falstaff characteristically replies to one of Parson Evans's nearly incomprehensible but risible gibes: "Have I lived to stand at the taunt of one that makes fritters of English?" (v.v.143–44). The familiarity of the phrase—few who write on the play can keep from quoting it—indicates its general application. Virtually every one of the minor characters is distinguished by a trick of speech, in most cases mainly and in some cases only by this. The Welshman's "fritters" are matched by the gaffes of Doctor Caius, about whose diction Quickly forewarns us:

"Here will be an old abusing of God's patience and the King's English" (1.iv.4–5). She is hardly in a position to cast stones, for she too contributes some howlers, particularly her remark on the "erection" (direction) of Mrs. Ford's admirers. Pistol's bombastic phrases, while not as extreme as in *Henry V*, stand out even in this gallimaufry of styles, and Nym is famous for his addiction to the word "humour," a habit that leads the plain-speaking Page to remark, "Here's a fellow frights English out of his wits" (11.i.134–35).

The "ranting Host of the Garter" (as Page calls him) typifies the collective contribution of the minor figures. The affected, pleonastic style of his initial conversation establishes the passion for words that his every appearance will sustain.

> *Falst.* Mine host of the Garter!
> *Host.* What says my bully rook? Speak scholarly and
> wisely.
> *Falst.* Truly, mine host, I must turn away some of my
> followers.
> *Host.* Discard, bully Hercules, cashier: let them wag;
> trot, trot.
> *Falst.* I sit at ten pounds a week.
> *Host.* Thou'rt an emperor, Caesar, Keiser, and Pheazer.
> I will entertain Bardolph; he shall draw, he
> shall tap. Said I well, bully Hector?
> *Falst.* Do so, good mine Host.
> *Host.* I have spoke; let him follow. [*To Bard.*] Let me
> see thee froth and lime. I am at a word; follow. *Exit.*
> (1.iii.1–14)

The Host possesses a wild enthusiasm for the possibilities of language but lacks the taste to control it, and his eccentricities differ from Quickly's or Evans's in proceeding not from ignorance but from that more dangerous thing, a little learning. If a word is not repeated exactly ("trot, trot"), it is followed by a superfluous synonym ("discard . . . cashier"). Consciousness of style overwhelms the nominal subject: many of the sentences contain verbs concerned with speech ("says," "speak," "said," "have spoke"), and the speaker is always eager to observe the effect of his linguistic prowess ("Said I well?"). His obsession is not limited to his own words: he delights in mocking Caius with antonymous definitions, tells Simple that Falstaff will "speak like an Anthropophaginian" to him, and wonders if the Germans "speak English?"

Lack of discipline, whether with words or with imagination generally, is the source of virtually all the comic conflict and is the topic that unifies the major and minor plots and characters.[22] Evans's and Caius's understanding of English is about as accurate as Falstaff's understanding of himself or Ford's of his wife, and Mistress Quickly's skirmishes with her native tongue (not to mention Latin) work in the same way. The Host lacks the sense to restrain his speech; Slender has no imagination and therefore no conversation; the limitations of Nym's mind appear in his verbal fixation; and William's rote repetition of Latin signifies his childish lack of penetration. Shakespeare connects these various failings in a crucial place, at the end of the masque, where the errors are summarized and, insofar as is possible, every man is brought out of his humour:

> *Evans.* Sir John Falstaff, serve Got, and leave your
> desires, and fairies will not pinse you.
> *Ford.* Well said, fairy Hugh.
> *Evans.* And leave you your jealousies too, I pray you.
> *Ford.* I will never mistrust my wife again, till thou
> art able to woo her in good English.
>
> (V.v.130–35)

Words themselves are images of reality, and the misconstruction of both produces the chaos that produces the delights of *The Merry Wives*.

§III

Imagination is as surely the central theme in *Every Man In* as it is in *The Merry Wives*. That poetry is one of Jonson's chief concerns here is well known: indeed, the comedy may be regarded as Jonson's defense of poetry. But poetry alone is not the only issue, and critics who make it the primary subject must then pronounce much of the action irrelevant.[23] Many go on to argue that Jonson discovered his gift for satiric characterization while composing the work and was finally incapable of reconciling theme and method. But these alleged inconsistencies diminish if poetry is considered a branch of the larger topic of creativity and its various manifestations. Jonson places poetry in this context in the first lines of the opening scene, when Lorenzo Senior complains about his son's singleminded devotion to books:

My selfe was once a *student*, and indeede
Fed with the selfe-same humor he is now,
Dreaming on nought but idle *Poetrie:*
But since, Experience hath awakt my sprit's,
And reason taught them, how to comprehend
The soveraigne use of study.
(1.i.16–21)

The fond father's concern about his child's preoccupation, "the vayne course of study he affects" (line 10), illuminates the relation between poetry and dreams and, in Baconian language, introduces the judicial function of reason. The structure of the drama is arranged to display the rich bounty of fruits that imagination may yield—some wholesome, some poisonous, some deformed, some extremely tasty—and poetry is one of her choicest products.

In the gallery of characters whose actions represent these imaginative products, Lorenzo Junior occupies a central position, thanks to his passion for poetry.[24] But this aesthetic impulse is only one feature of his artistic sensibility and is accompanied by and related to an appreciation for physical beauty. It is significant that the young man courts a mistress and a muse, and in similar terms. He "stands very strongly affected towardes" Hesperida (IV.iii.110), just as he "affects" the study of verse (1.i.10). Still another dimension of the artistic sensibility, revealed in Lorenzo Junior's encounters with Matheo, Bobadilla, and Stephano, is his capacity for recognizing foolishness, for distinguishing between pretension and substance. By encouraging these *"Zanies,"* ridiculing them, and helping to expose their vanities, Lorenzo Junior and Prospero stand for the comic playwright, perceiving the gulls' foibles and developing them for the sake of amusement.[25] This motive is inherent in Prospero's invitation to Lorenzo Junior to join him in town—"I thinke I have a world of good Jests for thee" (1.i.153–54)—and the conversion of a group of fools into a world of jests constitutes an imaginative act equivalent to the transformation of words into poetry or action into theater. The two friends are surrogates for Jonson's audience as well, understanders and spectators; they are able to identify and judge the follies of a vain world and able at the same time to appreciate and learn from them, and the evidence of this process is scornful laughter. The artistic quality of their cony-catching appears in Lorenzo Junior's introduction of Stephano to Prospero: "Oh sir a kinsman of mine, one that may make our Musique the fuller" (II.iii.57–58).

The poet's opposite number is Matheo, whose most striking characteristic is imaginative penury. He is not utterly bankrupt, a distinction belonging to Stephano, for at least he has the wit to aspire, but his reach hopelessly exceeds his grasp. Matheo wishes to play the roles filled by Lorenzo Junior—poet, lover, and witty gentleman—but his attempts only expose his capacity for mimicry, affectation, and witlessness. At first there is a kind of naive charm about Matheo, like the sophomore who proclaims himself a "poet," and Jonson has fun with his postures. Calling on Bobadilla at Cob's house in I.iii, Matheo exhibits his odd vocabulary ("doest thou inhabit here Cob?"); warped syntax ("*Cob* canst thou shew me, of a gentlemen, one Signior Bobadilla, where his lodging is?"); affectation of foreign terms ("bastinado"); admiration for bad literature, particularly *The Spanish Tragedy,* especially the lines that had already become clichés; false humility covering pride and probably literary theft ("a toy of mine in my nonage"); love of fashion (his remarks about boots and hangers); and worship of a poseur ("He lodge in such a base obscure place as thy house? Tut, I know his disposition so well, he would not lie in thy bed if thould'st give it him"). That Matheo sets his amorous cap for Hesperida, whom Lorenzo Junior ultimately wins, points the contrast between lover and pretender, poet and poetaster.

Jonson links Matheo and Lorenzo Junior specifically in that Matheo's corruption of divine poetry— "Poetry? nay then call blasphemie, religion; / Call Divels, Angels; and Sinne, pietie"—prompts Lorenzo Junior's passionate justification of the real thing. The genuine poet identifies what Matheo lacks, the imaginative sources of poetic inspiration, when he describes poesie's "peculiar foode, / Sacred invention" (v.v.321–22). Doctor Clement's formal interrogation is designed to show not only that Matheo is incapable of poetic creation but also that he lacks the wit to steal what Jonson considered good poetry: he is attracted only to the most popular works of the age, *The Spanish Tragedy, Hero and Leander,* sonnet sequences, and ballads. By means of the jokes about "translation" (the fool's euphemism for theft), "invention" (Prospero plays on *invenire* [found] when he says "No this is invention; he found it in a ballad" [v.v.299]), and "conceit" (lines 300–303),

46

Jonson rehearses the theme of imaginative infertility. But for all the mirth Matheo inspires, he is finally shown to be a plagiarist, and Jonson, refusing to deal lightly with theft, lingers over his humiliation in the final scene.

Bobadilla, whom Matheo apes and with whom he is cast out of the play, puts vast imaginative energy to ridiculous use. The parallels between Bobadilla and Falstaff are almost as striking as those between Thorello and Ford: both are soldiers, braggarts, and cowards descending from the Plautine *miles gloriosus,* behave contentiously, take advantage of their hostesses, attract a retinue of followers with their charismatic personalities, display a monstrous vanity, and fascinate the audience with exceptional verbal dexterity proceeding from imaginations of almost limitless wealth. Falstaff—even Falstaff of *The Merry Wives*—is more various, fully realized, and dramatically imposing than his Jonsonian counterpart, but both serve their creators as representatives of creative talent gone bad. Bobadilla's way with words impresses not only those who idolize him but even those who see through him. The former wish to emulate him; the latter encourage him because they wish to hear more from the speaker whom Jonas A. Barish has called the "fountainhead of eccentricity," the embodiment of what Jonson refers to in *Discoveries* as "the wantonnesse of language" denoting "a sicke mind."[26] It is no accident, I think, that Bobadilla's most memorable speeches, those in which his mad creativity is given full play, are prompted by questions from the poetic "hero" of the comedy: Lorenzo Junior employs his artistic sense constructively, committing himself to poetry and to marriage, while Bobadilla squanders his verbal talent in vanity and fraud.

One of Bobadilla's gifts is an infallible ear. His sensitivity to nuance is established in his first conversation, when he queries Matheo's complaint that Giuliano has threatened to give him "the bastinado":

Bob.   How, the bastinado? how came he by that word trow?
Mat.   Nay indeed he said cudgill me; I tearmd it so for
       the more grace.
Bob.   That may bee, for I was sure it was none of his word.
       (1.iii.174–79)

Bobadilla catches the inconsistency because he possesses a dramatist's instinct for matching speech to speaker, and from it he has synthesized a unique style for himself out of hackneyed oaths and bits of jargon from the duello. The rhythms of his self-introduction to Stephano indicate that his bizarre style is dramatically conceived: "Signior, I must tell you this, I am no generall man, embrace it as a most high favour, for (by the Host of Egypt) but that I conceive you, to be a Gentleman of some parts. I love few words: you have wit: imagine" (II.iii.72–75). Such stylistic alertness governs his use of invective, as when he attacks the departed Cob as "A horson filthy slave, a turd, an excrement" (III.ii.117). The gulls are most impressed with his talent for swearing, and in a single scene (II.iii) he speaks the following oaths: "As sure as God," "as I have a soule to bee saved," "by *Phoebus*" (twice), "by the host of Egypt," "by Phaeton," "upon my salvation," and, most ironic, "as I am a gentleman and a soldier."

Bobadilla's persona of hero and worldling is self-created, a function of a theatrical sense that refuses to observe the distinction between fiction and experience.[27] His recitation of his exploits at "the beleagring of Ghibelletto," for instance, is an artistic creation forged apparently out of nothing.[28] His prodigious gifts of invention also produce the brilliantly delivered proposal for the defense of the state with (besides himself) a mere nineteen men:

Say the enemie were forty thousand strong: we twenty wold come into the field the tenth of *March*, or thereabouts; & would challendge twenty of the enemie; they could not in their honor refuse the combat: wel, we would kil them: challenge twentie more, kill them; twentie more, kill them; twentie more, kill them too; and thus would we kill every man, his twentie a day, thats twentie score; twentie score thats two hundreth; two hundreth a day, five dayes a thousand: fortie thousand; fortie times five, five times fortie, two hundreth dayes kills them all, by computation, and this will I venture my life to performe: provided there be no treason practised upon us. (IV.ii.74–86)[29]

The mechanical progress of the style suits the mathematical precision of the scheme, but the strategist's exactitude is subverted by arithmetical error, and his delicate structure rests precariously upon the uncertainty of the final subordinate clause. Bobadilla's imagination has run riot, inventing not only a vision of success and glory, but a style to express and a self to perform it. Fortunately Bobadilla commands the imaginative resources to shield himself from his own cowardice and to transform it, for the benefit of the credulous, into wisdom; he protects himself from the truth by drawing upon an enormous fund of vanity. As he says of the fencing masters, "They hate me, and why? because I am excellent, and for no other reason on the earth" (IV.ii.36–37). When threatened by Giuliano, Bobadilla responds by attempting to deny the evidence of the senses ("Its not he: is it?"), and unable finally to escape humiliation, he looks to the supernatural: "I cannot tell; I never sustayned the like disgrace (by heaven) sure I was strooke with a Plannet then, for I had no power to touch my weapon. *Exit*" (IV.ii.124–26).[30] This flat, matter-of-fact defense, another case of answerable style, is calculated to reduce the humiliation to an event of little significance.[31] It is also a Falstaffian maneuver. But for all the parallels, we must differentiate between the two braggarts. Bobadilla seems to lack Falstaff's knowing manner, the self-consciousness that almost always preserves the audience's good will. And Jonson finally ejects Bobadilla from the comedy; Shakespeare, in *The Merry Wives* at least, is more tolerant.[32]

Just as Bobadilla is a descendant of the Roman braggart, so Musco is Jonson's version of the clever servant. In adapting this figure Jonson clarifies the defense of wit implicit in the Plautine slave's ingenious plots. Musco's artistic bent first manifests itself when the trickster enters disguised as Portensio, the mendicant soldier, and comments on the irony: "S'blood, I cannot chuse but laugh to see myselfe translated thus, from a poore creature to a creator; for now I must create an intolerable sort of lies, or else my profession looses its grace" (II.ii.1–4).[33] Echoing the jokes in Prospero's letter about the poet as father of lies, the passage links the young master, the devotee of "divine poesie," with the servant who applies his imagination to a less exalted form of art. After deceiving both son and father as Portensio, Musco looks for "another tricke to act yet" (IV.i.55): in the last two acts he usurps Peto's role of Doctor Clement's clerk and then, as an officer, claims Giuliano at the suit of Bobadilla and Matheo, and arrests Stephano for stealing Giuliano's cloak. These last performances are peppered with short soliloquies, asides, and bits of stage jargon, and Lorenzo Junior even offers a theatrical review of Musco as Portensio, commending "so speciall and exquisite a grace, that (hadst thou seene him) thou wouldst have sworne he might have beene the Tamberlaine, or the Agamemnon of the rout" (III.ii.19–22).

Musco's caprices represent the sportful value of the imagination, its power to divert, since self-interest and profit mean less to him than pleasure in fantasy: he pawns the clerk's suit not for money but for a varlet's uniform to perpetuate the jest. One measure of Musco's thematic significance is that in his various roles he interacts with every male in the comedy, and Jonson arranges these encounters so as to juxtapose genuine wit with its counterfeit or its opposite. After easily baffling Stephano in the first scene, Musco makes his way to town where, as Portensio, he toys with Lorenzo Senior and thus exposes the shortcomings of the careful father's practical, pedestrian mind. (The most telling moment occurs when "Portensio" suggests that Musco might have given away the old man's scheme, a form of ironic self-revelation that presages the comic risks of *The Alchemist*.) He is one of the witnesses at Matheo's laughable courtship of Hesperida: although Musco speaks no lines, Jonson seems to have felt that his wit makes him a fit spectator at this display of stupidity, a worthy fellow of Lorenzo Junior and Prospero. "Portensio"'s recitation of military exploits ("I was twise shot at the taking of Aleppo") must call to mind the similar inventions that Bobadilla seeks to pass off, but with a difference: Bobadilla's heroic fiction is a desperate act of self-promotion, a wasteful product of pride, while Musco's tale of woe is consciously entertaining and its effect ultimately altruistic. With the possible exception of Thorello, Musco displays the most active imagination in the comedy. Whereas Thorello is the victim of his fancies, Musco is usually the master of his, but the thrill of success makes him careless. Jonson's unfailing sense of artistic discipline cannot allow such self-indulgence to flourish without limit; and thus, in the role of the officer, Musco loses control, must resort to a hectic improvisation in the episode of arrests and counterarrests, and admits to having "made a fayre mashe of it" (v.ii.74). At the same time the playwright's admiration for Musco's wit remains undiminished. This mixed response is reflected in Doctor Clement's sentencing him to a jail term and then pardoning him. Musco's offenses pale in light of his talent and its diverting achievements.

Jonson's concern with the uses of the imagination touches virtually every member of his cast. Prospero initiates the day's amusement, arranges the marriage of Lorenzo Junior and Hesperida, and conceives of the scheme to thwart the opponents of the marriage. His letter of invitation, written in an outlandish prose style which disgusts Lorenzo Senior, promises imaginative satisfactions in town and urges ingenuity in getting there: "*Sblood, invent some famous memorable lye, or other, to flap thy father in the mouth withall: thou hast bene father of a thousand,*

in thy dayes, thou could'st be no Poet *else*" (1.i.56–58). Prospero's elder
brother, Giuliano, is his opposite number in his taciturnity; his Folio
name, Downright, establishes his limitation.[34] He has no imagination,
wants none, cannot understand it. In the last scene he fails to see that
Matheo is being mocked: "Call you this poetry?" (v.v.304). Piso seems
equally obtuse, apparently failing to understand Thorello's elaborate
ruses for deceiving him. Cob's mind, to put it charitably, is merely
disordered, his recitation of his lineage an ingenious mess. Doctor
Clement is that ideal figure with whom Jonson would later dispense,[35]
but his presence here indicates that imagination in general, not just
poetry, is the overriding issue in *Every Man In*. Although he can twit
Matheo with doggerel and distinguish genuine poetic art from specious,
his most notable trait is his regulated imagination. All his judgments are
predicated on his respect for wit and creativity: fancy must be tempered
with reason. The justice's harshness with Bobadilla and Matheo is probably a function of Jonson's emerging didactic bent and artistic inex-
perience: the desire for a normative conclusion accounts for their ejec-
tion from the final scene. (In the Folio version, Jonson softens the
penalties.) The key to Jonson's theme is Clement's treatment of Musco.
The last lines of the comedy are given over to the justice's praise of the
ingenious servant, after which the two depart together, leaving us with
an image of imagination conjoined with judgment.

§IV

To find that Shakespeare and Jonson both treat the topic of imagination
is less surprising than to discover that they take almost the same attitude
toward it. *The Merry Wives* and *Every Man In* challenge our preconcep-
tions about each playwright's characteristic tone and the differences
between them. In both these comedies the primary dramatic effect is
Olympian irony, and the audience's response to each may be fairly
described as mirth with a generous quotient of scorn. This brand of
irony is uncharacteristic for Shakespeare: having placed the audience in
a superior position, he has discouraged sympathetic involvement with
his characters and emphasized, even magnified, the ridiculousness of the
action.[36] I do not wish to revive the familiar taxonomic debate (is the
play a farce or not?), a problem whose answer depends almost entirely
on the definition of terms.[37] Nevertheless, we recognize a fundamental

difference between our reaction to this comedy and, to choose a contemporary text, *Much Ado About Nothing*. The tone of *Every Man In*, similarly, is almost thoroughly ironic, and for the same dramatic reasons: at almost every point our awareness of events and their implications surpasses that of most of the characters. The major benefit of our complicity with Musco in the execution of his schemes is scornful laughter at the gulls. Jonson thus creates the kind of ironic distance that Shakespeare flirts with in *The Merry Wives* and that will be essential to the success of Jonson's great middle comedies. But whereas Shakespeare's tone is more ironic and derisive than we might expect, Jonson's is more tolerant and positive than it will become.

The tonal resemblance is a function not only of the dramatists' manipulation of ironies but also of their having subordinated the romantic strain in the stories they tell. For Shakespeare, such a tactic was a major departure from his usual approach: the only courtship that matters in *The Merry Wives* is Falstaff's grotesque attempt on the wives. Anne Page is most valuable as the object of Slender's preposterous affections, not Fenton's, for the genuine lover uses his imagination not to rhapsodize on his beloved but to devise a trick to steal her. Their "love scene" (III.iv) is almost perfunctory: its twenty-one lines are given mainly to the young man's laments about parental objection and to Anne's cautious answers; his one amorous declaration is a brief financial metaphor, " 'tis the very riches of thyself / That now I aim at" (lines 17–18). Significantly, Fenton's "wooing" quickly dissolves into the buffoonery of Slender's advances. The love story adds one more disguise plot to the collection of entertaining masquerades; more than anything else it provides an excuse for the elopement of Slender with a "lubberly boy" and Caius with "un paysan, by gar, a boy." The marriage in *Every Man In* receives equally minor treatment: Lorenzo Junior's courtship of Hesperida matters less theatrically than Matheo's idiotic effort. And yet this love story, insignificant though it is, is given more attention than in most of Jonson's plays. For all the irony, the two courtship plots function positively, illustrating the triumph of natural affections over irrelevant parental claims and providing a standard against which to judge the buffoons. Jonson follows Shakespeare in contrasting genuine amorous feelings with improper motives: Lorenzo Junior is to Fenton as Matheo is to Slender. Although the two fools woo the young ladies for different reasons—Matheo because fashion dictates and Slender because his uncle shoves him—their attempts are similarly illegitimate and risible. Elizabethan comedies ended in marriages, and the young Jonson was not yet an iconoclast, but the marriage is not merely a fulfillment of a convention: the attraction of Lorenzo Junior and Hesperida represents an imaginative impulse that Jonson recognizes and approves, even if he is not much interested in it.

Its subject makes *The Merry Wives* congruent with Shakespeare's contemporary work. In *A Midsummer Night's Dream* the failure of figures such as Theseus and Bottom to appreciate the power of the imagination promotes the creative value of fantasy. *Love's Labor's Lost* (which the Chamberlain's Men apparently revived in 1597) confronts the problem of affectation, with inflated language signifying an exalted sense of one's own powers. And each work in the Great Tetralogy—on which Shakespeare seems to have interrupted work to write *The Merry Wives*—encourages multiple perspectives on the values and perils of imagination in politics.[38] Around the same time also comes *Much Ado*, in which the issues of imagination, language, fidelity, self-deception, and pride are carried even further. But the critical tone makes *The Merry Wives* distinctive. Here the major figures are fools, and irony attends virtually every member of the cast except Mrs. Ford and perhaps Anne. The constructive power of wit rests chiefly with the wives themselves, whose merry schemes bring on recognition and apology but cannot efface from our consciousness the foolish and ugly delusions of Falstaff and Ford. Although it has been asserted that this work represents an important stage in the "feminization" of Shakespearean comedy,[39] these "heroines" scarcely bear comparison, in wit or charm or any other such gifts, with a Rosalind or Viola. In *The Merry Wives* the imagination is mainly deceptive, and while Shakespeare balances the many instances of abused imagination with implicit reference to his own brilliant performance, he is less interested in the creative power of the mind than in its liability to perversion. This is hardly a dark comedy or a problem play, but the view of imagination urged upon us is noticeably more qualified, less optimistic, less reassuring than we expect from Shakespeare. His normal tonal balance has not been upset completely, but there is more scorn than usual. Perhaps it is not too much to say that *The Merry Wives* may be seen, as *Much Ado* or *2 Henry IV* must be seen, as a station on the way to the tragedies, where the hazards and rewards of great imagination receive their most sophisticated and meaningful treatment. And even if this reading is too dark, we must admit that the comic style in *The Merry Wives* is un-Shakespearean: the usual subject of the comedies is courtship, and when we look at who is courting whom and consider the result, we see that this play represents something of a digression.

If Shakespeare's tone is unusually scornful, Jonson's is uncharacteristically positive. Jonsonian comedy usually puts imaginative abuse or duplicity at center stage. Puntarvolo's medieval-romantic fantasy of courtship, Captain Tucca's bizarre and compelling speech, Sejanus's deadly manipulation of his enemies, Volpone's multiple impersonations (invalid, mountebank, officer, dead man), Sir Epicure's pornographic visions of pleasure—these are the memorable portraits of imagination in action. The representatives of disciplined creativity (Crites, for instance) fade next to their dazzlingly wicked counterparts, as Jonson recognized when, after *Poetaster*, he abandoned virtue for virtuosity. *Every Man In* applauds the properly managed poetic impulses of its young hero and the benevolent impostures of his servant, and it asks us to endorse the final concord. Thus, it stands apart from the main corpus of Jonson's work. For example, the only real point of resemblance between *Every Man In* and his next effort, *Every Man Out*, is their titles. The first is a humour comedy, the second a comical satire, and they have almost nothing else in common. I do not mean to depreciate Jonson's doubts about his fellow beings or to deny the force of his comic attack, for he is nothing if not critical, even in *Every Man In*. The final scene suggests, perhaps in spite of itself, that Jonson himself is dubious about the promise of reform, and he is harsh with those he thinks truly incorrigible. One senses a tension, less crippling than in *The Case Is Altered* but palpable nonetheless, between Jonson's inchoate satiric perceptions and Elizabethan comic fashion, as if he is of two minds about his happy ending. But there is no denying the mirth that the play creates. The ironies are less sharp than they might be, the attacks less ferocious than they will become, and the point of view admits hope and even geniality.

§ V

Reading these two plays together discloses the limitations of the orthodox categories of romantic and satiric comedy.[40] The connections and resemblances I have described suggest that these rubrics probably ought to be replaced with a horizontal scale at the opposite ends of which would stand Shakespeare's most romantic comedy, perhaps *As You Like It,* and Jonson's most critical, almost certainly *Volpone.* This kind of sliding scale would reflect more faithfully the scope of which both artists are capable and would allow greater precision in the placement and description of comedies where the artistic emphasis or method is undeveloped or simply odd. Predictably, the works that might float near the center of a horizontal line are those neglected by critics seeking to define either comic style: a great many books on Shakespearean comedy omit or make short work of *The Merry Wives,* and much criticism of *Every Man In* concerns itself with Jonson's later efforts to revise it in light of his mature practice. A more fluid system of description would be useful in reducing our critical prejudices. Although Shakespeare's versatility has rarely been challenged, his reach toward the critical is sometimes underrated; and in Jonson's case, "flexibility" and "balance" are not the first words that come to mind. Removing the old barrier between the two styles of comedy gives greater definition to the actual borders and also brings to light distinctive properties of individual works.

That neither comedy ranks with its author's greatest achievements is hardly news: both dramatists, for whatever reasons, were attempting something different from what they did best. Jonson was hoping to establish himself with audiences who knew what they wanted, and he did not yet know his own mind. Shakespeare's brief detour from the path of romantic comedy is somewhat harder to explain. Perhaps in light of the recent hypothesis about the Garter celebration, the old-fashioned idea that he was fulfilling a royal request is not so far-fetched after all.

CHAPTER 3

Unstable Forms

1599–1604

The turn of the seventeenth century marked the beginning of a transitional phase for Shakespeare and Jonson. The artistic visions of both
playwrights began to darken appreciably, and their changing views were
accompanied by major revisions in their mimetic strategies. Between
1599 and 1603 Jonson moved from the qualified affirmation of *Every
Man In* to the almost unrelieved pessimism of *Sejanus*, a shift that
amounts to a movement from youth to maturity, since the "vision" of
the early dramas is incompletely developed. His medium for this passage was comical satire, that mixed form combining disgust at human
weakness with hope for amendment. Shakespeare at roughly the same
time (say from 1600 to 1604) proceeded from the comic to the tragic
phase of his career, advancing through a series of tragedies and dark
comedies, each displaying the influence of the complementary mode.
His darkening vision, by contrast, represents an exchange of one mature
conception for another, the affirmation of the romantic comedies for the
skepticism of *King Lear* and *Macbeth*. This period of experiment was
characterized by an intense concentration on the means of representation: works as different as *Cynthia's Revels* and *Hamlet* are plays with
much to say about, among other things, plays. Changing views led the
two artists to consider many of the same themes: the weaknesses of
mortality, especially the perils of pride and nearly irresistible claims of

56

the flesh, the ease with which evil overwhelms or traduces virtue, the baselessness of hope, and the corruptibility of language. This gradual disillusionment produced a series of unstable dramatic forms devised to accommodate the developing points of view. A host of internal and external forces must have inspired these shifts in artistic direction— Jonson's artistic growth, Shakespeare's exhausting the possibilities of romantic comedy, the War of the Theaters, demands of the box office, biographical circumstances, the new philosophy, politics (particularly the matter of succession), Jonson's skill as a self-promoter, the available personnel, both artists' reading, and any number of factors we can know nothing about. I do not offer to suggest causes. But the texts created during this phase record that Shakespeare and Jonson were both impelled towards new forms of expression by an increasingly negative appraisal of the human creature and its capacity for error and evil.

§ I

About 1599 the work of both playwrights begins to manifest an extraordinary self-consciousness, a reflexivity suggesting a reconsideration of the purposes and value of dramatic fiction in human affairs.[1] The theory of the theater and the ways of the imagination had always been matters of concern to both artists, but beginning with *Every Man Out* and perhaps *Henry V,* Jonson and Shakespeare appear to think more critically about their own imaginative endeavors, considering more frequently and intensely what they did for a living, the best way of doing it, and the value of doing it at all. Jonson for the first time indulges his passion for extradramatic features—inductions, prologues, plays-within-plays, stage commentators, authorial spokesmen, epilogues— all tactics calculated to guide the audience's response towards the actions and persons represented. Shakespeare, ever the more reticent artist, discloses his self-scrutiny more obliquely, by means of metaphors, internal performances both formal and informal, and digressions that do not seriously damage the dramatic illusion. The principle that texts with a high degree of self-consciousness tend to emerge from periods of literary experiment and change is as true in little as it is at large: a work with a high degree of self-referral suggests that its creator is engaged in a reconsideration of artistic means.[2] Moreover, such dense commentary on the dramatist's craft is consistent with the formal innovations, mixed modes, and oscillation between kinds that distinguish both playwrights' work at the time.

The abundance of extradramatic devices accompanying *Every Man Out, Cynthia's Revels,* and *Poetaster* is mainly responsible for our impression of Jonson as egoist, moralist, and didact. While such devices permit remarks on any number of topics, their primary concern is drama itself, its proper forms and functions. The mode of comical satire, a product of Jonson's powers of moral and dramatic invention, was new to audiences, and so in *Every Man Out* Jonson used the introductory matter and choric intrusions to defend the play's unprecedented style and to orient the audience morally and aesthetically.[3] The induction establishes the illusion that two playgoers await a performance of a new work called *Every Man out of His Humour,* and this frame contains several sections: the commentators' discussion with Asper (the "presenter"); their conversation, after Asper's exit, about the history and kinds of dramatic comedy; their dispute with a character called "Prologue" over who will introduce the play (ironically, nobody does); the appearance of Carlo Buffone, who talks about the author but then becomes a fictional character; a summary of these events by Cordatus and Mitis; and notice of "your envious man."[4] By the time Macilente takes the stage for the first scene proper, some 370 lines and about fifteen minutes of playing time have passed, most of it devoted to Jonson's justification of his form and cultivation of an atmosphere of criticism.[5] As the play develops, the repeated interjections of Mitis and Cordatus sustain this critical climate and keep before us the problem of satiric mimesis.

In *Cynthia's Revels* neither induction nor epilogue is as copious or complex as in *Every Man Out,* but here too the primary topics are Jonson's artistic standards and his contempt for dramatists who do not share them. The lengthy preparatory scene introduces a child who, purporting to speak for the spectators, defends the unconventional dramatic structure; this cunning piece of flattery is especially meaningful, since *Cynthia's Revels* was Jonson's first effort for the private theater.[6] The peculiarly Jonsonian combination of confidence and suspicion appears in the epilogue also. The speaker announces that his creator is "jealous, how your sense doth take / His travailes," and after dismissing possible reasons for the audience's disfavor, repeats "what I have heard him say; / By (———) '*tis good, and if you lik't, you may*" (lines 3–4, 19–

20).[7] The play itself, even more than its predecessor, promotes the expository and corrective powers of art. The boy actors in the induction having promised a kind of pageant, Jonson delivers a panorama of courtly follies annotated by figures who mingle with and comment on the fools. The dramatic language reiterates the theatrical dimension of all experience: shadow is distinguished from substance, acting from being, and virtually all the actions serve to develop the multiple meanings, specious and substantial, of words such as "play," "acting," and "courtship." The concluding masque, composed by Crites at the request of the idealized monarch, is an image of the play in which it appears, Cynthia's Revels in *Cynthia's Revels,* and succeeds as Jonson hopes his pageant will succeed, exposing and curing narcissism and stupidity.

Poetaster, the most intensely self-conscious of the three, is a poetic fiction about poets and poetry in which the artists and pretenders of antiquity stand not only for all poets and poetasters but also for Jonson and his theatrical competitors. As Jonson's final blast in the War of the Theaters,[8] *Poetaster* attests to his obsession with the effect of his work, although the personal dimension has probably been overrated. The "poeticall banquet" of gods and goddesses, at which the poetasters and their ladies amuse themselves in act 4, illustrates the abuse of literary gifts even as it proves the power of drama to uncover truths about human nature (when Albius, Tucca, and Chloe enact Vulcan, Mars, and Venus). But the personal and theoretical were never far apart in Jonson's thinking about the theater, a point demonstrated in Captain Pantilius Tucca's encounter with the Roman actor. Depending upon quotations from contemporary plays, gibes at companies such as Pembroke's, the Admiral's, and the Chamberlain's Men and at individual members, and a host of in-jokes, the episode reinforces Jonson's high seriousness about drama even as it lets fly at his enemies:

TUCC. And what new matters have you now afoot, sirrah? ha? I would faine come with my cockatrice one day, and see a play; if I knew when there were a good bawdie one: but they say, you ha' nothing but *humours, revells,* and *satyres,* that girde, and fart at the time, you slave.

HIST. No, I assure you, Captaine, not wee. They are on the other side of *Tyber:* we have as much ribaldrie in our plaies, as can bee, as you would wish, Captaine: All the sinners, i' the suburbs, come, and applaud our action, daily. (III.iv.187–96)

With a deft, ironic hand Jonson differentiates, tendentiously of course, between his own moral art in the private theaters and the attractions of the popular Bankside companies (although it is instructive to recall that *Hamlet* was then being acted across the Thames). The self-absorption that sounds throughout the comical satires reaches its climax in an audaciously original form, the "Apologeticall Dialogue" spoken after one performance of *Poetaster*.[9] Jonson here dispenses with surrogates or agents and, even though the Author's part was presumably spoken by an actor, puts himself on the stage to defend himself and his satiric method. This appendix provides a fitting conclusion to the series of comical satires. *Every Man Out* had begun with a lengthy playlet contrived to introduce and justify Jonson's new dramatic form; the "Dialogue" supplies clarification and further defense. Neither piece of apparatus seems to have worked, as the immediate direction of Jonson's career indicates, but this last effort at self-justification offers final evidence, if any is necessary, that the most important topic in Jonson's comical satires is comical satire. Sometimes critics seem to believe all art to be concerned mainly with art, but in Jonson's work at the turn of the century the claim is incontestable.

Shakespeare's dramatic self-consciousness at this time is, characteristically, less obvious than his colleague's, especially since Jonson was then engaged in some of the most vigorous self-promotion of his career. Beginning about 1599, however, the idea of *theatrum mundi* comes to inform Shakespeare's works even more significantly than before, and self-referring devices such as prologues and epilogues, plays-within-plays, schemes discussed in theatrical terms, and metaphors of playing become more abundant and prominent.[10] Fabian's famous joke in *Twelfth Night*—"If this were played upon a stage now, I could condemn it as an improbable fiction"—is the most pointed instance of a strategy that supports the play's obsession with role-playing, affectation (conscious and unconscious), and counterfeit words and feelings.[11] *Troilus and Cressida*, in the process of revising one of the most famous episodes in Western literature, bombards its audience with deflationary histrionic metaphors, offering characters who play parts, devise plots or miniature dramas, describe the spectacle of processions and battles, and remark disparagingly on the performances of others.[12]

> Sometime, great Agamemnon,
> Thy topless deputation he puts on,

> And like a strutting player, whose conceit
> Lies in his hamstring and doth think it rich
> To hear the wooden dialogue and sound
> 'Twixt his stretch'd footing and the scaffoldage,
> Such to-be-pitied and o'er-wrested seeming
> He acts thy greatness in.
> (1.iii.151–58)

Although the dramatics here are conscious, the play's theatrical texture is devised primarily for the benefit of the audience, as in Cressida's surrender to Diomedes: the lovers are secretly observed by Ulysses and Troilus, who are witnessed by Thersites, who is seen and heard by the audience. By such reflexive means *Troilus and Cressida* questions the correspondence between art and truth and thus subverts its own mimetic potentiality. Such explicit concentration on the theater is nowhere more noticeable than in *Hamlet*—from the initial distinction between feeling and playing through the gravediggers' division of an "act" into three kinds, to the final concern for the onlookers, the "mutes and audience to this act"—but in this respect *Hamlet* is only typical of the phase in which it was composed.[13]

Such passionate interest in the theory of dramatic art indicates concern about its function and worth. In this phase of Shakespeare's career, the vocabulary of the theater, which in earlier works resembles any other metaphor—say, of disease or duelling—now becomes an essential element in the meaning of the drama. Another way of putting it is to say that Shakespeare has become as interested in the vehicle of the metaphor as in the various tenors to which it is applied, so that the distance between subject and means begins to diminish and dramatic art ceases to be merely a way of elucidating a topic but becomes itself a part of the topic. Much the same might be said of those Jonsonian fictions which address themselves directly to the problems of faithful representation and which are supplemented by prologues, interloping scenes, and other such commentary. Shakespeare's thinking about his medium never seriously endangers the theatrical worlds he constructs, whereas Jonson, at least in this period, rarely allows his fiction to assume enough life to endanger his pronouncements on fictional art.

Once it is granted that Shakespeare was searching for a new artistic path and Jonson was struggling to find his way professionally, a major distinction is still to be made between their attitudes towards their art. A corollary to the difference between Jonson's relative newness to the theatrical scene and Shakespeare's considerable experience in it, this distinction is simple but perhaps surprising: around 1600 Jonson's faith in the possibilities of drama seems much firmer than Shakespeare's. All the Shakespearean texts in these years stress the perils of imagination and the limitations of the "unworthy scaffold." Helena in *All's Well* or Vincentio in *Measure for Measure* may use imaginative means to bring order to chaos, and there is a sense in which the dramatic artifact itself— the story of Hamlet as passed on by Horatio—furnishes imaginative reassurance.[14] At the same time, however, evidence of alarm repeatedly asserts itself, in Iago's frightening abuse of histrionic ability, in Claudius's skill at dissembling, and even in the ambiguous imaginative faculties of Hamlet and Othello themselves. The performances within plays at this period are almost all unsettling, from Hamlet's antic disposition to the bed tricks to Ulysses' stunt against Achilles. Such acts and the works that contain them imply that the successful playwright, with ten years of experience and numerous masterpieces behind him, may have begun seriously to doubt the revelatory and constructive powers of fiction. His junior colleague, meanwhile, is full of zeal for his art. The virulent anatomy of human folly for which the comical satires are notorious coexists with an active faith in the heuristic capacities of the stage. Jonson is well aware of the dangers of play-acting, as the strutting of his fools indicates, and yet each of the dramas moves confidently towards affirmation. The various artistic stratagems employed in *Every Man Out*, the masque in *Cynthia's Revels*, and the virtues embodied by a few of the Romans in *Poetaster* attest to the dramatist's positive thinking about his medium. This is what Gabriele Bernhard Jackson means when she writes about the "mandatory optimism of satire."[15] Jonson has yet to accept the distinction between art and life acknowledged in Miss Prism's account of her own novel in *The Importance of Being Earnest:* "The good ended happily, and the bad unhappily. That is what Fiction means." In their views on the theater at the end of the Elizabethan era, Shakespeare seems closer to the conventional description of Jonson, and vice versa.

§11

The darkening visions suggest themselves immediately in the subjects picked for dramatic treatment. Shakespeare turns with increasing frequency to tragic stories. Even in his late efforts at comedy, however, a new emphasis on failure and weakness distinguishes these tales of love and courtship from those dramatized in *Dream* or even in *Much Ado*. Whether the play is *Othello* or *All's Well*, tragedy or comedy, the audience is forced to concentrate on obstacles to love, the frailty of the flesh, the failure or perversion of reason, and the potency of evil. Although virtue may finally be rewarded, as it is in *All's Well* and *Measure for Measure*, the uncertainty of the "happy endings" means that all comic values, even marriage itself, are scrutinized with a skeptical eye. Although Jonson relies more upon portraiture than dramatic narrative, the skits and tableaux that make up his plots present extreme forms of the follies that absorbed Jonson everywhere, from *Every Man In* to the antimasques of his royal entertainments to the *Epigrams* and lyric poems. Both dramatists create a series of commentators—Thersites, Macilente, Lavatch, Crites, Lucio, Buffone, Iago, even Hamlet—who appraise their fellow beings in tones of doubt and even contempt and who dwell on similar issues: the prevalence of self-absorption, pride, and hypocrisy; the force of bestial instincts, particularly the sexual; the inadequacy of idealism in the face of physical truths; the unreliability of language; and the liability of the imaginative faculty to abuse. Shakespeare reveals a new fascination with death, which invades even the comedies of this period and presses itself upon the spectator as it has not done in earlier plays. Jonson at the same time creates powerful images of death-in-life. Both dramatists lament the tendency of man's baser instincts to tyrannize the nobler. Speaking of *All's Well*, G. K. Hunter describes an "intimate connection (and not only in this play) between the theological view of man as a fallen creature . . . and an uninhibited revelling in the sordidness of his fallen state."[16] Such a divided response to human failings informs virtually all the plays of both authors around and just after the turn of the century. Their caustic observers speak partial truths, for neither Shakespeare nor Jonson had abandoned belief in the potential dignity and spiritual power of mankind. But the eloquence of the doubtful voice implies grave difficulty in maintaining that faith.

The increasing prominence of the physical is apparent, to take a simple instance from *All's Well*, in the remarks of Lavatch, whose trick is scatological equivocation: Parolles is "a pur of Fortune's" (a piece of animal excrement or the knave in a pack of cards) and a "carp" (a fish bred in a manured pond); the message he brings is "a paper from Fortune's close stool." Their exchange (v.ii) owes its nastiness to Lavatch's contempt for Parolles, but throughout the play Lavatch offers an estimation of mankind that, while neither as topsy-turvy as that of Lear's fool nor as viciously set forth as that of Thersites, is very grim indeed. Through him Shakespeare stresses the qualities that cause man, this time in Parolles' words, to be "muddied in Fortune's mood, and smell strong of her displeasure" (v.ii.4–5). This conception of the human dilemma, if not quite as brutal, is akin to the mechanistic philosophy of Iago.[17] Both in comedy and tragedy, the reductive viewpoint is given strong expression; it manages to hold its own against the contrary view and such exemplars of that view as Helena, Desdemona, and the heroes; it is and is not the view of Shakespeare himself. There is a sense in which even Hamlet, whatever else he may be, is the "quintessence of dust." Like Shakespeare's observers, Jonson's satirists sometimes embody depravity even as they expose it. Macilente describes Buffone as

> an open-throated, black-mouth'd curre,
> That bites at all, but eates on those that feed him.
> A slave, that to your face will (serpent-like)
> Creepe on the ground, as he would eate the dust;
> And to your back will turne the taile, and sting
> More deadly then a scorpion:
> (*EMOH*, 1.ii.231–36)

Envious motive cannot negate the truth of this ugly portrait, and the variety of bestial metaphor bespeaks a conception of humanity that will receive its most thorough expression in *Volpone*. Crites, unmistakably an authorial surrogate, usually addresses himself to particular courtly vanities but occasionally rises to an eloquent, general assault:

> O how despisde and base a thing is a man
> If he not strive t'erect his groveling thoughts
> Above the straine of flesh! But how more cheape
> When, even his best and understanding part
> (The crowne, and strength of all his faculties)
> Floates like a dead drown'd bodie, on the streame
> Of vulgar humour, mixt with commonst dregs?
> (*Cynthia's Revels*, 1.v.34–39)

Most men do not so strive. In other, more familiar words, "Godlike reason" tends "to fust in us unused" (*Hamlet*, IV.iv.38–39), and moral will is dominated by the claims of the body.

Sexual urges become more and more insistent in the lives of Shakespeare's characters at this period, and in Jonson, although sex is often a matter of power, the physical dimension is not unimportant. Even with Shakespeare's virtuous heroines, Helena and Isabella and Desdemona, suggestions of physical passion are strong.[18] Uncharted sexual regions exist even in the chaste Ophelia, as the lyrics of her mad scenes imply. And these are the innocents. As for the others, Bertram is "very ruttish," and though the phrase is Parolles', the action proves it; Angelo's seeming rectitude conceals a lubricious imagination; Hamlet's image of "the bloat king" "paddling in [Gertrude's] neck with his damned fingers" characterizes speaker as well as subjects; to Iago love is "merely a lust of the blood and a permision of the will"; and Cressida's "wanton spirits look out / At every joint and motive of her body" (IV.v.56–57). In *Measure for Measure*, Pompey will not be talked out of his trade, knowing as he does that the youth of Vienna "will to't"; his candid view of sexual desire is a synecdoche for appetite in general and is consistent with the views of most other Shakespearean and Jonsonian commentators. If Jonson's attention to the spiritual damage wrought by lust is more obvious elsewhere—say, in *Volpone*—the social emphasis of the comical satires brings into focus the ancillary foolishness associated with sexual desire. Fallace and Chloe, the wanton wives of *Every Man Out* and *Poetaster*, are less eager for physical gratification than for the fine clothes and social cachet that a love affair could bring, motives which are perhaps even more deplorable than if the ladies were driven by real passion. And yet Jonson acknowledges the naughtiness of their behavior by larding their speech with nasty puns. Fallace sends Fungoso to Fastidious Briske to warn him "of my husbands malitious intent; & tel him of that leane rascals trechery: O hevens! how my flesh rises at him!" (IV.ii.91–93). Chloe endlessly hectors Albius, her doting husband, for "poking at" her and for wanting to put his "spoke in [her] carte"; and when the banqueters go off to prepare for the masque, Chloe, picked for Venus, is eager to perform: " 'Tis very well; pray'lets goe, I long to be at it" (IV.iii.152). Shakespeare seems most concerned with the physical urges themselves, whereas Jonson deplores the absurdity they can foster; in both cases their alarm signifies gathering doubt about the full range of mortal weakness.

If reason is inadequate to control the power of the will (a noun associated with desires of the flesh), then words, the medium of reasonable discourse, have also become suspect. Both Shakespeare and Jonson begin seriously to question the reliability of language, the very means by which they convey their visions. The abuse of words, one of the central themes in each of Jonson's comical satires, is associated explicitly or implicitly with nearly every important episode of every play. Crispinus's vomiting his intolerable vocabulary is the most damning proof of his many literary crimes:

> HORA. *Barmy froth, puffy, inflate, turgidous,* and
> *ventositous* are all come up.
> TIBU. O, terrible, windie words!
> (v.iii.495–97)

Puntarvolo's application of romantic terms to the most pedestrian events represents everyone's tendency to clothe himself in unsuitable garments, literal and figurative. The trivial word games in *Cynthia's Revels* signify the waste of verbal talent, especially the circular "*A thing done,*" of which Phantaste says, "This play is cal'd the *Crab,* it goes backward" (iv.iii.175–76). The linguistic profusion of the comical satires—these are wordy plays—is to some degree a function of the fools' verbal prodigality, and no one is more self-indulgent than Captain Tucca. Here is his summons to the passing player:

A player? Call him, call the lowsie slave hither: what, will he saile by, and not once strike, or vaile to a *Man of warre?* ha? doe you heare? you, player, rogue, stalker, come backe here: no respect to men of worship, you slave? What, you are proud, you rascall, are you proud? ha? you grow rich, doe you? and purchase, you two-penny teare-mouth? you have *fortune,* and the good yeere on your side, you stinkard? you have? you have? (*Poetaster,* iii.iv.120–27)

Paradoxically, Jonson's gift for words impresses us with their danger. We remember the verbal outrages above all else, and yet we also remember that Jonson himself is responsible for their effectiveness.

The same ironic truth applies to Shakespeare, who begins to express grave doubts about the slippery quality of language. He parodies Hamlet's unparalleled eloquence in Polonius's foolish figures, and he brings Othello's sumptuous account of his adventures near enough to rodomontade to disturb many modern readers. Even more unsettling is

Iago's talent for verbal manipulation. Parolles, whose name tells us as much, is all words and no actions, and the emptiness of his boasts, of his speech in general, is emphasized in the humiliation the French lords devise for him:

> First Sold. Boskos thromuldo boskos.
> Par.   I know you are the Muskos' regiment,
>   And I shall lose my life for want of language.
>   (IV.i.68–70)

The lameness of Bertram's couplet in the last moments—"If she, my liege, can make me know this clearly / I'll love her dearly, ever, ever dearly" (v.iii.309–10)—tends to stimulate fears, not allay them, about the felicity of the ending. We cannot be sure that what we hear corresponds to what is. Sometimes we cannot even be sure what we hear, as in the final scene of *Measure for Measure:*

> Mariana. My lord, I do confess I ne'er was married;
>   And I confess besides, I am *no* maid;
>   I have *known* my husband; yet my husband
>   *Knows* not that ever he *knew* me.
>
>   . . . .
>
> Ang.   Charges she moe than me?
> Mariana.   Not that I *know*.
> Duke.   No? You say your husband.
> Mariana. Why just, my lord, and that is Angelo,
>   Who thinks he *knows* that he ne'er *knew* my body,
>   But *knows*, he thinks, that he *knows* Isabel's.
>   (v.i.185–88, 199–203; italics mine)

The multiple homonyms raise epistemological problems. Can we know the truth? Can we know ourselves? Angelo does not know whom he knew in his midnight tryst. The ear can be as deceptive as the eye.

Shakespeare's growing distrust of referentiality reveals itself in a comparison of cognate passages from *Twelfth Night* and *Troilus.* When Viola asks Feste at the beginning of act 3, "Dost thou live by thy tabor?" the Clown replies with a sanctimonious example of antanaclasis, "No, sir, I live by the church" (III.i.2–3), explaining that his house stands near the church. Words may sound alike or look alike but mean different things, just as Viola and Sebastian look alike but are very different people. In this comedy the puns are calculated to amuse, and Providence has supplied identical lovers to square the apparently hopeless love triangle. At the same central point in *Troilus* Shakespeare replays the routine:

> *Pand.* Friend, you, pray you, a word: do you not
> follow the young Lord Paris?
> *Serv.* Ay sir, when he goes before me.
> *Pand.* You do depend upon him, I mean.
> *Serv.* Sir, I do depend upon the Lord.
> *Pand.* You depend upon a notable gentleman, I must needs
> praise him.
> *Serv.* The Lord be praised!
> (III.i.1–8)

This exchange continues for some forty lines, offering similar puns on several topics and ending with the Servant's comment on Pandarus's language, "There's a stewed phrase indeed" (lines 40–41). Here the disjunction between sign and referent, unlike that in *Twelfth Night,* is potentially threatening: the endless puns obfuscate truth and quickly grow tedious. Similarly, in the narrative, the two Cressidas, Troilus's and any man's, are contained in one woman. Variations of this *schtik* occur in *Hamlet* (the gravediggers' banter) and *Othello* (the Clown's puns on "lie"), and such playing suggests that words are as likely to conceal as to convey meaning, and that the consequences of misreading may be tragic. Antanaclasis carried to such extremes as in *Troilus* exposes the vulnerability of the word.

Words are decayed because humans are degenerate, and Shakespeare's and Jonson's loss of faith in humanity and its language appears in the experience of their fictional idealists. Shakespeare repeatedly challenges or destroys the illusions of such figures, among the most memorable of whom are Angelo and Isabella, misled by naive faith in their own goodness.[19] Isabella's wish for greater rigidity in the order of St. Clare implies a commitment not simply to physical purity but to a more comprehensive, metaphysical chastity as well: she yearns for an immaculate world. So does Angelo, whose moral absolutism prompts him to enforce the ancient statute. Helena's unrelenting pursuit of Bertram may be grounded in physical desire, but she is also propelled by a faithful, optimistic sense of herself and her fellow creatures, an attitude reinforced by her mysterious gift of healing. Her faith is finally vindicated, but she must perform some sordid trickery to get her way; moreover, the denouement undermines the value and durability of her triumph. Troilus's disillusionment, on the other hand, is fierce. His heroic ideals manifest themselves most forcefully when he urges continuation of the war, describing its object as "a pearl / Whose price hath launch'd above a thousand ships" (II.ii.82–83). Helen's entrance in act 3 contradicts his characterization, for she appears to have strayed into the scene from one of Jonson's comical satires. The young man's illusions about Helen are recapitulated in his relations with Cressida: the world shatters his callow belief in true love and heroic action. Between the extremes of Troilus and Helena stand Hamlet and Othello, each of whom loses his illusions about human nobility but is able, in the last instant, to rebuild a more solid structure of values, including a reconsidered version of such faith. Othello comes to recognize the fact of Desdemona's purity, but he also discovers the nature and power of evil, an epiphany that modifies his comprehension of the good. The tones of idealism are clear and appealing in all these plays, regardless of mode, and Shakespeare asks his audience to respond to such stirring music. Finally, however, those tones are either silenced or modulated into dissonance.

Most of Jonson's gulls and eccentrics also may be said to subscribe to an ideal creed: their pride and solipsism convince them that the world is sure to go their way. Such optimism underlies Puntarvolo's chivalric idealization of his wife and her gentlewoman, as well as his arrangement with the Notary for the projected journey to Constantinople and back: "Neyther shall I use the helpe of any such sorceries, or enchantments, as unctions, to make our skinnes impenetrable, or to travaile invisible by vertue of a powder, or a ring, or to hang any three-forked charme about my dogges necke, secretly convey'd into his collar: (understand you?) but that all be performed, sincerely, without fraud, or imposture" (IV.iii.31–37). Magic is unnecessary, as long as there is no foul play; Puntarvolo is absolute in his confidence of success. Virtually all the fools and hypocrites—the courtiers in *Cynthia's Revels* come to mind—think of themselves with similar assurance, and all are roundly disabused. The absurdity of Puntarvolo's games is exposed when Fungoso enters to announce that the knight's dog has been poisoned: "O, sir PUNTARVOLO, your dogge lies giving up the ghost in the wood-yard" (V.iii.56–57). But still the idealist clings to his courtly manner: "O, my dog, born to disastrous fortune!" (v.iii.59). Ironically, Jonson also depicts a few idealists who are not disillusioned, the satirists who succeed in puncturing the false hopes of the fools. The distance between what the world is and what it ought to be accounts for the violence of their initial responses to the folly of their peers. Asper, Crites, and Horace believe deeply in the powers of reason and art, and Jonson grants them their triumphs. Yet the negative forces against which they struggle are so potent that we can hardly endorse their hope, and this apparent contradiction reflects the uncertainty of their creator. The one Jonsonian idealist who flatly refuses to abandon faith in man's corrigibility is Ben Jonson. Despite all the pessimistic evidence that the artist has imagined and exhibited, he is loath to concede that man will never be guided by higher instincts. That will not come until *Sejanus* and, accompanied by greater artistic assurance, *Volpone*. But throughout the period of the comical satires Jonson cannot fully acknowledge the implications of his growing vision of evil. Like his surrogates, he clings to hope in himself and his work.

The kinds and extent of Shakespearean and Jonsonian evil grow more pervasive and serious. Follies often become crimes. Shakespearean fools such as Parolles, Lucio, and Ajax become more dangerous than their predecessors, and in the tragedies they can be, like Roderigo and Polonius, serious if unwitting threats. Major figures are problematic too. Shakespeare's comic heroes were never his most attractive lot: at times Bassanio, Claudio in *Much Ado,* and Orsino seem unworthy of the heroines who win them. Now this difficulty is compounded. Any actor playing Bertram, no matter how young and good-looking, will be hard pressed to win the audience's sympathy; and while we may not want to go as far as Clifford Leech in his famous hatchet job on Vincentio, his argument raises troubling questions, particularly in light of the Duke's summoning Isabella to the altar in the final minute.[20] We need not linger over the iniquity of Claudius or the motiveless malignity of Iago. As for Jonson, Carlo Buffone's advice to the social-climbing Sogliardo will illustrate the playwright's understanding of how—and how far—humanity has gone wrong.

Nay, looke you sir, now you are a gentleman, you must carry a more exalted presence, change your mood, and habit, to a more austere forme, be exceeding proud, stand upon your gentilitie, and scorne every man. Speake nothing humbly, never discourse under a nobleman, though you ne're saw him but riding to the *Starre-chamber*, it's all one. Love no man. Trust no man. Speake ill of no man to his face: nor well of any man behind his backe. Salute fairly on the front, and wish 'hem hang'd upon the turne. Spread your selfe upon his bosome publikely, whose heart you would eate in private. These be principles, thinke on 'hem, I'le come to you againe presently. (*EMOH*, iii.iv.101–12)

The concerns are familiar: self-interest, affectation, pride, fraud, faithlessness, hypocrisy, social cannibalism. Such behavior, as even the rhythms indicate, leads perforce to isolation ("Love no man. Trust no man.") and destroys the social bonds that even beasts require. Such instruction might have come from Parolles or Lucio, even from Edmund, for that matter, and it is presented and enacted in play after play, by character after character, Shakespearean and Jonsonian. There are degrees of adherence to these stipulations, to be sure, for "These be principles": not everyone can live by them. But numerous characters seek to. The dual vision of man as god and beast was a familiar tenet of Renaissance thought, and we see Shakespeare and Jonson adjusting the focus of this vision between 1599 and 1604.

§ III

A register of Shakespeare's and Jonson's disenchantment with their human subject is provided by the fluctuations in dramatic tone that occur at this period. Jonson's attitude towards his characters and their actions alters radically in 1599, when the genial ironies of *Every Man In* are replaced with the loudly proclaimed satire of *Every Man Out*:

> I looke into the world, and there I meet
> With objects, that doe strike my bloud-shot eyes
> Into my braine:
> (1.i.16–18)

Macilente enters forecasting the kind of behavior to be represented and the response it ought to elicit. There are degrees of satiric reaction, of course, and such vitriol is not appropriate to every figure and situation in the three comical satires. For example, Macilente is more than just an authorial mouthpiece: his unbridled rage and envy make him a satiric target as well.[21] But the sharp tone of *Every Man Out* and the two subsequent plays is distinctive and easily apprehended. Shakespeare, as everyone knows, was not caught up in the enthusiasm for dramatic satire that swept through the London theatrical scene at the turn of the century, but it is wrong to suppose that his work was not affected by it. His growing fears about human frailty coincided with the rise of a literary fashion devoted to mockery and exposure of man's weaknesses. The strains of bitterness and disgust found in *Hamlet, Troilus,* and *All's Well* correspond to the satiric tones found in the contemporary texts of Jonson, Marston, and others. Just as we must not overestimate the importance of satire in Shakespeare's middle plays, so we must not overlook its contribution. The rise of dramatic satire probably aided Shakespeare in making the transition from comedy to tragedy.

The tone of Jonson's comical satires, implicit in the name of the mode, is immediately audible. Indeed, so insistent and distinctive is the derisive strain that it has come to dominate criticism of Jonsonian drama, has been made an identifying feature of his style, and has been associated with texts (such as *The Alchemist* and *Bartholomew Fair*) to which it is scarcely germane.[22] But the familiarity of the label "satire" has prematurely closed the case. In fact the audience is made to feel a good deal more than simple outrage. In the first place, a major point of difference among the three comical satires is their tonal emphasis: *Every Man Out, Cynthia's Revels,* and *Poetaster* are not just three versions of the same play. The first, thanks to its immense length, an unparalleled assortment of fools, and the presence of at least two satirists (three if Asper is counted), is the fiercest. There, Jonson's critical fervor seems barely under control, almost in danger of crossing the boundary into moral hysteria; no one escapes the satiric lash. *Poetaster,* by contrast, suggests that the author has mastered his contempt for the errors he depicts: the tone is much less truculent, and the dramatist's Horatian surrogate easily triumphs by appealing to the reasonable authority of Augustus. *Cynthia's Revels* marks the mid-point in Jonson's progress from Juvenalian fury to Horatian detachment.[23]

The range of tones evident throughout the series reflects the tonal mixture found in each play. None of them is purely satiric. The importance of the adjective "comicall" should not be neglected, particularly in *Cynthia's Revels* and *Poetaster.* In each text, according to R. B. Parker, the dramatist "experiments with combinations of comedy and satire and gradually shifts the emphasis between them."[24] Moreover, each text reveals the variety of emphasis available within satire itself. It is a commonplace that satire arises from a combination of contrary impulses: disgust at the weaknesses of the flesh, and faith in the power of reason to identify and correct them.[25] Most great works of satire—*The Dunciad* and *Gulliver's Travels,* for example—are known by the harshness with which their authors excoriate human error and the detail with which they expose folly. And yet these satires invariably include a countermovement to such an attack, an explicit or implied model of behavior in which the author invests his confidence that the corruption observed is neither universal nor inevitable and that his work is worth writing. The satirist, in other words, is both critic and idealist, his idealism generating and buttressing his critical perceptions.[26] The comical satires offer the first full exposition of this characteristic Jonsonian duality.

Every Man Out provides little in the way of positive example and small ground for hope: in its effort to "strip the ragged follies of the time / Naked as at their birth," the play's action emphasizes the ludicrous and contemptible sides of humanity. Within the fiction itself there is little relief from the dark mood of invective. Balance is supplied from without, by the critical acumen of Asper, the positive guidance of Cordatus, the critical awakening of Mitis, and the healthy, scornful laughter of the theater audience. The conclusion of the action, the bringing the characters out of their humours, is often felt to be artificial or external, in that the purgation is less an inevitable result of what has gone before than an act of authorial prestidigitation. Clearly Jonson wills his fools into recognition and correction, as the metamorphosis of Macilente into Asper implies, and the artificiality of the ending must have been even more striking in the original staging, in which a figure representing Queen Elizabeth shocked Macilente out of his envy and into an epiphany:

> Envie is fled my soule, at sight of her,
> And shee hath chac'd all black thoughts from my bosome,
> Like as the sunne doth darkenesse from the world.
> My streame of humour is runne out of me.
> (original ending, lines 4–7)

After five very long acts that concentrate on pride, greed, lust, stupidity, vanity, meanness, triviality, envy, and witlessness, we suddenly see the evaporation of these errors. The air is cleared; fools have learned their lessons; art works wonders. We are asked to exchange doubt for faith, despair for hope, contempt for charity. Many have felt that this trade is unearned. Although one mood succeeds another with great speed, the replacement of a pessimistic with an optimistic tone is not merely a Jonsonian quirk. It is inherent in the nature of the kind.

The combination of tones is smoother in *Cynthia's Revels* and *Poetaster* because Jonson sets within the illusion characters who anchor his faith in reason and virtue. The evils represented—narcissism and courtly affectation in Cynthia's court and literary pretension in Augustus's—make the plays less panoramic than *Every Man Out,* but the author's attitude is no less critical for being more concentrated and disciplined. The dissipation of follies and of the censure they demand is carefully prepared for, however. Crites and Horace are Jonson's representatives, and his founding the action upon a struggle between these exemplars and the fools who besiege them prepares the audience for a positive resolution and minimizes the disjunction felt at the end of *Every Man Out*. The endings here are just as artificial; indeed, Jonson insists that they be regarded as "made." Crites is a scholar rather than an artist, but he displays his enemies' fatuities in a masque; Horace is a poet, and his triumph over Crispinus is explicitly presented as a work of imagination. In these two later plays, particularly *Poetaster,* Jonson seems to have gained control of his moral fervor by concentrating his disgust upon a few offenders and subjecting them to the forces of reason and virtue. Still, this control cannot completely disguise the inherent tensions between hope and outrage, doubt and faith, and comedy and satire.

Even Jonson himself appears to have felt and regretted the uneasy mixture of pessimism and optimism in the comical satires. The "Apologeticall Dialogue" to *Poetaster* implies a reassessment of the power of art to illuminate and alter the ways of the truly incurable.[27] The "Dialogue" is by no means a repudiation; indeed, it is a defense. But it plainly exposes the dramatist's doubts about the efficacy of art, an impression confirmed by the immediate direction of Jonson's career. Apparently his first task was a hack job for Henslowe, to compose additional material for another revival of *The Spanish Tragedy.* Returning to serious composition, he tried his hand at tragedy in *Sejanus,* working with an unidentified collaborator on the first version; joined Chapman and Marston to write the almost completely satiric *Eastward Ho!;* and then shifted his attention to satiric comedy, as opposed to comical satire, in

74

Volpone. Ironically, the tonal shift from satire to comedy signifies not greater hope but more intense pessimism, resignation to the ubiquity of human folly that the endings of the comical satires seek to will away.[28] These three comical satires are not great works of dramatic literature, and while there are many explanations for their failings, one of the most plausible is Jonson's unsettled opinion of art and its place in human experience. The tonal uncertainty throughout the series exposes an important tension in Jonson's way of looking at the world, and it is the resolution of that conflict in favor of the negative that determines his artistic course and prepares for the creation of his masterpieces.

The tonal variations of the comical satires are slight compared to the immense range in Shakespeare's work of the same period. Individually and as a group, the plays from *Twelfth Night* through *Othello* and *Measure for Measure* exhibit a great variety of tonal effects: purely comic or tragic, romantic, gently or fiercely ironic, critical, even satiric, and combinations of all. Just as the degrees of satiric fervor in Jonson attest to his shifting and ambiguous assessment of his subject, so the vastly greater range of tones in Shakespearean comedy and tragedy is a reliable index of Shakespeare's unsettled and sometimes paradoxical thinking about humans and their place in the world. In *Twelfth Night*, the blend of romance, farce, liberal irony, and mild satire makes it a kind of plateau.[29] After it, Shakespeare seems unable or unwilling to sustain an optimistic or predominantly sympathetic view of human nature. His essays in a darker mode of comedy are enriched by, and also serve to enrich, his simultaneous interest in the tragic mode. Moreover, the comedies and tragedies of these years are distinguished from his earlier work by occasional intrusions of an intensely harsh, even satiric tone. Whether the dramatist's changing view of experience influenced his choice of mode, or whether his interest in new forms prompted a change in his view of the world, the darkening tones of his drama after 1600 indicate that this is a crucial moment in the development of Shakespeare's art.

Twelfth Night, the last of the great romantic comedies, may also be seen as pointing the way towards the tragedies. Shakespeare usually began his work in a given mode by concentrating on a single kind of effect, and as he gained experience in that mode, gradually widened the range of tones. In other words, as he contemplated the kinds of action that a dramatic mode could represent, he expanded the possible responses to various kinds of behavior. In *The Comedy of Errors*, for instance, he mainly exploits the risible consequences of mistaken identity and mostly neglects the romantic possibilities. One of the characteristics that makes *A Midsummer Night's Dream* his first comic masterpiece is the tonal variety resulting from the several lines of action. The multiplication of tones continues, most notably in comedies such as *Merchant* and *Much Ado;* then in *As You Like It* and *Twelfth Night,* Shakespeare brings these contrasting tones into a nearly perfect suspension. The oppositions of *Twelfth Night* are immediately perceptible in its scenic juxtaposition: the languor of the opening tableau yields to the brisk mood of Viola's arrival; the sympathetic interview between Orsino and Cesario (II.iv) gives way to the broad humor of Malvolio's letter scene; and the range of effects is felt powerfully in the final moments, when the joy of the several unions is modified by the melancholy of Feste's serenade. At times we are led to laugh scornfully at human vanity and self-absorption; at others we sympathize with the ironic disappointments of the winning heroine; elsewhere we smile wistfully at the deception and absurdity that love can generate. The comedy's darker strains imply Shakespeare's growing concern with the dangerous side of man's nature and thus give a sense of the direction his career will take. Earlier comedies such as *Much Ado* reveal an awareness of such threats; later ones such as *Measure for Measure* exploit them.

Tonal poise seems to me one signal that Shakespeare has come close to fulfilling, if not exhausting, the possibilities of a given mode.[30] After *Twelfth Night* his approach to comedy becomes more restricted, less inclusive. The stories he selects to dramatize and the features he chooses to stress are more somber and their ramifications more discouraging than before. His treatment of Boccaccio's story of Gileta of Narbonne in *All's Well,* for instance, tips the balance in an opposite direction: although the scenes with the Old Countess furnish an elegiac quality, the dominant tone is critical, at times profoundly so. *Twelfth Night* and *All's Well* both tell stories of a woman's successful pursuit of the man she loves, but the progress of the chase and the implications of her victory are decidely different. The confusion and humiliation that Viola suffers, including even a death threat from her beloved, provoke mirth and pleasure; Helena's disappointments are rarely humorous and often disturbing. Moreover, Viola's winning of Orsino promises happiness, whereas Helena's triumph leads us to doubt whether the prize is worth the struggle. Most of the plays written after the turn of the century encourage unfavorable responses to situations that in earlier works have produced pleasure. In *Much Ado* Claudio only thinks that he sees his mistress dallying in the dark with another man, whereas Troilus actually witnesses such an encounter. Orsino is devoted to an abstract idea of love, and his ignorance of genuine passion is the object of considerable fun; Angelo in *Measure for Measure* is committed to an abstract idea of justice, and the consequences of his self-deception are nearly disastrous for all Vienna. Another such parallel might be drawn between Malvolio and Angelo, both of whom would deny the world its cakes and ale and both of whom prove to be hypocrites. Malvolio is never given free rein, whereas Angelo is able for a time to wield and abuse the power that Malvolio only imagines. The most telling contrast is that between Ford and Othello: the comic husband only dreams of torturing an "errant" wife; the tragic figure murders his.

The critical tone that makes itself felt in every play Shakespeare wrote between 1600 and 1604 occasionally becomes sharp enough to be called satiric, a term very rarely associated with his drama. It has become axiomatic that satire was foreign to Shakespeare's natural temper, that its effects appealed to him less than to other playwrights, that its contribution to his comedies and tragedies is negligible.[31] Certainly Shakespeare never gave himself over completely to the vogue for satire, but he was thinking seriously about the topic as early as 1599, and his interest deserves careful assessment.[32] *As You Like It* presents an early version of the Elizabethan satirist, the social critic whose distaste for universal human weakness has become an obsession. Jaques's colloquy with Duke Senior in II.vii addresses the theoretical problem of satire that his contemporaries were debating in their dramatic prefaces and inductions.[33] Jaques takes the same line that Jonson would later adopt in answering charges of libel and personal attack: the satirist lambasts folly, not fools; his aim is constructive, not vicious; although his means may seem base, his point of view is purely moral:

> Invest me in motley. Give me leave
> To speak my mind, and I will through and through
> Cleanse the foul body of th'infected world,
> If they will patiently receive my medicine.
> (II.vii.58–61)

This is Jonsonian in spirit and diction, but Jaques's argument is complicated by dramatic circumstances. He turns out to be a satirist without proper targets. The famous anatomy of the span of life, ending as it does with abhorrence at blind senility, is contradicted by the immediate entrance of the generous spirited old Adam carried on the back of the sympathetic Orlando. The world he calls infected is shown to be relatively sound, if sometimes a little unbalanced or unfair. Still, some of his barbs stick, particularly his fleering at Orlando's romantic naiveté. As David Bevington puts it, "A satirical voice in the forest of Arden offers a valuable if limited contribution to the many-sided view of humanity there represented."[34] If Shakespeare dismisses most of Jaques's conclusions in this play, he endorses the satirist's right, even his duty, to express them. And within two years the playwright himself would imagine, in *Hamlet*, a world consistent with this malcontent's description.

The world of Illyria can hardly be thought of as infected, but Malvolio, a kind of humour character "sick of self-love," is Shakespeare's first important target of satire. (Sir Andrew, debilitated by stupidity, occasions derisive laughter, but Shakespeare's treatment of him is too gentle to be called satiric.) The scheme devised to trap Malvolio might have been imagined by Jonson himself, since his immense self-absorption is made the means of his discomfiture.[35] Malvolio's irredeemably unpleasant nature separates him from earlier fools such as Dogberry or Bottom, and his charmlessness deprives him of much sympathy from the spectators. Shakespeare's depiction of the hypocritical steward indicates growing fears about the consequences and meaning of human foolishness, especially in Malvolio's inability to learn from his humiliation and his minatory departure from the last scene. Shakespeare leaves open the chance of reconciliation,[36] and he permits his audience a pang of compassion amid the cruelties of the exorcism scene (IV.ii). These qualifications put a kind of Shakespearean brand on the satiric method, but the crucial point is that the scenes with Malvolio constitute satire of a Jonsonian kind.[37] They exist within a play not thoroughly satiric in mood, but they contribute to the tonal complexity that Shakespeare has begun to seek and will continue to explore.

Shakespeare in his last two comedies, *All's Well* and *Measure for Measure*, displaying what might be called Jonsonian indignation at some of the vices he represents, seems to have assimilated some of the techniques of the comical satires. He treats his fools very harshly, particularly Lucio and Parolles. Although they descend from earlier Shakespearean clowns, they are more sinister, less engaging, and their follies are familiar from contemporary satire. Both are pretenders. They claim to be valiant, wise, and superior; in fact they are arrogant, hypocritical, and cowardly. The First Lord describes Parolles to Bertram in a passage that applies to Lucio also: "a most notable coward, an infinite and endless liar, an hourly promise-breaker, the owner of no one good quality worthy your lordship's entertainment" (III.vi.9–12). Lucio's exposure—he *"pulls off the friar's hood and discovers the Duke"*— comes off with a Jonsonian ironic justice: it occurs at the moment of apparent triumph, when his humour of pride, courtly intimacy, and self-righteousness is at its most expansive. The gulling of Parolles seems virtually Jonsonian in the richness of symbolic meaning attached to the episode.[38] In deceiving him into recapturing the lost drum, symbol of regimental honor, the soldiers appeal to his false courage, and the bogus language with which they terrorize their captive is as empty as the words he uses to create his own false reputation. Touches such as Parolles' regimental assignment, beating his own drum, as it were, and his role as Bertram's tutor in cowardice, infidelity, and immaturity suggest that Jonson's practice may have influenced Shakespeare directly: one thinks of the shaming of Bobadilla, the sealing of Carlo Buffone's lips, and the emetic punishment of Crispinus. The presentation of Lucio and Parolles is not as narrow as Jonson's employment of his fools, in that Shakespeare's characters contribute to a larger narrative, as well as moral, pattern. Further, Parolles does not merely evaporate after his explosion but retains "a further layer of existence, the bedrock of the irreducible human,"[39] and Lucio can eloquently sympathize with Isabella. Lucio and Parolles, in other words, exhibit distinctive Shakespearean markings, but their Jonsonian relations and their satiric functions plainly declare themselves.

His integration of such figures into the texture of the plays indicates how Shakespeare's comic point of view has been shaped and altered by his satiric perceptions of experience. In *Twelfth Night*, Malvolio is thematically related to the other would-be lovers, wanting what he cannot have and humiliating himself in pursuit of it, but the satiric reaction he evokes—laughter of scorn—mostly sets him apart from the rest of the *dramatis personae*. The tones associated with Malvolio are complementary, adding variety to romantic comedy, whereas the satiric figures in the darker comedies supply consistency. Shakespeare attacks Lucio for the same errors of which the major figures are also guilty: he is a "seemer," like Angelo and, in perhaps a more benign sense, like the Duke himself; Lucio's faithless treatment of Kate Keepdown corresponds to Angelo's of Mariana; his forswearing his crime is parallel to Angelo's lying about his use of Isabella; his sexual appetite is replicated in others; and some would say that his imperious abuse of the "friar" in the final scene resembles the Duke's pleasure in power. Parolles likewise draws attention to the faults endemic to the world depicted. As friend and counselor to Bertram, he shares his master's egoism, immaturity, lechery, and faithlessness. Parolles betrays his friend and his regiment, Bertram his wife and mother; both betray themselves. Parolles has given himself a name for valor and honor, but is hollow within; Bertram has little more than his family name. "A past-saving slave," a "damnable both-sides rogue," Parolles is not always distinguishable from Bertram. At the conclusion we feel that, for all Helena's strength and virtue, Bertram may be past saving. Both master and companion are "crushed with a plot." Diana says that if she were Bertram's wife, she "would poison that vile rascal" Parolles, and Bertram's behavior almost makes one want to do the same to the young lord. Although *All's Well* and *Measure for Measure* are not finally satiric in effect, they present a series of repellant minor actions carefully connected with the whole, and this unity indicates a development in Shakespeare's art and thought. The dramatist has darkened his tones and in so doing has absorbed some essential features of the contemporary Jonsonian style.

The satiric point of view contributes to the tragedies of this phase as well as to the comedies, although the mutual effect of satire and tragedy is more difficult to identify. The scorn and ridicule associated with satire proceed naturally from a critical comic perspective, while the moral indignation characteristic of the mode serves to augment the representation of a tragic environment. This is how Shakespeare channels his satiric impulses into *Hamlet*. Surely a kinship exists between Hamlet and Macilente, although we should not press the resemblance too far. Jonson's malcontent is a "black fellow," "a Scholler," and "a Soldier," one who shares Hamlet's disgust at the injustice of the world and the partiality of fortune. His remarks on the meeting of Buffone and Sogliardo strike a familiar chord:

Who can endure to see blinde *Fortune* dote thus?
To be enamour'd on this dustie turfe?

> This clod? a whorson puck-fist? O god, god, god, god &c.
> I could runne wild with griefe now, to behold
> The ranknesse of her bounties, that doth breed
> Such bull-rushes;
> (1.ii.157–62)

Even so brief a passage calls to mind the rhetoric of Hamlet's most celebrated speeches—"who can endure," "god, god, god, god . . . ," and "ranknesse." The prince seems acquainted with the current literature of satire ("the satirical rogue says here . . . "), and he and Macilente ruminate on the same topics: bestiality, hypocrisy, unjust preferment, sexual license, female treachery, and general corruption.[40] Both become intriguers, laying plots in an effort to relieve the causes of their "grief." The differences between the two characters are so much greater than the parallels that they need not be enumerated, but the similarities exist because Shakespeare and Jonson are looking at the same phenomena. Their different angles of vision produce different responses: Jonson considers the capriciousness of fortune and the weakness of the flesh from a scornful, highly ironic standpoint, while Shakespeare addresses these topics with tragic sympathy as well as scorn. But the chronological proximity of the plays and the parallels between protagonists, their meditations, and their language, not to mention the relative abundance of topical reference in *Hamlet,* all suggest that Shakespeare took notice when *Every Man Out* was produced at the Globe in 1599 and that his thinking and technique may have been guided by its satiric content and style when he took up the problem of human disillusionment and gave it its greatest artistic embodiment.

Satiric feeling finds its way into *Othello,* although very little of it is associated with the tragic figure himself.[41] That many readers see the Moor as a satiric butt attests, I think, to the potential connection between the satiric and the tragic points of view. Yet satire, like comedy, is ultimately subsumed into the tragic vision. One of Shakespeare's principal techniques for dramatizing Cinthio's novella of the misled soldier is his reference to the stock figure of the jealous husband in Elizabethan comedy, Thorello in *Every Man In,* Labervele in Chapman's *An Humorous Day's Mirth,* and Shakespeare's own Master Ford. Audiences knew how to read this figure, with scornful hilarity, and Shakespeare drew upon this conventional reaction in depicting Othello's tragic *agon.*[42] In other words, the playwright has moved beyond the satiric or comic interpretation of an action to examine its tragic meaning. Othello may behave at times like an object of satire, but the audience finds a scornful response proscribed by his nobility and idealism, feels itself directed to a higher level of understanding by the hero's difference from the conventional satiric victim. The great spokesman for the satiric conception of human action is Iago, in his cynical tutelage of Roderigo, his misogyny, and his envious raillery on his own bad fortune in the opening moments. Satire is ultimately swept aside by the hero's tragic experience.

Troilus and Cressida is the one play in which the satiric response appears not to have been assimilated into a more capacious comic or tragic vision, the play in which Shakespeare allows indignant and bitter tones to dominate all others. The primary source of indignation is Thersites, the censorious expositor with an eye for hypocrisy, folly, roguery, stupidity, and cant.[43] His invective is so pertinent to what we see and so memorably phrased that it exerts a potent influence on our attitude towards the drama. His most savage attacks are directed at Ajax, the "elephant" who surely merits the succession of insults; his attacks on Achilles and Patroclus, only slightly less biting, are borne out by the behavior and language of these "heroes." His cynical, vulgar assessment of Troilus and Cressida themselves—"Will a swagger himself out on's own eyes?" (v.ii.135); "Any man may sing her, if he can take her clef: she's noted" (v.ii.10—11)—is not the only possible interpretation, certainly. The audience is invited to feel some sympathy for Troilus's disenchantment and even perhaps for Cressida's inability to control her acknowledged passions. In his famous summary of the war and its participants—"Lechery, lechery, still wars and lechery! Nothing else holds fashion" (v.ii.193—94)—Thersites does not necessarily speak for his creator, but his is an eloquent and frightening voice. Like Jonson's Macilente, Thersites is not only the purveyor of satire but also the object of it. Both speakers see nothing about them but incontinence and self-delusion, and their reactions to these monstrosities are so violent that they are unable to retain their venom. Thus they participate in the very world that disgusts them and are included in the picture they cannot bear to look upon.[44]

It is the tone of *Troilus and Cressida* that sets it apart from the rest of the canon: the familiar and popular tale is subjected to critical and even contemptuous scrutiny. In dramatizing this most glorious of legends,

Shakespeare emphasizes cowardice, betrayal, self-delusion, and triviality, thus revealing the unreliability and inaccuracy of the fictions that people use to dignify their history. The unusually harsh tone must have been governed to some extent by the audience's familiarity with the legend, through Chaucer and the Elizabethan versions of Homer.[45] Satire is written to debunk, to correct man's deluded view of himself, to strip the pleasing mask from the deformed face, and this above all is what *Troilus* does—to Achilles, Helen, and Ajax most notoriously, but also to Ulysses, Hector, Troilus, and virtually every worthy in the tale. And for those figures whose masks had already been cracked by history or literature, particularly Pandarus and Cressida, this version displays their deformity in the harshest possible light. Some of the most celebrated persons in literature are presented as mercilessly as any in the Shakespearean corpus.

The abundance and sharpness of satire in *Troilus* should naturally lead us to connect it to the theatrical climate and to the work that Jonson was doing at the same time. To notice such parallels returns us to the old thesis, proposed by O. J. Campbell, that *Troilus* is a slavish imitation of the Jonsonian form.[46] In fact, Campbell devised his theory to rebut Chambers's conception of "a disillusioned Shakespeare," thus hoping to replace psychobiography with historical analysis.[47] A synthesis of these two interpretations probably offers the fairest account of Shakespeare's actual practice. Certainly his vision was darkening, and his increasingly skeptical view of human conflict strongly influenced his choice of sources and his dramatization of them. Moreover, the theatrical milieu in 1601–2 offered a suitable style for expressing this negative assessment of experience. Shakespeare found it convenient to experiment with the Jonsonian method, and while this practice does not make him into a satirist or his works into satires, it does give most of them a satiric edge.

§ IV

Expression of these changing visions required the creation of some complex dramatic architecture. One of the most revealing properties of Shakespeare's plays just after the turn of the century is their formal instability. The dramatist alternates between comedy and tragedy as if in search of a proper vehicle to convey his ambiguous view, and each mode is enriched and complicated by the assumptions and conventions

83

of the other.[48] Virtually all the plays from *Hamlet* through *Measure for Measure* illustrate the connection between comedy and tragedy that has intrigued literary theorists since Socrates:

> Comedy and tragedy alike are imitations of the actions of men, and the crucial fact about man is his dual nature. His duality makes him an incongruous figure, and if there were nothing incongruous in the human condition, there would be nothing to dramatize. The union of a spiritual essence and a corporal existence poses the initial incongruity, and from this all others flow. Infinite aspirations are subject to a finite capacity for achievement; immortal longings break upon the fact of mortality; the rational purpose gives way to irrational impulse. Incongruities such as these are the warp and woof of human experience, and the fabric of human life reveals a pattern shot through with discrepancies: the discrepancy between the ideal and the reality, between the intention and the deed, to name those which subsume all others. To dramatize these is the purpose of tragedy and comedy alike, and this is the reason that the true artist in one will be an artist in the other as well.[49]

The intensity of a dramatist's perception of discontinuity governs the choice of mode. Around 1600 Shakespeare and Jonson are both subject to conflicting perceptions. Shakespeare recognizes that while the human creature offers much to admire, its estimable qualities are fragile and easily overwhelmed by the penchant for evil, whether passive or aggressive. Jonson, his disgust at much human behavior notwithstanding, refuses to abandon his faith in reason and art.

Jonson in this phase does not move back and forth between comedy and tragedy but combines the stuff of both into the hybrid form of comical satire, which Cordatus describes as "strange, and of a particular kind by itselfe" (*EMOH*, "After the second Sounding," lines 231–32).[50] What is important here is that *Every Man Out, Cynthia's Revels,* and *Poetaster* occupy a kind of middle ground between comedy and tragedy. As Alvin Kernan has shown, "Pure satire is far rarer than the mixed kinds in which after a time the satiric stasis is broken and the characters, both satirists and fools, are swept forward into the miraculous transformations of comedy or the cruel dialectic of tragedy."[51] Virtually any satiric text, in other words, will be an unstable structure. In these three it is easy to discern the conflicts and ambiguities that signify the author's shifting attitudes towards human frailty, attitudes that throughout the rest of Jonson's career find expression in the more familiar forms of comedy and, on two occasions, in tragedy. Even more striking is that each play reveals a fundamental uneasiness—we might even say contradiction—between form and content. Jonson's moral imagination responds indignantly, with an almost tragic intensity, to the conditions of a lapsed world, and yet the comical shape of the action promises that reason and especially art can rectify the fallen creatures in it. This series of plays ends with Jonson's admission that the moral and artistic impulses generating such forms might find a more suitable outlet in tragedy. And our sense of formal instability in these works, of their transitional status, is reinforced by the awareness that they are bordered chronologically by a comedy and a tragedy of more familiar generic properties, *Every Man In* and *Sejanus*.

Shakespeare's artistic imagination at this time is divided between revulsion at the skull beneath the skin and attraction to the loveliness of the skin itself, a tension that gives the dark comedies and the tragedies their distinctive forms and flavors. Audiences have little trouble perceiving the tragic shape and effect of *Hamlet* and *Othello,* despite critical maneuverings to claim the former as a problem play or to make the latter over into a satire. Familiar comic patterns are converted for tragic use, and familiar actions and characters appear in a grave new context. Shakespeare's metamorphosis from a primarily comic to a primarily tragic dramatist is marked by his investigation of the alarming implications of material formerly regarded as amusing. Susan Snyder has persuasively argued, for example, that *Hamlet* challenges directly the value of that flexibility which it is comedy's usual business to promote: the prince is tortured by the "multiple perspective" which in Shakespearean comedy is almost always desirable.[52] And in *Othello,* as I have suggested, the dramatist consciously exposes the limitations of the comic point of view by removing the usual safeguards and depicting the tragic form of jealous imaginings. *Othello* was performed at court on November 1, 1604, and shortly thereafter, on February 2, 1605, the company revived *Every Man in His Humour* for the new king, who would not have seen its original production. Perhaps the King's Men, having pleased their patron with the tragedy of jealousy, sought to delight him with the comic version of the same emotion. Even if the repetition of *Every Man In* was coincidental, *Othello,* and indeed all the tragedies, must be read as critiques of comic conclusions.

Shakespeare's contemporary comedies are less conventional, more experimental, much less formally grounded than the tragedies, for the influences of the complementary mode disrupt the traditional comic harmonies. The difficulties presented by these plays are manifested in the continuing debate over what to call them: *All's Well* has been described as "farcical comedy, sentimental romance, romantic fable, serious drama, cynical satire, and a thematic dramatization."[53] *Measure for Measure* has inspired "no single agreed formulation of what the play actually does or how well it does it. . . . The ambiguities are almost countless, and increased familiarity only serves to emphasize that one conception is inseparable from another."[54] And Swinburne described *Troilus* as a "hybrid and hundred-faced and hydra-headed monster."[55] *All's Well* and *Measure for Measure*, for all their complexity, are predominantly comic, and *Troilus* should probably be regarded as nearer to comedy than tragedy. Whatever we choose to call these plays, the descriptive problems attest to the contradictory elements out of which they are formed.[56]

Serious consequences exist potentially even in the earliest and lightest of Shakespeare's comedies, but at this period the playwright insists upon the dangers these possibilities represent to the comic way of thinking. In *All's Well* and most especially in *Measure for Measure,* a comedy set mainly in a prison, the gravity of the dramatic narrative often seems at odds with comic convention, and Shakespeare seems to have wanted it that way. He has established and emphasized a contest among forms and the responses associated with them; he has arranged the action so that the spectator is urged toward a tragic reaction and then pulled back toward comedy. Within particular episodes or in a series of scenes this motion may tend in either direction, but in the play as a whole the final push is toward comic resolution. Bertram's struggle against marriage until just twenty-one lines before the end, when his forced capitulation is made the occasion for rejoicing, is typical of the way these narratives resist the comic progress toward felicity. The tonal effect of the conflict is even more pronounced in *Measure for Measure,* which seems especially close to tragedy, since it shares many central concerns with *King Lear.*[57] But the comedy's serious conflicts are resolved positively when Providence supplies appropriately ironic means, the head of a diseased pirate who happens to resemble Claudio; and the conclusion is a triumph of comic intricacy, replete with disguises, discoveries, and happy surprises for the characters, played before an audience blessed with an omniscient advantage. This uneasy absorption of tragic impulses into a comic mode is neither inept nor accidental. Arthur Kirsch is surely correct in asserting that "the various disjunctions in [*All's Well*] are deliberate and part of a self-consciously paradoxical conception."[58] In other words, the taxonomic confusion is not an obstacle to be surmounted so that the play can then be interpreted, evaluated, and appreciated. Effect and meaning depend upon the formal uneasiness built into these works. Northrop Frye nicely captures the relation of contrary structures when he comments that *Measure for Measure* is notable for "the way it contains, instead of simply avoiding, a tragic action."[59] This attempt at containment is the most telling feature of *All's Well* and *Measure for Measure*, and it is an inherently unsettling process. If it were easily accomplished, these comedies would be much less meaningful than they are.

The contest of forms is best illustrated by *Troilus and Cressida*. Kenneth Palmer, the editor of the recent New Arden text, puts the matter of formal designation this way: "Comedy, tragedy, satire, tragic farce, and the rest have been propounded and justified; *and all are right*."[60] The various components seem to have been assembled and displayed without a controlling point of view, as if Shakespeare has reached an ideological and therefore a formal standstill (a word relevant both to the story chosen and the dramatic treatment of it). Neither of the familiar dramatic structures is adequate to represent the world imagined in *Troilus*. Whereas in the surrounding plays the complementary mode is invoked, often ironically, to complicate the tragic or comic response, here both comedy and tragedy are overwhelmed by irony. Shakespeare has organized *Troilus* so as to engage not our sympathies but our critical faculties. Thus, it is marked by an uncharacteristic stasis and a relative neglect of plot. The military story is mainly about inaction, about Achilles' neglect of his duty, and most of the scenes are given over to some kind of talk—debate, invective, speculation, plans, and wordplay.[61] The play emerges as a kind of showcase, a gallery in which persons, ideas, postures, and habits are displayed for evaluation and criticism. Pandarus and Cressida comment on the Trojan heroes passing in review; the initial group scenes in the Greek camp and among the Trojan officers (i.iii and ii.ii) turn upon major, extended debates; Helen, the *casus belli*, appears only once, in the center of the play, and the episode demands that we doubt whether she is "worth what she doth cost the keeping"; the onlookers' dramatic annotations of Cressida's submission to Diomedes are as important as the tryst itself. Shakespeare's presentational style entails constant reference to the dramatic agency through which the world of the play is mediated.[62] The audience is regularly admonished that it is watching a play, that this is an artificial arrangement of scenes from history, not a straightforward imitation of experience.[63] The effect of the prologue and epilogue—Shakespeare's use of both in one play is relatively rare—is to establish the drama as a spectacle to be judged or wondered at. Neither delight nor pity and fear will be appropriate, especially since we are kept at several removes from the action. Although we may briefly succumb to the impulse to sympathize with Troilus, we are conscious of his misplaced faith even before we enter the theater. Establishing aesthetic distance is one of Shakespeare's primary goals, and so the conflicts of this play engage us less than those of any other in the canon.[64]

The presentational style and the cultivation of judgment set *Troilus* apart from most of Shakespeare's work and make it seem nearly satiric, almost Jonsonian. Jonson's comical satires, especially *Cynthia's Revels* and *Poetaster,* are organized according to the principles that govern the construction of *Troilus.* Intermediaries and presenters keep the audience at several removes and guide critical responses. Since the stories exist as a way of exhibiting characters' failings, scenes are based on games, schemes, demonstrations, skits, and disputes, encounters which prompt the viewer to analyze and criticize.[65] The courtiers' games in *Cynthia's Revels,* the masque that Crites prepares for his foolish enemies, the costume party in *Poetaster,* the exemplary punishment of Crispinus, the plots in which all take part—these are not so firmly rooted in a story as are their equivalents in *Troilus,* but they are similarly directed toward the judgment. The symmetry often discerned in *Troilus* functions as in Jonson's dramas, to juxtapose persons, compare related actions, and promote ethical and intellectual distinctions. The fact that very little "happens" in both *Troilus* and its Jonsonian counterparts has thematic ramifications in both cases. Everyone has noticed in *Troilus* what one critic calls "devices of discontinuity": the failure of plans, the interruption of dialogue, the contradiction of oaths, the perversion of intentions, and the dashing of hopes. Such theatrical discontinuity is everywhere to be found in these Jonsonian texts.[66] Failure (in every sphere) is only one of many shared themes: pride, lust, naiveté, linguistic abuse, and self-delusion.

Troilus is much more than a dramatic exercise in the Jonsonian style. Shakespeare's dramatic situation is taken from legend, while Jonson's are gotten up for the moment, and *Troilus* lacks any authorial surrogate or figure of authority, a Crites or an Augustus. Characters express points of view with which the playwright surely concurs, Ulysses most obviously, but Ulysses cannot be considered a satirist nor even an agent of the order he so eloquently propounds: his scheme for flushing Achilles out of the tent is a flop. Shakespeare has left his naifs, schemers, dolts, liars, and Myrmidons with neither an earthly nor heavenly force to organize or control them,[67] and he has similarly deprived the audience of structural guidance. The pessimism of *Troilus*, anomalous and temporary though it is, cannot and should not be explained away or forgotten, even though it interferes with the consistent and unified vision that some critics wish to ascribe to Shakespeare. This text presents a world as dark as any that Jonson imagined for the stage, as dark as that of *Sejanus*, which was probably staged in the following season. Those who come to conclude, with Peter Alexander, that *Troilus* is not itself a cynical play but instead Shakespeare's "medicine for cynics,"[68] have identified yet another parallel with Jonson's vision and technique. The comical satires offer some relief from the ugliness they depict by enabling the audience to recognize and deplore it, and this may be Shakespeare's hope for *Troilus*. But we need not apologize for our uncertainty, for Shakespeare has removed the usual formal guides in this most unstable of his plays.

Jonson's shift from comedy (*Every Man In*) to tragedy (*Sejanus*) to dark comedy (*Volpone*) is recapitulated in the disjunctions of each of the intervening comical satires. The moral imagination recoils (satirically) from the overwhelming evidence of human folly and corruption, and yet the artistic sense still asserts (comically) that man's lapses can be exposed and remedied. This tension is most explicit in *Every Man Out*:

MIT. . . . I must tel you, signior (though I was loth to interrupt the *Scene*) yet I made it a question in mine owne private discourse, how he should properly call it, *Every man out of his Humour*, when I saw all his actors so strongly pursue, and continue their humours?

COR. Why therein his art appeares most full of lustre, and approcheth nearest the life: especially, when in the flame, and height of their humours, they are laid flat, it fils the eye better, and with more contentment. How tedious a sight were it to behold a proud exalted tree lopt, and cut downe by degrees, when it might bee feld in a moment? and to set the axe to it before it came to that pride, and fulnesse, were, as not to have it grow.

MIT. Well, I shall long to see this fall, you talke of. (*Grex*, IV.viii.161–74).

Jonson thus admits the problem inherent in his satiric conception, confessing it at the point where the fault line is most visible, just before the denouement. The use of an impersonated Queen to complete the transformation of the play's deviants is Jonson's radical solution to the problem of balance—she is the axe that fells the mighty trees—and even though forced to alter the original ending, Jonson imagined new versions of the episode in the two subsequent plays. Still, the ease with which these resolutions are achieved contradicts the sense of incorrigibility and intransigence that the actions have so persuasively conveyed.[69]

Jonson's perception of human shortcomings is so intense, and his skill at recreating them so dramatically sure, that the triumphs of this phase are the portraits of the fools: Puntarvolo, Asotus, Philautia, Tucca, and Crispinus, among many others. As Jonson's vision of the relation between good and evil begins to darken, his imaginative concentration on self-love and disorder virtually overwhelms his interest in the corrective process that is the formal basis for the action. "Jonson's success," as Gabriele Bernhard Jackson puts it, "is invariably to be gauged by the strength of the anti-norm. His greatest plays succeed not by enforcing a concept of balance but by impressing upon us the overwhelming force of imbalance."[70] In the comical satires, the gravity and tenacity of the characters' errors begin to dominate a dramatic structure designed to contain them but finally inadequate to do so. *Poetaster* makes its way towards the proposition that folly can be exposed and shamed into amendment, moves towards the climax in which Horace, applauded by Augustus, Virgil, and the court, administers the medicinal purge to Crispinus and elicits an apology for the fool's literary crimes. But this conclusion, brilliant as it is, does not seem commensurate with the mass of nonsense that has preceded it. A much more revealing scene, one crucial to our comprehending the problem of the comical satires, is the encounter between poet and poetaster (III.i), the episode in which Crispinus attaches himself to Horace and refuses to be shaken off. Horace invents excuses, tries insults, pleads business across the Tiber, curses under his breath, and finally prays for divine intervention:

> Archer of heaven, PHOEBUS, take thy bow
> And with a full drawne shaft, naile to the earth
> This PYTHON; that I may yet run hence, and live:
> Or brawnie HERCULES, doe thou come downe,
> And (though mak'st it up thy thirteenth labour)
> Rescue me from the HYDRA of discourse, here.
> (III.i.280–85)

Aristius enters but does not rescue Horace because, like the audience, he relishes the poet's discomfort and Crispinus's folly, so the suffering artist is saved only by chance. Placed at the very center of the play, this confrontation represents more faithfully than the denouement Jonson's developing sense of the actual relation between folly and reason: the rational man is powerless either to elude the fool or to bring him to a consciousness of his deplorable state. On the street, in the real world, fools and villains have the advantage. Reason and art can scarcely defend themselves, much less reform or even control their adversaries.

The triumph of virtue, Jonson's notion of a happy ending, can occur only in a privileged realm such as the court of Elizabeth or Cynthia or Augustus—or in the world of a play. Jonas A. Barish makes this point in suggesting why the end of *Poetaster* seems unsatisfactory: "The Rabelaisian purgation inflicted on Crispinus leaves him, as a character, nonexistent, and it leave us, as auditors, doubtful of the possibility of any real conversion, in view of the fact that Caesar's tribunal exists only in Jonson's longing fantasy and not in the actual world."[71] The imperial court represents the world for which Jonson wishes, the charmed locale in which the lamp of reason can illuminate man's baser instincts and the power of art can master them. But most of his dramatic actions take place outside these privileged spaces, in the outer reaches of Cynthia's palace or the streets of Rome or the aisle of St. Paul's; only at the end do the characters move to the beneficent spot. These two settings signify the competing ideas in Jonson's conception of experience.

After *Poetaster* the ideal world disappears from Jonsonian drama, at least explicitly, and the playwright devotes himself to the world as it is.

Accordingly, virtuous surrogates like Horace and Crites vanish too. The artists become the great con-men, Volpone and Mosca, Subtle and Face, and the early fools and rogues are reincarnated in the magnificent madmen of the great plays—Sejanus, Corvino, Morose, Sir Epicure Mammon, Zeal-of-the-Land Busy. A major difference between the early and middle plays, apart from the greater skill in portraiture that Jonson gradually attains, is that the mature Jonson admits the fact of human incorrigibility and accommodates his dramatic structures to this discouraging truth. The response he elicits may be comic or tragic, depending on the nature and degree of the characters' villainy: Sejanus provokes horror, Mammon scornful laughter. But the later figures spring from a dark, skeptical view of human behavior. *Sejanus* is the first mature product of this new comprehension of man's limitations, *Volpone* the first wholly successful one. But in the comical satires Jonson still believes that the imagination and depiction of a model world might bring it into being, and this desire contradicts his certitude about the vast gulf between that world and this.

This tension in the comical satires between pessimism and optimism, between consciousness of limitation and hope for improvement, corresponds to Shakespeare's divided attraction to comedy and tragedy. The dubious endings of the comical satires are comparable to the problematic conclusions of *All's Well* and *Measure for Measure*. Carlo Buffone and Crispinus are very different persons from Bertram and Angelo, of course; in general Jonson's men and women are conceived almost solely in terms of their weaknesses. But in none of these plays can we escape the problem of reformation or dispel the doubts that impinge upon the final reconciliations. Jonson attempted to eliminate such fears with the *coups de théâtre* that finish off his comical satires, but he could not do so entirely. We cannot know the extent to which Shakespeare wished us to doubt the final harmonies of his comedies or how skeptically he wished us to regard his tragic figures. The answers to these questions constitute the range of criticism on these comedies and tragedies. But we should worry over such matters: the deliberately compound forms attest to an unsettled vision, a combination of doubt and hope both tragic and comic.[72] Shakespeare moves haltingly towards tragedy, using his experience in comedy to fortify and color his efforts in the new form, and continues meanwhile to experiment with new styles of comedy, shading the traditional forms with new tragic insights. Jonson at the same time is attempting to contain the ambiguities of his vision within the mixed and unstable form of comical satire. Eventually, and at about the same time, each of the playwrights committed himself to a more coherent and settled view of man in the world, and the new certainty fostered a formal assurance that issued in the creation of *Volpone* and *King Lear.*

§ v

These transformations of vision and technique occurred during one of the most dynamic periods of English drama, one that included that much-discussed phenomenon the War of the Theaters. Whatever the Poetomachia actually was—a personal feud between Jonson and Marston, a competition between public and private companies, a commercially motivated publicity stunt—Shakespeare was aware of it, and Jonson was at the center of it. Nobody needs another rehearsal of the charges and countercharges or a search for identities beneath the satiric portraits, but some notice must be taken of the possible effect of this episode upon the development of Shakespeare's and Jonson's work.

Jonson, for all his arrogance and contempt for his dramatic rivals, appears to have been the loser in the Poetomachia. Indeed, he seems to have surrendered. *Cynthia's Revels,* with its glorification of Jonson as the scholar-satirist-artist Crites and its attacks on Marston and Dekker as Hedon and Anaides, provoked a counterblast from Marston: in *What You Will* Jonson (as Lampatho Doria) is held up to blatant personal and professional ridicule. In turn, Jonson, upon learning that Dekker was preparing a similar shot, rushed *Poetaster* onto the stage in late spring or summer of 1601 as a preemptive strike, a mighty engine intended to rout his enemies and insure his moral and artistic supremacy. But *Poetaster* seems to have backfired, for Dekker took up its principal characters—Horace, Crispinus, Demetrius, and Tucca—and used them as ammunition against Jonson himself in *Satiromastix.* As Dekker puts it in his prefatory remarks, "To the World," "*neyther was it much improper to set the same dog upon* Horace, *whom* Horace *had set to worrie others*" (lines 37–39).[73] Although *Satiromastix* is a patch job, a curious hybrid in which the collection of satiric portraits is only tenuously related to the inconsequential story of threatened love, Dekker's characterization of Jonson is rather subtle, something more than simple insult. Here is the passage in which Demetrius begs Horace to come down from his satiric high-horse:

> out of our loves we come
> And not revenge, but if you strike us still,
> We must defend our reputations:
> Our pens shall like our swords be always sheath'd,
> Unlesse too much provockt, *Horace* if then
> They draw bloud of you, blame us not, we are men:
> Come, let thy Muse beare up a smoother sayle,
> Tis the easiest and the basest Arte to raile.
>
> (1.ii.249–56)

This might be taken as the satirist's conventional self-justification and denial of self-interest, but throughout the comedy Horace is shown to be his own worst enemy, a talented poet who wastes his gifts in personal slurs, posturing, and self-promotion. Dekker's disgust seems to arise from disappointed admiration.[74]

Although Jonson never admitted as much, he took Dekker's advice. The "Apologeticall Dialogue" to *Poetaster* was intended to be an apology for the satiric method, a scarcely disguised riposte from the poet to those who had misconstrued him. The paradox of this appendix is its unstated acknowledgment that Jonson's art has failed him: the satirist has found that the general is not clearly visible in the particular, that reason and poetry have been unable to bring the foolish to a consciousness of their error, that the voice crying in the wilderness is only an annoyance. The fissure discernible in the comical satires between Jonson's doubts about humanity and his confidence in the power of art has become an irreconcilable split. The announcement that the satirist would next seek his fortune in tragedy was probably not meant as an admission of defeat, but that is surely how the lines must be taken. The comical satires have failed to bring his enemies out of their humours; the "mighty axe" described by Cordatus has struck its blows, and the forest of fools still stands. Jonson's disenchantment with the power of his art is further revealed in Manningham's note of February 1602 that "Ben Jonson the poet now lives upon one Townesend, and scornes the world."[75] Moreover, between *Poetaster* and *Sejanus* he undertook *Richard Crookback* and additions to *The Spanish Tragedy*. This awareness of his misplaced confidence in satire appears to have led to a further darkening of his vision and, paradoxically, to a more congenial form. Recognition of the limitations of drama, one effect of the War of the Theaters, liberated Jonson to create some of the greatest plays in the language.

Shakespeare did not engage in the fracas, at least not as actively or publicly as Jonson, Marston, or Dekker. We know that he was conscious of it, we may guess from the relevant lines in *Hamlet* that he was bored by it, but whether he engaged in a skirmish or two we are unable to tell. In this, as in most matters, Shakespeare kept his own counsel. It will usually be admitted that the armed prologue who introduces *Troilus* must glance at Jonson's use of the device in *Poetaster* and that the disclaimer "I come / . . . not in confidence / Of author's pen or actor's voice" (lines 22–24) refers slightingly to Jonsonian self-promotion. As I have suggested, the claims that *Troilus* might be the "purge" referred to in *The Return from Parnassus II* or that Ajax might be a personal swipe at Jonson remain unproved. But most criticism reflects a desire to keep Shakespeare a neutral party in the War of the Theaters, an impulse that preserves his image as above the common lot. His apparent unwillingness to squabble publicly does not preclude familiarity with or distaste for or interest in his contemporaries' work, however, and insofar as possible this connection ought to be pursued, not minimized or dismissed.

It is difficult to suggest meaningful relations between plays such as *Hamlet* or *Troilus* or *All's Well* and the major documents or issues in the Poetomachia. Certain specific references—the "little eyases," for example—present themselves at once, but there is not much to say once they have been cited. O. J. Campbell's overstated thesis about *Troilus* generated immediate, furious refutations and later fostered a tendency to underrate Shakespeare's connection to his professional milieu. That Shakespeare may have wanted to trade on the popularity of satiric drama should not embarrass us. Jonson's *Every Man Out,* whether or not it was an evasion of the June 1, 1599, prohibition against poetic "*Satyres* or *Epigrams,*" attests to the kind of taste emerging among the *literati* and at least a portion of the public theatergoers. And Shakespeare the professional was always conscious of what his fellows were doing and what the public was demanding: he tried his hand at Senecan tragedy, composed Ovidian poetry, played with sonnets, took a cue from Kyd and others in dramatizing the story of Hamlet, and helped to create and satisfy the taste for Jacobean tragicomedy. The distinctive qualities of *Troilus* may owe something to the probable circumstances of its composition, as a presentation for the literate young lawyers at the Inns of Court.[76] Even if it was only another Globe play, the audience there was certainly acquainted with recent developments on the theatrical scene: *Satiromastix*, after all, was a Chamberlain's play. At the beginning of the new century Shakespeare's attitude towards his art was developing at the same time that the theatrical market was changing, and in much the same direction. His diminishing estimate of human character and misgivings about the mimetic fidelity of comic forms coincide with his contemporaries' expression of disgust at man's baseness and inclination to err. The personal satire which fueled the War of the Theaters and for which it is mostly remembered was finally, as its major participants claimed, less important than the general anatomy of corruption, hypocrisy, and self-interest. The dramatization of such themes must have engaged the attention of Shakespeare, who was then seeking out new dramatic means of embodying an increasingly critical view of experience. His plays from 1600 to 1604 display ideas and strategies congruent with those of Jonson, Marston, and other dramatists. If it is difficult to prove that such consistency is more than accidental, it is far more difficult to imagine that Shakespeare was unaffected by the new style and the conception of humanity it presupposed.

CHAPTER 4

Dreamers

Jonson's Middle Comedies and
Shakespeare's Mature Tragedies

My analysis thus far has been concerned largely with the fringes of each career, not the main fabric: although *Hamlet, Othello,* and *Measure for Measure* have received attention, the emphasis has fallen on lesser works of both dramatists. Shakespeare has been represented by some of his least representative comedies, notably *The Merry Wives,* and coverage of Jonson's career has ended with *Poetaster* (1601) and a reference or two to *Sejanus* (1603). This chapter enlarges that narrow focus. In it I propose to examine Jonson's great comedies and Shakespeare's major tragedies under the same lens and to argue that the actions of these mature and representative works suggest visions of experience that are arrestingly similar. Artistic maturity coincides with the emergence of new and darker attitudes toward humanity in both Shakespeare and Jonson.[1] Gone are the confident progressivism of Shakespearean romantic comedy and the sense of corrigibility implicit in Jonson's comical satires. The visions that displace them, while reflecting to varying degrees the tensions apparent in the transitional phase I have just discussed, are for the most part skeptical about the efficacy and endurance of human virtue and idealism. The central feature of each is the inevitability of human error, limitation, and failure.

A telling way to study these Shakespearean and Jonsonian visions is through the authors' visionary characters, those whose conflicts with this world impel them to imagine "a world elsewhere." It is unusual, certainly, to link such characters as Othello, Antony, Lear, Timon, Coriolanus, Hamlet, and Macbeth with Volpone, Morose, Sir Epicure Mammon, and Zeal-of-the-Land Busy, and yet these memorable figures share certain fundamental traits: they are imaginative, solipsistic, inflexible, larger than life. The better lives they envisage, for all the variations in detail, are similarly impressive and unattainable, and the worlds they seek to alter or escape are likewise of a piece. In each play containing such a character, his conception of an ideal clarifies the imperfections of the actual against which the ideal is set. The playwright's interpretation of this clash between a harmonious vision and a corrupt world produces the two forms of dramatic action: Shakespeare conceives of the confrontation as tragic, Jonson as comic.

Even more interesting, however, is the ambivalence that both authors display toward their dreamers' visions. Shakespeare, insisting finally on the impossibility of sustaining an ideal, stresses its great beauties. Jonson, admitting the potential attractions of another realm, firmly repudiates the fool who clings to it. Yet Jonson can portray the unreal world in highly sensual terms, may even linger over its seductive attractions, and Shakespeare fiercely destroys any hope of fixing that ideal. Beauty and grandeur may be found in the fantasies of a mad knight, folly and delusion in the dreams of a sensitive prince. Such ambiguities are found in all the plays I shall examine: *Hamlet, Othello, King Lear, Timon of Athens, Macbeth, Antony and Cleopatra,* and *Coriolanus;* and *Volpone, Epicoene, The Alchemist,* and *Bartholomew Fair.* Investigation of these imaginative visions, characters' and creators', discloses connections between tragedy and nonsense, sublimity and absurdity, nobility and delusion, and heroism and foolishness. It is this ambiguity that helps to account for the artistic complexity and multiple significance of these major texts.

The related actions and ideas that will emerge raise tantalizing questions about the philosophical or even religious convictions of the architects of these works;[2] and such speculations lead naturally to further questions about the relations of plays and playwrights to the spirit of the age that produced them. It is tempting to connect the skeptical conclusions about human nature that arise from dramas such as *Volpone* or *Othello* with the ontological uncertainty that had begun to manifest itself in philosophy and science. We have learned, rightly, to be skeptical about the prevalence of skepticism in the early years of the seventeenth century: modern efforts to identify the nature, specify the origin, and estimate the prominence of the "new philosophy"[3] have properly modified the notion that the thinkers and writers of Renaissance England exchanged theistic optimism for doubt and pessimism as they mourned the queen and became acquainted with the king. It can be argued, for example, that the beginning of James's reign, the very period that fostered the texts I shall examine, was marked by a sense of political hope and enthusiasm.[4] And yet, for all the restraint and qualification, there is ample evidence that the philosophical tone of the Jacobean age differed significantly from that of the Elizabethan.

Whether Donne or Shakespeare or Jonson was actually engaged in the intellectual and scientific turmoil growing throughout Europe is not the issue; the fact is that such a doubtful phase had begun and was becoming more widespread as the years passed. Richard H. Popkin, the leading historian of Renaissance philosophical skepticism, summarizes the contribution of one of its most important proponents: "Montaigne discerned the relativity of man's intellectual, cultural and social achievements, a relativity that was to undermine the whole concept of the nature of man and his place in the moral cosmos."[5] This is a fair statement of the intellectual atmosphere that had begun to settle over England at the beginning of the seventeenth century. Herschel Baker, describing the new philosophy, identifies its two principal forms, "Baconian empiricism" and Cartesian "mechanistic philosophy": "As strategies for interpreting man's place in nature both were radically incompatible with the sacramental view of nature which the Renaissance had inherited from the Middle Ages, and both resulted from the fracturing of that uneasy synthesis which had subsumed the tradition of Christian humanism."[6] The greatest works of the two greatest playwrights of the age stimulate just the sort of doubt that these scholars discern in its intellectual history.

I shall not argue that either Shakespeare or Jonson was seriously affected by such philosophical weather or that their plays resulted from or contributed to it;[7] my analysis is chiefly aesthetic, not philosophical or historical. Also, it is worth remembering that both dramatists were capable of looking at the world in other ways. In the same years that Jonson was writing his comic masterpieces, he was also composing his court masques, those celebratory spectacles in which doubts about authority and order are vanquished in the twinkling of an eye; and Shakespeare would soon go on to the renewed affirmation of the late romances. But it would be perverse to deny that *King Lear* and *The Alchemist* are documents that at least reflect the philosophical tensions of their age. Intellectual history at the beginning of the seventeenth century records a movement towards disillusionment, and in little, this is the experience depicted in Jonsonian comedy and Shakespearean tragedy. The visionary character is made to surrender his idealistic and optimistic conception of man and the world, and by the end of the struggle, the spectator has lost his illusions as well.

§I

Certain major figures in Jonson's comedies and Shakespeare's tragedies are created on a similarly grand scale. All are magnificent creatures, superb in their strength or error or folly. The "greatness" of the Shakespearean hero, so familiar that it hardly requires additional comment, is a property he shares with all genuinely tragic figures, especially those of contemporary playwrights: Tamburlaine, Faustus, Bussy D'Ambois, and the Duchess of Malfi. Jonson created his two great villains, Sejanus and Catiline, according to such proportions. This tragic magnitude has its comic equivalent in the enormous scale on which Jonson's rogues and fools exhibit their wit or delusion. If Othello is larger than life, so is Sir Epicure Mammon. Although Jonsonian comedy does not concentrate, as does Shakespearean tragedy, on the *agon* of a single great personage, it nevertheless presents certain grand figures, such as Volpone or Busy, who stand out from the rest of the *dramatis personae* and who compel our attention by virtue of their elaborate speech, forceful personality, obsession, solipsism, intransigence, or prodigious imagination. They attract notice for many of the same reasons that the Shakespearean charismatic hero fascinates his audience. In them, Jonson depicts trickery or foolishness on a heroic level.

Shakespeare's most effective method of signifying a heroic nature is the verbal idiom he creates for his protagonist. Each speaks a language that is expansive, hyperbolic, and immediately identifiable:

Whip me, you devils,
From the possession of this heavenly sight,

Blow me about in winds, roast me in sulphur,
Wash me in steep-down gulfs of liquid fire!
O Desdemona, Desdemona dead,
Oh, oh, oh.
(*Othello*, v.ii.279–83)

And thou, all-shaking thunder,
Strike flat the thick rotundity o'th'world!
Crack Nature's moulds, all germens spill at once
That makes ingrateful man!
(*King Lear*, iii.ii.6–9)

Then fly, false Thanes,
And mingle with the English epicures:
The mind I sway by, and the heart I bear,
Shall never sag with doubt, nor shake with fear.
(*Macbeth*, v.iii.7–10)

Let Rome in Tiber melt, and the wide arch
Of the rang'd empire fall! Here is my space,
Kingdoms are clay:
(*Antony and Cleopatra*, i.i.33–35)

Who dares, who dares,
In purity of manhood stand upright,
And say this man's a flatterer? If one be,
So are they all, for every grise of fortune
Is smooth'd by that below: the learned pate
Ducks to the golden fool; all's obliquy;
There's nothing level in our cursed natures
But direct villainy. Therefore be abhorr'd
All feasts, societies, and throngs of men!
His semblable, yea himself, Timon disdains.
Destruction fang mankind!
(*Timon*, IV.iii.13–23)

But out, affection!
All bond and privilege of nature break!
Let it be virtuous to be obstinate.
(*Coriolanus*, v.iii.24–26)

The voice audible in these familiar speeches and common to all the protagonists is the voice of an "overstater."[8] True, each speaker exhibits particular verbal turns that individualize him or reflect his distinctive nature, such as Othello's exotic diction or Lear's propensity to curse. But the differences are in detail; the outlines of their speeches are similar and the tonality is unmistakable. Modern criticism, thanks (or no thanks) to Caroline Spurgeon, has placed inordinate stress on the contribution of imagery to the creation of magnitude, but in fact the means differ from play to play. Prosody, diction, and syntax are usually as important as metaphor, and in parts of some plays much more so. In thinking of the tragic figures we hear reverberations of the spacious line ("smooth as monumental alabaster"), passionate interjection ("Howl! Howl! Howl!"), stark imperative ("Give me my robe, put on my crown"), and intimation of infinity ("Oh, I could tell you—"). But whatever the particular poetic means, the protagonist's magnificent language is Shakespeare's main instrument for suggesting universality and heroic scale.[9]

Jonson too is capable of writing in Ercles' vein. Morose rises to it: "Oh, the sea breakes in upon me! another floud! an inundation! I shall be orewhelm'd with noise. It beates already at my shores. I feele an earthquake in my selfe, for't" (*Epicoene*, III.vi.2–5). At an especially calamitous moment Mosca becomes an overstater:

> if my heart
> Could expiate the mischance, I'ld pluck it out.
> Will you be pleas'd to hang me? or cut my throate?
> And i'le requite you, sir. Let's die like *Romanes*,
> Since wee have liv'd, like *Grecians*.
> (*Volpone*, III.viii.11–15)

Zeal-of-the-Land Busy utters his nonsense with something like vatic grandeur: "Downe with *Dagon*, downe with *Dagon*; 'tis I, will no longer endure your prophanations" (*Bartholomew Fair*, v.v.1–2). The sounds of these outbursts are similar to those of Shakespeare's heroes; the difference, of course, is in the nature of the speakers, their circumstances, and their ludicrous causes. An obsessed old miser and a clever servant lament their fortune as if it were the stuff of tragedy: Morose seeks cosmic correlatives for the verbiage of the Collegians, and Mosca, placing Volpone's failed rape in an exalted historical tradition determines that he and his master should put an end to their miseries "after the high Roman fashion." Busy's oracular outburst proclaims his heroic stand against a trunk of puppets.

What Jonson provides here and elsewhere is a ridiculous version of Shakespearean eloquence. He is aware that the extravagance upon which the grand style depends is potentially risible. Puttenham emphasizes the ironic possibilities of hyperbole when he names it "the over reacher right with his originall or [lowd lyar] & me thinks not amisse."[10] But the effect of such linguistic exaggeration in the Renaissance was not necessarily subversive: hyperbole could be used straightforwardly, as "a common figure of the inexpressibility topos."[11] The key to interpretation is context or, putting it another way, dramatic mode. In Shakespeare, the protagonist's manifest nobility and capacity for heroism ensure that the audience accepts and appreciates his speech.[12] Since Jonson does not admit heroes into his comic universe, the language he creates in this vein properly strikes the auditor as inflated and overwrought. And this is precisely the point. By assigning a grandiose dialect to a race of impostors, the playwright exposes the distance between sound and sense. Shakespeare, on the other hand, allows such eloquence to mark the distance between the hero and the ordinary men around him. Yet this opposition of technique ought not to be oversimplified. An overtone of bombast often sounds in the speeches of Shakespeare's heroes, as even a cursory acquaintance with Othello (or Othello criticism) reveals; and Jonson's raging fools, absurd though they be, occasionally achieve a grandeur not easily dismissed, as the arguments about the generic classification of Volpone indicate.

This exalted language, in both its Shakespearean and Jonsonian forms, signifies breadth of vision and strength of will. Hamlet and Sir Epicure and Antony—indeed, virtually all the major figures in these plays and some of the minor ones, particularly in Jonson—possess an active imaginative faculty. They speak differently from their fellows, at least in part because they see differently. Even such a figure as Othello, often considered the least sensitive of the major tragic heroes, conceives of and therefore speaks of his military experience and his marriage in a style that may be called imaginative, idealized, and even artistic. He demands perfection of his wife, his officers, and himself, and this vision of perfection is representative of the dreams of the Shakespearean hero in general. It is also germane to the imaginative designs of the Jonsonian fool and rogue. Harriet Hawkins speaks of the "wild and peculiar power" of Volpone's language, comparing the sensual grandee to Marlowe's intellectual idealist: "Volpone's imagination roves the world and its myths, commandeering them with a privateer's bravura, making all the glittering spoils his own. 'Then I will *have* thee.' 'None but thee shall be *my* paramour.' Volpone and Faustus both want to grasp, to seize, to possess, to summon and command their visions of delight in the forms they most desire."[13] The sumptuous language spoken by Jonson's great imaginative figures is an appropriate medium for the contents of their visions. Even the undeniable tendency of the verse to mock itself, which represents Jonson's use of hyperbole for *meiosis,* depends upon the relation of ridiculous language to the genuine article, and the undercutting does not cancel the powerful imaginative appeals that this kind of speech can set forth. Jonson allows the poetry or prose to forecast the eventual collapse of this vision of beauty or harmony or fulfillment—he twits the speaker in mid-career—but the hyperbolic quality testifies also to the imaginative fertility of the dreamer's mind.

Although Shakespeare does undermine his heroes' eloquence from time to time, the immediate and main effect of their heightened rhetoric is to signify greatness of heart. The connection of Volpone and Faustus is relevant to Shakespeare as well, who must have noted the connections between language and vision in the plays of Christopher Marlowe. Most efforts to locate specific Marlovian echoes center upon Shakespeare's earliest productions, but it seems likely that at the height of his career the wish to develop an appropriate tragic idiom led Shakespeare to recall not only the sounds he had heard at the Rose in the early 1590s but also the principles underlying them.[14] The most fundamental of these is Tamburlaine's identification of language with power: the aspiring mind expresses itself in soaring speech. Madeleine Doran contends, after quoting "Let Rome in Tiber melt," that Antony's hyperbolic style springs from his "large and generous imagination," and this same identification between verbal power and imaginative fecundity obtains for all the characters under scrutiny here.[15] Generosity is peculiar to Antony and perhaps to Hamlet—we would certainly except all of Jonson's characters and Macbeth and Coriolanus—but in scale and force of desire they are all related.

Each of Jonson's and Shakespeare's imaginists invents and seeks to realize an ideal state of being. Although each vision originates in personal desire, such as Morose's insistence on quiet and Hamlet's reverence

for truth, the dreamer's solipsism and strength of will lead him to generalize, to expand that wish into a great silent empire or a Denmark,
indeed a world, set right. The most important feature common to each
vision is that it is unattainable, and the imaginist's commitment to it
brings about his undoing.

The imagination of an ideal world, or at least the hankering after a
better lot in this one, is a constant and fruitful topic in Jonsonian
comedy, and the touchstone for such activity is found in the ruminations
of Sir Epicure Mammon:

> I will have all my beds, blowne up, not stuft:
> Downe is too hard. And then, mine oval roome,
> Fill'd with such pictures, as TIBERIUS tooke
> From ELEPHANTIS: and dull ARETINE
> But coldly imitated. Then, my glasses,
> Cut in more subtill angles, to disperse,
> And multiply the figures, as I walke
> Naked betweene my *succubae*. My mists
> I'le have of perfume, vapor'd 'bout the roome,
> To loose our selves in; and my baths, like pits
> To fall into: from whence, we will come forth,
> And rowle us drie in gossamour, and roses.
> (*Alchemist*, 11.ii.41–52)

These roses are without thorns, of course, for this is Sir Epicure's conception of an earthly paradise, of the way life ought to be lived. Yet the
private chamber here described is only a minor province in the "novo
orbe" that the lubricious knight promises Surly, the "free state" he
imagines for Dol. He sees beyond the tawdry precincts of Blackfriars to a
world of harmony and pleasure. Indeed, his elaborate speech, while
conveying a sense of infinity and perfection, transforms the vulgar present. Come projection, no longer will

> The sonnes of *sword*, and *hazzard* fall before
> The golden calfe, and on their knees, whole nights,
> Commit idolatrie with wine, and trumpets:
> Or goe a feasting, after drum and ensigne.
> No more of this.
> (11.i.18–22)

Mammon's imagination is so perfervid that it converts the crude realities of London nightlife into an elaborate and impressive-sounding ritual. But Sir Epicure's fantasies are not merely ridiculous; they are also expressions of a desire for transcendence, even for salvation.[16] Although his personal obsession is physical pleasure, the speculations in which he indulges essentially represent the desires shared by all the clients in *The Alchemist*. They wish for something novel, for liberation from the mundane, for distinction, for metamorphosis. It may seem inappropriate to regard the dim Dapper as a visionary, but his dreams become more and more ambitious as his fortunes seem to improve. When Face assures Doctor Subtle that the young lawyer's request is modest, Dapper is quick to escalate his hopes:

> *Fac.* Y'are mistaken, Doctor.
> Why, he do's aske one but for cups, and horses,
> A rifling *flye:* none o' your great *familiars.*
> *Dap.* Yes, Captayne, I would have it, for all games.
> *Sub.* I told you so.
> (1.ii.82–86)

Each dreamer regards the "cunning man" as a source of secret knowledge, power, and change: "the tongues of carpes" and "camels heeles" are to Mammon what customers are to Drugger or knowledge of the duello is to Kastril. Sir Epicure's highly developed fantasy is unique but not unrepresentative; it is simply the most detailed expression of Jonson's concern throughout the comedy with human aspiration.[17]

This vision of a better world, of "nature, naturiz'd 'gainst all infections," is not limited to *The Alchemist*, of course. Volpone's appeals to Celia are based upon Epicurean impulses—he offers her the milk of unicorns—and the histrionic gifts he shares with Mosca constitute another route of imaginative escape into other, better realms:

> my dwarfe shall dance,
> My eunuch sing, my foole make up the antique.
> Whil'st, we, in changed shapes, act OVIDS tales,
> Thou, like EUROPA now, and I like JOVE,
> Then I like MARS, and thou like ERYCINE,
> So, of the rest, till we have quite run through
> And weary'd all the fables of the gods.
> (*Volpone*, III.vii.219–25)

Even the theatrical transformation of himself into a dying man is an ironic avenue to power and distinction: "I gaine / No common way" (1.i.23). In *The Silent Woman*, Morose proposes to model his household after the court of a Turkish potentate, with all commands given in sign language (11.i.29–38). One of the most astonishing and horrifying visions in Renaissance literature is Morose's anticipation of debasing Dauphine (11.v.98–131), the lengthy passage beginning "O my felicity! how I shall bee reveng'd on my insolent kinsman, and his plots, to fright me from marrying!" When Zeal-of-the-Land Busy is put in the stocks, he comforts Dame Purecraft by describing his punishment as an honor: "Peace, religious sister, it is my calling, comfort your selfe, an extraordinary calling, and done for my better standing, my surer standing, hereafter" (*Bartholomew Fair*, 1 v.vi.119–21). Such visions of heaven, earthly and otherwise, represent Jonson's most effective dramatic means of presenting the wholesome and poisonous fruits of the human fancy and will. Alvin Kernan's description of the imaginative talent of Volpone and Mosca places it in an instructive context:

They are thus the spokesmen for progress, the kind of progress based on increase of material possessions and rugged individualism. And in this they are one with such titans as Tamburlaine, Faustus, Richard III, Edmund, Lady Macbeth, and Milton's Satan, who all express—before coming to tragic awareness—the optimistic Renaissance view:

The mind is its own place, and in it self
Can make a Heav'n of Hell, a Hell of Heav'n.
(*Paradise Lost*, 1.254–55)

We cannot help being moved by the power of such a belief, and a comic figure such as Volpone, as well as a defiant Satan thundering from the depth of hell, has a magnificence about him, a gusto for experience and a turbulent vitality that is attractive.[18]

The visionary propensities of the tragic hero, although not so colorfully displayed as those of a Mammon or a Morose, contribute to his tragic standing and his tragic fall. The conflict in each of Shakespeare's great tragedies, as in Jonson's comedies, may be described as a collision between the world as it is and the world as the protagonist imagines it.[19] The great tragic figures impress us with their commitment to some kind of truth or perfection. Our response to this vision alters from play to play: we endorse Hamlet's devotion to right action, but deplore Macbeth's vision of the perfect crime. Bernard McElroy writes that "Shakespeare's four mature tragedies, *Hamlet, Othello, King Lear,* and *Macbeth,* all embody at least one essential experience in common, the collapse of the subjective world of the tragic hero. . . . that view is based upon a few assumptions that are as natural to the character as his heartbeat, that are so basic, in fact, that he does not, in the ordinary course of things, question them. All values to which the hero subscribes and by which he judges himself and others flow naturally from his subjective world-picture."[20] Since the business of each tragedy is the destruction of the unrealistic vision, or the hero's awakening to the limits of mortality, Shakespeare does not always give to the ideal conception the elaborate expression that Jonson does. Sometimes the initial attachment to an absolute world-view is implied in its opposite, as in the second scene of *Hamlet,* where the Prince's expressed contempt for the mutability and corruption of the present suggests his devotion to the lost realm of benevolence and order symbolized by his father. Such a commitment to an ideal domain is always present, however, a concomitant of the hero's exceptional imagination and force of will, and it is both the source of his greatness and the cause of his ruin.

The relation between the heroic Shakespearean vista and the specious Jonsonian paradise is most evident when the tragic protagonist, usually as the pressures of the fallen world become most intense and its limits most restrictive, offers a pure expression of the visionary impulse. Coriolanus so indulges himself when he stands before the multitude and finds himself unable to satisfy the demands of custom:

> Better it is to die, better to starve,
> Than crave the hire which first we do deserve.
> Why in this wolvish toge should I stand here,
> To beg of Hob and Dick that does appear
> Their needless vouches? Custom calls me to't.
> What custom wills, in all things should we do't,
> The dust on antique time would lie unswept
> And mountainous error be too highly heap'd
> For truth to o'erpeer. Rather than fool it so,
> Let the high office and the honour go
> To one that would do thus.
> (*Coriolanus,* II.iii.112–22)

This solipsist has devoted himself to his imaginative understanding of a just society, a state in which merit is absolute, not subject to the constraints of form or ceremony. Coriolanus is often said to be unlikable, and his ideal government is so closely tied to his unpleasant nature that connections between his vision and those of the earlier tragic figures may be hard to discern. But all the heroes conceive of the world in similarly extreme ways. And the crucial ambiguities of the tragedies depend upon a conflict of opposites like that evident in this passage.

It is his idealism, above all else, that makes the Shakespearean hero a compelling figure.[21] The hero makes his entrance committed to his own ideal construction of experience, a vision as erroneous as it is attractive; he bears a firm conviction that the world functions as he understands it. To describe this habit of idealization as simply as possible, we may say that he believes in a perfect correspondence between the way things are and the way things appear to him. Most of the qualities commonly associated with the tragic figures—hubris, solipsism, tenacity—either support or arise from these ideal conceptions. The heroes' attempts to impose this personal vision upon the recalcitrant world (and, when this fails, to sustain it for themselves against fearsome opposition) make up the action of the tragedies.

The heroic conception is normally marked by a radical simplicity. In the opening scene of *King Lear*, for instance, the plain formality of the divestiture illuminates Lear's childlike faith in his own interpretation of his kingly role, his family, and himself. This is a version of the Cinderella story, and the audience's certainty of what is what, a function of intuition and the familiarity of the tale, makes the king's subjective interpretation all the more arresting.[22] The king is ague-proof, the ultimate arbiter of value, a believer in the absolute identity of words and meanings. He imagines a future in which he can "retain / The name and all th'addition to a king" (1.i.135–36). Like Lear, most of the tragic heroes are distinguished by an extraordinary naiveté. Even Hamlet, the most intellectually able and sophisticated of the lot, shows a youthful confidence in his ability to find the truth and act rightly upon it.

> Haste me to know't, that I with wings as swift
> As meditation or the thoughts of love
> May sweep to my revenge.
> (1.v.29–31)

Perhaps Shakespeare even implies that his heroes exist in a state of innocence.[23] That Othello has often been considered a simpleton—as one of my students put it, "Othello is not the brightest bulb on the porch"—is partly a function of his devotion to an elementary and clearly defined sense of honor, honesty, loyalty, and conjugal love. His famous credo, "To be once in doubt, / Is once to be resolv'd" attests to his uncomplicated ethical system, a mode of behavior appropriate to his naive understanding of human intercourse:

I'll see before I doubt, when I doubt, prove,
And on the proof, there is no more but this:
Away at once with love or jealousy!
(III.iii.194–96)

The aural effects of the verse attest to the hero's magnificent simplicity. The logical process of discovery and decision is compressed into a single line (every word except "before" is a monosyllable) and is followed by the swift and inevitable result. So it is with love: "My life upon her faith."

The other heroes' ideal visions are equally prominent. Brutus's conception of nobility makes the swearing of an oath seem degrading:

Swear priests and cowards, and men cautelous,
Old feeble carrions, and such suffering souls
That welcome wrongs; unto bad causes swear
Such creatures as men doubt; but do not stain
The even virtue of our enterprise,
Nor th'insuppressive mettle of our spirits,
To think that or our cause or our performance
Did need an oath.
(*Julius Caesar*, II.i.129–36)

Perhaps this passage is unrepresentative, for in it Brutus rejects the idea of ceremony; his characteristic strategy is to dignify the conspiracy by ritualizing it.[24] But the point is the same: Brutus converts what might have been "a savage spectacle" into a noble act, a sacrifice essential to his ideal vision of government. Timon is committed to the benevolence of humanity and to himself as the first exemplar of that virtue. According to G. K. Hunter, "The whole behaviour of Timon shows the curious paradox of the man, superlatively endowed and favoured by Fortune, who thinks that it is his privilege to move through society like an earthly god. . . . He dispenses largesse with an open, undiscriminating hand; he never counts the cost."[25] Macbeth, although it may seem wrongheaded to refer to the "dwarfish thief" as an idealist, acts upon a faith in his own strength and privilege. He believes that he can move directly from the "happy prologues" spoken by the witches into the "swelling act," can exert absolute control over his own destiny. If only Fleance had not escaped, Macbeth "had else been perfect; / Whole as the marble, founded as the rock, / As broad and general as the casing air" (III.iv.21–23). Finally, Mark Antony imagines himself as capable of balancing responsibility and desire, public and private life.

This commitment to a noble ideal is not as simple as it may sound, however. Shakespeare takes pains to indicate simultaneously the glorious appeals and the dangerous unreality of the ideal vision. The visionary hero who sees this world of beauty and harmony is also hubristic, self-absorbed, and blind to the potential dangers of his conception. His devotion to a heroic view of the world is predicated upon his location at the center of that world. When the ideal is threatened, the hero's identity is imperiled, and he responds with a violence that exposes the dark underside of heroic commitment. McElroy describes the reactions of Hamlet, Othello, Lear, and Macbeth in just these terms: "They demand that the world conform to what they desire it to be, and, when it refuses, they attack furiously, procuring their own destruction."[26] The volley of curses with which Lear meets Cordelia's reading of the filial bond represents the efforts of the self to preserve its identity. The ideal is lovely, but the attempt to retain it can be horrifying.

In every one of the tragedies Shakespeare insists that the audience recognize the ambiguous combination of beauty and danger. The tonal differences from play to play depend to a large extent upon Shakespeare's adjustment of this balance, and we respond far differently to the integrity of Hamlet's vision than to Macbeth's idea of a peaceable kingdom. These differences may seem less disturbing if we glance briefly at another "idealist" who fails to make the world conform to his wishes— Malvolio. Maynard Mack, after quoting the steward's explication of Maria's letter, notices that "the attributes of the comic alazon and the tragic hero" are mutually illuminating: "The deception to which Malvolio here falls victim, by 'crushing' the simulation a little, is not far different from that which victimizes Macbeth, when he too crushes to his will the riddling speeches of the Witches; or what King Lear allows to happen when he reads duty in the flattering phrases of his elder daughters, ingratitude in the blunt speaking of Cordelia; or what takes place in Othello when his whole vocabulary begins to shift and slide, as from some hidden rock-fault, under the pressures of Iago's insinuations."[27] We react to Malvolio's self-delusion with scornful mirth, but the form of his imaginative activity approximates that of the great heroes. All of them attempt "to crush this a little," to impose their will upon resistant reality, and thus our response to them is inevitably mixed. Othello calls himself an honorable murderer: he is honorable, but he is also a murderer; he is a murderer, but he is also honorable.

These Shakespearean visions lead us, with the aid of Malvolio, back to Jonson, whose comic protagonists also maintain deluded conceptions of themselves and their relation to other men. The connection should be clear between Shakespearean idealism and the visionary tendencies of the great Jonsonian gulls such as Morose and Mammon, whose naiveté and fertile imaginations reach virtually heroic proportions. All the clients in *The Alchemist,* for example, exhibit what Face refers to in Mammon as an "itch of mind" (IV.v.93), and their will generates a sublimely innocent confidence:

FAC.   Doctor,
When must he come for his *familiar?*
DAP. Shall I no ha' it with me?
(I.ii.141–43)

Typically, Dapper believes that he can purchase his gambling fly ready-made.

These parallels between alazon and tragic figure are easier to discern than the resemblances between the Shakespearean heroes and Jonsonian rogues, whose cunning and manipulative skill would seem to link them with such scoundrels as Edmund and Iago. (In fact, this is a tenable connection also.) Whereas the Shakespearean hero pursues his ideal in innocence of the fallen world, the Jonsonian shark is alert to its corruption and seeks to profit thereby. And yet such schemers as Mosca and Subtle and Face, for all their clear-sighted understanding of man's penchant for folly, imagine *themselves* to be exempt from the general weakness. Plague or no plague, the alchemist and his agents have created a private sphere in which the dross of society may be converted into gold.

When the "explosion" sends Mammon away empty-handed and disappointed, the rogues are exultant:

> SUB. Is he gone? FAC. Yes, and as heavily
> As all the gold he hop'd for, were in his bloud.
> Let us be light, though. SUB. I, as balls, and bound
> And hit our heads against the roofe for joy:
> There's so much of our care now cast away.
> (*Alchemist*, IV.v.96–100)

This is analogous to the sense of liberation expressed by Sejanus in his expectation of triumph—"My roofe receives me not; 'tis aire I tread: / And, at each step, I feele my'advanced head / Knocke out a starre in heav'n!" (V.7–9)—and such unbridled faith in the self should remind us of the attitudes of Lear and Macbeth and Timon. In *Epicoene* the three gallants revel in their intellectual and social superiority, particularly their special powers of wit. Truewit especially considers himself a man immune to the stupidity of such gulls as Sir John Daw and Sir Amorous LaFoole, and yet the play's final revelation leaves him as humbled and incredulous as the rest.

Volpone illustrates better than any other Jonsonian figure this mixture of insight and blindness, of earthy smarts and high-flown imagination. The temptation among some critics and directors to consider him a tragic figure implies yet another link with Shakespeare's tragic protagonists. He shares with them, as with Face, an *amour propre* that gives him absolute faith in his own judgment and an immensity of will that proscribes compromise. This pride in cunning characterizes virtually everyone in *Volpone*. The hapless Sir Pol boasts of exceptional perspicacity: the whale in the Thames is a "project" "either sent from *Spaine*, or the *Arch-dukes!* / SPINOLA'S whale" (II.i.50–51); Mas Stone, the fool, was "one of the most dangerous heads / Living within the state" (II.i.65–66); the Italian mountebanks "are the onely-knowing men of *Europe!*" (II.ii.9).[28] Considering himself a man "of wisdom and of reach," Sir Pol plays Polonius to Volpone's Hamlet, a parodic embodiment of the central figure. All the Jonsonian rogues and would-be rogues are simultaneously cunning and naive. Volpone's arrogant view of himself as the champion among tricksters requires that he divulge his identity to the court rather than be outfoxed by Mosca. Like Othello or Coriolanus, he will sustain the ideal regardless of the cost.

"You are too absolute," says Volumnia to her son in a phrase that elucidates the dilemma faced by both tragic and comic extremists. A supremely powerful will is coupled with the wealthy imagination, but the world invariably resists transmutation or control. Maynard Mack contends that "Brutus, Othello, Lear, Timon, Macbeth, Antony, Coriolanus . . . have an heroic, single-minded commitment to some absolute in themselves or in the sum of things, or both, to which their hyperbolic speech is vehicle; and against them, characteristically, are ranged all the personalities and forces which favor a less intransigent address to life."[29] It will be noticed that Hamlet is absent from Mack's list, but even he, "the least engaged of all the Shakespearean heroes, because disengagement is in a sense his problem, is made to seem heroically engaged when placed against the extreme detachment of Horatio."[30] In Hamlet's jesting with the gravedigger in v.i, the clown's puns prompt Hamlet to comment "How absolute the knave is!" (v.i.128). The gravedigger's "equivocation," his mock-precision about "lying" in the grave and whose grave it is, constitutes a parodic comment on Hamlet's own absolute commitment to truth and to right action. All these visionaries find themselves undone by their absolute commitment to a subjective view.

Shakespeare emphasizes the tragic failure and waste that attend the hero's devotion to his sense of how the world operates: each of the protagonists is betrayed by the force of his will. Even when it becomes clear that the ideal conception cannot be sustained, the hero insists upon fulfilling its conditions. Othello in committing suicide judges himself by the same standards he has applied to others. Antony must meet Caesar in the most heroic and challenging manner possible ("By sea, by sea"), and when this fails, he adopts an even more quixotic approach:

Ant.   I dare him therefore
To lay his gay comparisons apart
And answer me declin'd, sword against sword,
Ourselves alone. I'll write it: follow me.
[*Exit Antony and Ambassador.*]

Eno. [*Aside*] Yes, like enough! High-battled Caesar will
Unstate his happiness, and be stag'd to the show
Against a sworder! I see men's judgments are
A parcel of their fortunes, and things outward

> Do draw the inward quality after them,
> To suffer all alike, that he should dream,
> Knowing all measures, the full Caesar will
> Answer his emptiness; Caesar, thou has subdued
> His judgment too.
> (*Antony and Cleopatra*, 111.xiii.25–37)

Enobarbus's sympathetic critique of Antony's self-assessment captures nicely the mixture of pity and admiration we are encouraged to feel towards the uncompromising idealist. Even Macbeth, resolving that he will "bearlike . . . fight the course," retains some of our sympathy. Such rigidity is self-destructive, of course, but it ennobles the tragic hero in the same way that his vision magnifies him. Both the will and the object of that will provoke an ambivalent response and contribute to Shakespeare's exploration of the tragic paradox.

The comic version of heroic intractability appears in Jonson's portrayal of the rampant human will, especially where his emphasis falls upon the relentless pursuit of absurd desire. The great fools exhibit the most obviously rigid attachment to their hopes, as when Mammon finds ways to accommodate each of Surly's objections to the alchemical operation. Subtle's defense of the process for Surly's benefit reassures the expectant knight and evokes from him cries of enthusiasm: "Well said, father! / Nay, if he take you in hand, sir, with an argument, / Hee'll bray you in a morter" (11.iii.176–78). Morose's first entrance depicts the extremity of his attempts to create and secure his silent realm: the servant who has "fastened on a thicke-quilt, or flock-bed, on the outside of the dore" and oiled the locks and hinges must announce that he has done so only with nods of the head, shrugs, and bows, as Morose maniacally reminds him before every rejoinder. Other lesser figures display the same kind of monumental stubbornness. Ananias, the younger and more zealous of the Puritans who deal with Subtle, is so full of new religious fervor that he wishes to dictate even the terms of conversation with the alchemist:

> SUB. And, then, the turning of the Lawyers pewter
> To plate, at *Christ-masse* — ANA. *Christ-tide,* I pray you.
> SUB. Yet, ANANIAS? ANA. I have done.
> (*Alchemist*, 111.ii.42–44)

This portrait of religious fanaticism constitutes a sketch for that most extreme of Jonson's Puritan zealots, Zeal-of-the-Land Busy, who cannot restrain himself from "prophesying" against the corruption of Smithfield. Busy's hypocrisy complicates the matter somewhat, for when he cannot prevent the Littlewits from sampling the delights of the fair, he manages to endorse the venture and even to justify his own participation: he resolves "by the publike eating of Swines flesh, to professe our hate, and loathing of *Judaisme*, whereof the brethren stand taxed. I will therefore eate, yea, I will eate exceedingly!" (*Bartholomew Fair*, I.vi.95–97). Yet even with the obvious inconsistency, Busy represents the irony of absolutism, his rigid devotion asserting itself regardless of the position taken. Indeed, such a violent shift of commitment corresponds to the passage from love to hate in a figure like Lear.

It may seem inappropriate at first to describe as intransigent those great Jonsonian intriguers who thrive by means of their protean talents. Adaptability—here a wicked *sprezzatura*—is the main subject of Mosca's boast in his famous encomium to the genuine Parasite, who can

> be here,
> And there, and here, and yonder, all at once;
> Present to any humour, all occasion;
> And change a visor, swifter, then a thought!
> (*Volpone*, III.i.26–29)

Ironically, however, flexibility is the one point on which the schemer is dogmatic. Volpone's insistence upon the supremacy of his wit, the instance already cited, is characteristic of all the Jonsonian rogues. Their capacity for being all things to all men is central to their hubristic view of themselves and their world, and it is the one value they will never alter or compromise. The quarrel in the opening scene of *The Alchemist*, with each contestant claiming that his role is the more important, is a dispute over precedence; and even though the two knaves agree to disagree, neither yields his position because it is not in his nature to do so. Dol accuses them both of being madmen, and their rigid self-images collide at every lull in the action.

Busy virtually becomes a comic madman in the last act of *Bartholomew Fair*, disputing with a puppet whether dramatic representation should be considered profane. Similarly, Morose is said to have "run out o'dores in's night-caps, to talke with a *Casuist* about his divorce" (*Epicoene*, IV.v.3–4). If such fits do not constitute madness in the strict sense, they do at least represent the disorientation that occurs when the dreamer is awakened and his vision dispelled or shattered. Much of the "humourous" behavior in the earlier plays is sufficiently aberrant to be called madness; the danger of the *idée fixe* was one of Jonson's earliest concerns.[31] And when the idea is as grand or as fixed as those cherished by the great Jonsonian fools, the destruction of it creates a comic explosion. In *The Alchemist* that explosion is literal: "[*A great crack and noise within*]." When Mammon returns in the last act and finds that he has been bilked, he declares that he "will goe mount a turnep-cart, and preach / The end o'the world, within these two months" (*Alchemist*, v.v.81–82). The unyielding mind snaps under the pressure of failure or denial and spins into confusion, to the delight of the audience and often of the stage spectators.

In tragedy such dislocation produces a horrific insanity. The boldness and beauty of the hero's dreams invite assault from the malign forces of the tragic universe, an attack which his mortality cannot withstand: the result is the raving of Lear, "the lunatic king," in act 4, or Hamlet's brutal treatment of Ophelia in the nunnery scene. Even when the hero is not literally demented but merely out of control, like Othello in the latter half of the play or Antony in his assault upon Cleopatra and Thidias, the wild actions and fragmented language create a similar impression. As events combine to challenge him, the hero clings all the more tenaciously to his vision, and the ensuing tension creates an outburst corresponding to the fit of comic dementia. "Each tragedy portrays a tremendous struggle to hold onto the self in the face of hostile forces. The hero seeks to realize an ideal image in opposition to an invading environment. So great is the tension between an inner will and outer world that the former seems able to maintain itself only by denying all other reality or by laying the world to waste."[32] Charles Frey thus describes the collision I have been studying and cites several examples, the most valuable being Hamlet's words to Laertes:

Was't Hamlet wrong'd Laertes? Never Hamlet.
If Hamlet from himself be ta'en away,
And when he's not himself does wrong Laertes,
Then Hamlet does it not, Hamlet denies it.
Who does it then? His madness.
(*Hamlet*, v.ii.229–33)

According to the tragic paradox, the hero's great power of will takes him beyond himself into insanity.

§ 11

The imagined worlds to which the Jonsonian and Shakespearean characters madly cling are of a piece: they are realms of infinite possibility.
Particular details vary, of course, according to the character and taste of
the dreamer, from Volpone's quest for exotic physical sensations to
Lear's hope that he may "Unburthen'd crawl toward death" (1.i.40),
and the audience's response varies accordingly. Still, each vision implies
an easy leap beyond the limits of the fallen world. It is in many respects a
version of the golden world realized at the conclusion of Shakespeare's
festive comedies, but without the questions or tinges of darkness. Since
certain of the tragedies have been shown to portray the stage of experience inevitably succeeding the happy ending,[33] we may think of the
tragic hero—Othello comes immediately to mind—as attempting to
maintain single-handedly that state of bliss and harmony. In the first act
of *Volpone*, just before Voltore begins the parade of *captatori* into the
chamber, Mosca imagines what the vulture must be imagining:

> VOL. Give me my furres. Why doest thou laugh so, man?
> MOS. I cannot choose, sir, when I apprehend
> What thoughts he has (without) now, as he walkes:
> That this might be the last gift, he should give;
> That this would fetch you; if you dyed to day,
> And gave him all, what he should be to morrow;
> What large returne would come of all his venters;
> How he should worship'd be, and reverenc'd;
> Ride, with his furres, and foot-clothes; waited on
> By herds of fooles, and clients; have cleere way
> Made for his moyle, as letter'd as himselfe;
> Be cald the great, and learned Advocate:
> And then concludes, there's nought impossible.
> (*Volpone*, 1.ii.97–109)

Although Mosca is contemptuous of Voltore, the fly will indulge in such
speculation on his own behalf. Anything may be. The limitations of
mortality will be forgotten, quotidian cares banished, the grandest desires for self and state easily gratified. Or so the imaginist sees things.

So Shakespeare would like things to be. He encourages his audience
to assent to the beauty of the vision, first by supporting the natural
dramatic bond between dreamer and spectator, and second by contrast-

ing the appeals of the imagined world with the brutality and malevolence of the hostile tragic environment. The audience's sympathy with the tragic figure is connected with its willingness to endorse the attractions inherent in the heroic vision, unreal though it is. It is tempting to contemplate the kind of world Othello believes in, where "Certain, men should be what they seem," and this desire for certainty and consistency is an alluring feature of most of these heroes' visions. I would contend that Shakespeare even invites limited approval for Coriolanus's dedication to an ethic of merit at the same time that he ironically subverts that commitment in his depiction of Martius's arrogance and inhumanity. An audience is probably less inclined to sanction Macbeth's mistaken conception of experience, for this idealistic and courageous hero rapidly becomes a criminal, and most of the action is given over to the consequences of his villainy. Nevertheless, it is possible, early in the tragedy, to sense the seductive power of Macbeth's wishes: if only this were a world where power could be achieved and secured by an "easy" act, where "it were done, when 'tis done," where a little water could clear one of the deed. But in this context *Macbeth* differs from the other tragedies because the emphasis is unusual: Shakespeare dwells upon the hideous personal and political effects of the imaginist's subjective view. *Antony and Cleopatra* illustrates more persuasively than any other play the powerful lure of the hero's vision. Since Alexandria is an actual location, not just an imagined state of being, the audience participates more directly in that glittering, sensual world. Although the physical temptations give to Egypt a particular flavor and texture, it nevertheless can stand for the idealized world to which the Shakespearean hero commits himself, and our response to Egypt guides us in reading the other versions of that world.[34] Somewhere in all the tragedies our own imaginations are teased, and the reaction is rather like Jake Barnes's at the end of *The Sun Also Rises:* "Isn't it pretty to think so?"

Even Jonson, despite his reputation as a moralist, betrays some sympathy for his dreamers' fancies. Although the moderate in him regularly subverts these imaginative flights with irony and finally condemns the solipsists and voluptuaries, the great passages given over to the realms of gold are too prominent, impressive, and memorable to be scorned and dismissed. Kernan shows that "the brilliance of phrase and urgency of rhythms in such speeches as Volpone's praise of his gold and his temptation of Celia guarantee that Jonson himself responded powerfully to this [Renaissance] optimism."[35] We may, while admitting the risks of such a position and the need for interpretive restraint, suggest that the pleasures of the imagined world are—temporarily, fleetingly—sometimes even celebrated. Jonson's attraction to extremism and excessiveness, what one writer calls his "fascinated respect for the eccentric and absurd,"[36] is a primary determinant of his comic method in all the plays. We remember the dreamers and their dreams, and it seems clear that these visionaries have captured the imagination of their creator.[37] Is it not possible that his success at articulating the desires and aspirations of his most imaginative figures is a measure of his own capacity to respond to such fantasies?[38]

The poet, after all, is responsible for having imagined and set down these visions of power and pleasure. Harriet Hawkins suggests as much when she writes that "Volpone's imagination seems notably comparable to that of his creator, who, whether his vision be of beauty or evil or folly, will set out to capture, to shape and to hold that vision, and to pass it on to others. . . . So Jonson summons up characters who will act out his own fantasies, embody his own visions. He thus recreates Volpone's erotic fantasies, and, for that matter, Sir Politic's idiotic schemes, with all the creative energy at his disposal."[39] Jonson invents such fantasies, fixes them permanently in dramatic form, and, what is more, allows the audience to respond to their temptations. Just as his management of the intrigue in the major comedies is designed to trap his spectators in the fun of morally dubious plots, so his exhibition of physical delights leads them to share the yearnings of libertines and buffoons. Like Shakespeare, Jonson seeks to win his audience over to an appreciation of the characters' ideals: the difference is that in the comedies we are seduced by meretricious satisfactions, by nothing more substantial than Sir Epicure's air mattresses.

Jonson and Shakespeare construct these visions only to destroy them. The dramatic action, both comic and tragic, is calculated to disillusion the idealist. Just as we notice resemblances among dreamers and their visions, so we may discern similarities among the agents of destruction and their approaches to the world. In Shakespeare these destroyers are the villains: Iago, Edmund, Claudius, perhaps Octavius. In Jonson they are the intriguers who invent the "plots": Volpone and Mosca, Subtle and Face, Truewit and Dauphine, Quarlous and Winwife. The parallels here are admittedly inexact. Shakespeare usually separates dreamer and villain into opposing figures; Jonson, although he may depict a purely foolish imaginist such as Mammon, most often makes his protagonists both visionaries and realists. I have shown how the idealism of characters like Volpone makes them resemble the Shakespearean idealists, and they resemble the villains in that the action depends upon their ability to identify, exploit, and shatter the unrealistic hopes of others. In Shakespeare and in Jonson, the agents of disillusion are, above all, rationalists, clear-eyed individualists who comprehend and seek to profit from vain imaginings.

This conflict between idealism and pragmatism is one of Shakespeare's oldest and most useful: we see it in Richard II and Bolingbroke, and in Brutus and Cassius. Such a conflict is central to *Hamlet, Othello,* and *King Lear.* Yet for all the cynical villainy of an Iago or Edmund, there is also a sense in which they, like their victims, possess a kind of faith in their own powers and a confidence about their prospects: "I grow, I prosper." The division between pragmatist and idealist, in other words, is not completely clean, just as it is not with figures like Volpone or Face. *Macbeth* is a fascinating variation on the pattern, for Shakespeare unites idealist and cynic in a single figure and, in so doing, complicates immensely the moral dynamics of the tragedy. This strategy appears to me comparable to Jonson's fusion of rogue and fool in Volpone and others, a parallel supported by the argument that Shakespeare seduces the viewer into dramatic collusion with Macbeth, even in the last horrifying acts.[40] In other words, Shakespeare forces us—allows us?—to participate in the experience of crime just as Jonson does in the con games of the great comedies. This combination of impulses might be considered a characteristic of Shakespeare's later tragic figures: even more than Hamlet, Othello, or Lear, later protagonists such as Macbeth, Timon, Coriolanus, and perhaps even Antony seem to be their own antagonists.

The resemblance between comic chicanery and tragic villainy manifests itself most obviously in Iago's deception of Roderigo and destruction of Othello. Even in those tragedies with less evident comic connections, say *Hamlet* or *Lear,* it is not difficult to see that Claudius's manipulation of Laertes or Edmund's deception of Gloucester depends upon techniques fundamental to the comic schemers in *Volpone, Epicoene,* and *The Alchemist.* The Machiavels are quick to penetrate the idealism that insulates the heroes from awareness of the malign forces around them, just as the comic sharks prey upon the credulity of their gulls. Claudius assures his stooge that Hamlet will not suspect their confederacy because he is "Most generous, and free from all contriving"; Iago descries and takes advantage of the Moor's "free and open nature"; Edmund's prosperity depends upon "A credulous father, and a brother noble, / Whose nature is so far from doing harms / That he suspects none" (*Lear*, 1.ii.176–78); and the Soothsayer informs Antony, "thy spirit which keeps thee, is / Noble, courageous, high, unmatchable, / Where Caesar's is not" (*Antony and Cleopatra*, 11.iii.18–20). In Jonson, although the fools are neither noble nor good but merely self-infatuated, their similar naiveté serves as a handle with which they can be twisted. In both tragedy and comedy, the scheme depends upon the victim's unworldliness and his enemy's consciousness of it. As Subtle says of Mammon, "If his dreame last, hee'll turne the age, to gold" (*Alchemist*, 1.iv.29).

The two dramatists insist upon different responses to the practical-minded manipulators, just as they demand different judgments on the idealists. The main distinction is between villainy and roguery, according to the conventions and limitations of the two modes. The pragmatists in Shakespeare's tragedies are among his most sinister characters. Even though his treatment of the heroic vision is ambiguous, Shakespeare's depiction of the villainy which attacks that vision reveals the perils of aggressive individualism, one of these plays' greatest ethical themes.[41] Such selfish criminality is in fact an interesting variation on the single-minded nobility of such characters as Hamlet and Coriolanus, who cling stubbornly or heroically to a moral, ethical, or political position; and, as I have suggested, it is odd to find that the villains are all cynics about the world at large but idealists about themselves. Jonson too attacks selfish desire, evident in the hopes of the *captatori* or the indiscriminant wants of a Bartholomew Cokes, but best displayed in the scheming of his intriguers.[42] The compacts formed to entrap others inevitably break apart from the pressures of competition: the selfish motives that brought them into being necessarily fracture them. But these comically conceived manipulators are no villains, and we find ourselves in league with them. Our relationship with these types is thus determined chiefly by the mode: in the comedies we join with the realists, while in the tragedies our lot is with the dreamers. Such alignments correspond to the attitudes the two playwrights encourage towards their characters' grand visions: generally speaking, Shakespeare invites us to admire and to sympathize, Jonson to enjoy and to judge.

Although the comic or tragic action is a contest between visionary and realist, the conclusion is clear from the start. The idealist is defeated, undone not so much by his enemy's potency as by his own un-worldliness, his inability to adapt to the conditions of mortality. The tragic hero is responsible for his own fall, just as the comic butt must take the blame for his humiliation. As Sir Epicure laments when the explosion rips through the house, "O my voluptuous mind." The antag-onists merely assist in the process of debasement. Furthermore, the pragmatist cannot be said to win, for in helping to bring down the visionary he usually confounds himself as well. Just as the shapes of the struggles are identical, so their ends are invariably the same. Whether considered tragically or comically, the result is always failure.

All these plays convey to the spectator a profound sense of pessimism about the durability, and sometimes even the possibility, of human hap-piness, goodness, or achievement. Forgetting for the moment the ob-vious distinctions between modes and the tonal differences that attend them, we notice that the actions depicted arise from similar motives and take a similar shape: attempts to seize advantage, betrayal of fellows or family, the desire to satisfy the self at the expense of others, efforts to dominate or to dictate behavior, the destruction or infection of good by evil, engagement in losing battles. If the degree of villainy is more ex-treme in the tragedies, that is balanced by the ubiquity of folly and evil in the comedies. The repeated presentation of such actions naturally cre-ates in these texts a startling thematic consistency, both comedies and tragedies raising doubts about the human creature and its chances for happiness and fulfillment. Virtually all of them are concerned with the collapse of order, the lure and force of wickedness, the perils of hope, the prevalence of self-delusion, the susceptibility of strength to perversion, and the inescapability of human weakness and pride.

§ III

The nature and extent of these skeptical visions can be clarified by the recognition that these comedies and tragedies are all insistently antiromantic. Jonson throughout most of his career was distrustful, even contemptuous of romantic stagecraft, a bias that produced some of his most famous attacks on Shakespeare. Such pointed critiques as the commentary in the Induction to *Bartholomew Fair* are among the most familiar articles of Jonsonian theory, and thus the assaults on romantic illusion that constitute the actions of the major plays are predictable and consistent with the view of art that produced them. But Shakespeare is equally celebrated for his commitment to romance in the Elizabethan comedies. In plays such as *A Midsummer Night's Dream, As You Like It,* and *Twelfth Night* he adapted and contributed to the traditional store of romantic conventions, and in so doing he sanctioned the positive view of mankind such materials imply. (This is not to say that these plays ignore the problems of validity and reliability in such a vision; on the contrary, the equilibrium between doubt and acceptance contributes strongly to the impression of truth that distinguishes these works from lesser efforts.) The romantic comedies offer hope and warmth, and do so with standard devices: fortunate escapes from the sea, a devoted friend who rescues his "fellow" from a duel, benevolent spirits who favorably alter the course of love, charmed forests where mistakes are forgiven and amended, enemies or perfidious relations who repent or are vanquished, and a controlling Providence whose interventions are always benevolent and timely. Indeed, Shakespeare's fondness for such situations and themes has proved to be one of the major distinctions between him and his major contemporary.

Jonson, after finding his artistic footing, takes undisguised delight in ridiculing such irrational folderol and those who credit it, and episodes devoted to puncturing illusions are among the most entertaining in his canon. Of these, the introduction of Dapper to the Queen of Faery is perhaps the most familiar; its simplicity makes it one of the most illuminating. The young clerk, with his modest hopes for a means to success in the gaming houses, is a pedestrian version of the grand imaginists in Jonson and Shakespeare. The scheme to dupe him is specifically adjusted to his romantic turn of mind. Dapper is willing to believe Face's assurances that "a rare starre / Raign'd, at your birth"; that "There must a world of ceremonies passe, / You must be bath'd, and fumigated"; and that, finally, he will be presented to Her Grace. His suitability as a candidate for this romantic mumbo-jumbo appears in the preparatory ritual, when the "servants" of the "Queen" demand all his worldly goods:

> DAP. By this good darke, I ha' nothing but a halfe-crowne
> Of gold, about my wrist, that my love gave me;
> And a leaden heart I wore, sin' she forsooke me.
> FAC. I thought, 'twas something. And, would you incurre
> Your aunts displeasure for these trifles? Come,
> I had rather you had throwne away twentie halfe-crownes.
> You may weare your leaden heart still.
> (*Alchemist*, III.v.43–49)

This credulous hope brings on humiliating consequences: left alone and gagged in the privy, nearly overcome by the stench, and finally granted an interview with a punk whose "departing part" he is invited to kiss, Dapper rushes from the house illusions intact. So absurd and negligible is he that the audience need not witness his eventual enlightenment. Jonson repeats this pattern in all the comedies, exploding dreams of success, wealth, and distinction, and laying traps for those whose sense of privilege gives them unrealistic expectations.

So far I have refrained from identifying the distinctively romantic features of the imaginists' visions in these tragedies and comedies, but it should be clear that heroes and fools alike share to varying degrees a romantic conception of the world and their place in it. "To be romantic is to expect a great deal from life; to believe in ideals, like true love; to be regardless of limits; not to count costs until we have paid the price, at which we may then be everlastingly outraged."[43] Jonson's fools—and to some extent his rogues too—accept the conventions of romance literature and interpret the actual world accordingly. Theirs is a universe where "out of the first fire of meeting eyes, (they say) love is stricken" (Morose); where sons or other relations may be disinherited or debased at will (Corbaccio and Morose); where fortunes may be won with magic formulae (Mammon); where one need "trust no learning but inspiration" (Busy); where a fairy spirit selects and blesses her favorite (Dapper). Adam Overdo in *Bartholomew Fair* imagines himself carrying on the tradition of the disguised ruler, Justice at work in a world where folly and vice may be corrected by a cloak-and-dagger game. Such romantic inclinations are not always so concrete, however: even more telling is the air of romantic optimism common to all. Hope is unbridled in such a realm of luck, where miracles may occur at any time. The imagination, bolstered by pride and a sense of personal immunity, encourages sharks and dupes alike to disregard social circumstance, legal restraint, and even the laws of nature. This is a progressive attitude toward human life, and it is foreign to Jonson's conservative, classical temper.

Distrust of romance pervades *Volpone,* and Jonson's expression of that doubt is characteristically vigorous.[44] The extravagant language of the opening lines presents Volpone's gold as a religious object drawing pilgrims to worship: it is a "shrine," a *"saint"* visited by questers bringing sacrifices to "the dumbe god." Such a perilous pilgrimage is worth any hardship: "Who can get thee, / He shall be noble, valiant, honest, wise" (1.i.26–27). This "sacred treasure," in other words, has the power to transform the votary into "what he will" (1.i.28). The blasphemous symbolism signifies Jonson's dubious opinion of both tenor and vehicle: the playwright applies the terms of religious quest-romance to the metal of commerce, thus cheapening object and language. He is equally ironic about Volpone's inflated self-conception: the fox imagines himself as a kind of superman, a being exempt from the constraints of mortality and superior to his earthbound clients. Although Mosca is properly deferential to the high priest in the opening scene, he too thinks of himself in romantic terms, and it is worthwhile to recall his parasite soliloquy in this context as well. Mosca prides himself on his uniqueness: he is "a most precious thing, dropt from above, / Not bred 'mong'st clods, and clot-poules, here on earth" (111.i.8–9). He thinks of himself as something of a wizard specializing in a "mysterie," but his talent for buzzing through the air is one that he shares not only with an "arrow," a "swallow," and a "starre," but also with his namesake, the fly. This magician is a member of a lower order, an insect.

Volpone's quest for Celia is a perfect instance of the protagonist's misuse of his imagination to dignify and inflate his tawdry desires:

VOLP. O, I am wounded.   MOS. Where, sir?   VOLP. Not without;
Those blowes were nothing: I could beare them ever.
But angry CUPID, bolting from her eyes,
Hath shot himselfe into me, like a flame;
Where, now, he flings about his burning heat,
As in a fornace, an ambitious fire,

> Whose vent is stopt. The fight is all within me.
> I cannot live, except thou helpe me, MOSCA;
> My liver melts, and I, without the hope
> Of some soft aire, from her refreshing breath,
> Am but a heape of cinders.
> (*Volpone*, II.iv.1–11)

Jonson creates an action emphasizing the romantic origins of Volpone's posturing. Celia's unapproachability makes her all the more desirable: she is "a wench / . . . / Whose skin is whiter then a swan, all over! / Then silver, snow, or lillies" (I.v.108–11), and she is locked in a tower away from the world by a sadistic guardian. Her conventionally romantic name, which David Bergeron thinks comes from Spenser's House of Holinesse, and her dropping her handkerchief from the window complete the parody of the romantic beloved. Volpone's catalogue of his amorous wounds, expressed as it is in exaggerated terms of fire and air, prepares for the hyperboles of the seduction scene, in which the lecher seeks to transmute common lust into an act of transcendence. The romantic selves and experiences the protagonists fashion for themselves are only attitudes, and Jonson repeatedly exposes the beasts' pretensions.

He does so in large part by means of the Would-bes. Their surname encourages us to connect their posturing with that of the chief characters, and they also may be profitably seen as parodies of romantic figures.[45] Lady Would-be travels with a squire and ladies-in-waiting. She claims acquaintance with Italian romantic literature:

> Which o'your Poets? PETRARCH? or TASSO? or DANTE?
> GUERRINI? ARIOSTO? ARETINE?
> CIECO *di Hadria?* I have read them all.
> (*Volpone*, III.iv.79–81)

She studies art and music and prides herself on her uncommon sensitivity:

> There was but one sole man, in all the world,
> With whom I ere could sympathize; and he
> Would lie you often, three, foure houres together,
> To heare me speake: and be (sometime) so rap't,
> As he would answere me, quite from the purpose,

Like you, and you are like him, just. I'le discourse
(And't be but only, sir, to bring you a-sleepe)
How we did spend our time, and loves, together,
For some sixe yeeres.
(*Volpone*, III.iv.116–24)

The subtext of this passage, aided especially by the pun on "rap't," exposes the vulgar facts beneath the lady's image of intellectual intercourse. Her romantic self-description conceals only from herself a virago and a trull. Her husband is equally self-deluded. As John Creaser puts it, "Sir Politic's romantic obsession is his Utopia of Machiavellian intrigue and political manouevre."[46]

When Lady Would-be responds to Mosca's report that her husband has been seen with a courtesan in a gondola, she rushes out to apprehend him and takes with her Volpone's dwarf (Bergeron compares her to Una in quest of Redcross). The episode illustrates Jonson's application of irony to the conventions of romance. Lady Would-be, perhaps having seen too many Shakespearean comedies before her departure from England, knows very well not to be deceived by simple appearances; hence, she accuses Peregrine of being a whore in male disguise. The truth, however, is as ordinary as it seems. Sir Pol's experience is also humiliating, for the tortoise shell—his "ingine" or "device" for escaping "the torture," a defense which seems foolproof in theory—is a miserable failure. The Would-bes withdraw in shame: "she will straight to sea, for physick," and he resolves "to shunne, this place, and clime for ever" (v.iv.86–87). The collapse of their romantic illusions forecasts the denouement in the main plot and fills out Jonson's picture of romantic pretension.

Because Shakespeare deliberately evokes and then destroys romantic expectations, his major tragedies are virulently antiromantic. He puts the conventions of romantic comedy to new use, employing them ironically so as to question and criticize the progressive conclusions he has formerly endorsed. The romance machinery that has moved his own earlier works is thrown into reverse, and it functions most powerfully in *King Lear* although it is noticeable throughout the tragedies. As Leo Salingar has demonstrated in an important essay, "Romance in *King Lear*," Shakespeare scrupulously altered his sources for the play in order to clarify the connections with romance and so to emphasize the bleak

Dreamers

failure of romantic possibilities. The faithful servant, son, and daughter, the debased ruler, the disguises, the joyful reconciliation of parent and child—all are relics of the romance tradition, and their fleeting appearance in this savage world underscores their unreality. "A repeated consequence of Shakespeare's innovations in the plot is to set up a dialectic between expectations belonging to romance and those attached to tragedy, between inalienable hopes and the sternest moral realism."[47]

Instances of such thwarted expectations crowd the final scene of *King Lear,* one of the most notable being the entrance of Edgar as the unknown knight. The Herald who reads the challenge, the three blasts of the trumpet, the appearance of the anonymous challenger in the final moment—this is the stuff of fairy tale:

> *Her.* What are you?
> Your name? your quality? and why you answer
> This present summons?
>
> *Edg.* Know, my name is lost;
> By treason's tooth bare-gnawn, and canker-bit:
> Yet am I noble as the adversary
> I come to cope.
> (*Lear,* v.iii.118–23)

The audience is led to hope that the day might be saved, as it is in some of the sources. Shakespeare achieves the same effect in the deathbed confession of Edmund, whose intention to do some good seems to open the way for the rescue of Lear and Cordelia. Moreover, since the horrors of the last minute are hard to forget, it is worth reiterating that an audience seeing the play for the first time does not know, when Lear enters with Cordelia in his arms, whether "she's dead as earth" or "she lives." According to Bernard McElroy, "Bradley was unquestionably right when he said that the actor playing Lear should die with an expression of joy on his face, but that joy scarcely makes *Lear* a drama of personal redemption and fulfillment. Quite the contrary: Lear's joy is far more painful to witness than despair could possibly be. His joy is based upon hope, but his hope is groundless."[48]

In Shakespeare's transition from romantic comedy to antiromantic tragedy, familiar settings, characters, and situations assume different meanings. The enchanted forest is transformed into a heath or a dark island; benevolent sprites become deaf or inscrutable gods; swordfights continue to their bloody conclusions; joyful meetings, if they occur at all, are cut short by imminent disaster. The timing is wrong, but only just. Emilia knocks a minute too late. Cleopatra's final scheme for winning Antony back to her misfires:

> *Dio.* . . . she sent you word she was dead;
> But fearing since how it might work, hath sent
> Me to proclaim the truth, and I am come,
> I dread, too late.
>
> *Ant.* Too late, good Diomed.
> (*Antony and Cleopatra,* IV.xiv.124–28)

In cases such as these Shakespeare emphasizes the nearness of the miss, thus contrasting happy possibility with tragic fact. Indeed, in *Antony* he even dramatizes the brief, doomed reunion to depict what will not be. Where Shakespeare does not present characters or settings or actions associated explicitly with comedy or romance, he still insists upon the distance between vain hope and bitter truth.

At the center of the dialectic stands the visionary hero, who may be thought of as a romantic figure. He is a solipsist, an individualist, one willing to set himself against the furies of the world and sustained by a mysterious faith in his power to survive, even to triumph. For all the tragic grandeur he is able to suggest, his self-inflicted suffering is humiliating and frightening. Shakespeare organizes the actions of the tragedies to indicate the price of the hero's vision, to adumbrate the pain and misery it creates, to strip the characters of their romantic delusions, naked as at their birth. It would be difficult to deny the contention that Shakespeare's tragedies are "the greatest anti-romantic structures ever created."[49]

When romantic illusions are annihilated, the Shakespearean and Jonsonian worlds that remain are similarly stale, flat, and unprofitable. Always in the background are the inescapable penalties of the fall. The settings chosen, regardless of the action, suggest pollution, limitation, and danger: a savage heath (*Lear*), a decaying imperial city (*Volpone*), a dark and politically unstable island (*Othello*), a neighborhood afflicted by the plague (*Alchemist*), a barren cave near an isolated shore (*Timon*).

In *Antony and Cleopatra*, Rome is such a place.[50] The hostile world both fosters and dooms the wish for imaginative escape. This is clear in Face's description of Subtle's condition before the commencement of the scheme:

> you went pinn'd up, in the severall rags
> Yo'had rak'd, and pick'd from dung-hills, before day,
> Your feet in mouldie slippers, for your kibes,
> A felt of rugg, and a thin thredden cloake,
> That scarce would cover your no-buttocks—
> (*Alchemist*, 1.i.33–37)

And so it will be again after Dol and Subtle make their retreat over the back wall. Likewise, Shakespeare's visionaries are unwilling to accept the implications of man's fallen condition. The refusal to accommodate themselves to postlapsarian reality sentences all these imaginists to a comic or tragic reenactment of the Fall. The struggle is intensified by the other major group of characters—the serpents in these dramas—who embrace evil and seek to profit from it. Their trickery or villainy is an alternative response, equivalent to the idealists' wish for imaginative transcendence, another way of liberating the self from the constraints of the earth. For both Shakespeare and Jonson, the outcome of the struggle is certain, for the universe will tolerate neither escape nor exploitation. But their attitudes towards their characters' falls determine the very different kinds of plays they make from the same conflict.

§IV

A blunt statement of the distinction is this: Jonson regards the destruction of illusions with scornful amusement, while Shakespeare laments the waste of imaginative gifts. The difference here is related to the point of view each dramatist establishes, the bond he seeks to form between stage and audience. Shakespeare's creation of a sympathetic link between audience and visionary leads the spectators to assent to the attractions of the vision, to deplore the disillusionment and destruction of such an individual. In Jonson, on the other hand, the structure of the comic actions and the behavior of the characters leave the viewers no choice but to delight in the puncture of grandiose dreams. Both dramatists affirm the impossibility of realizing the dreamers' illusions—the denouements leave no doubt on this point—but the authorial responses to characters' myopia are in sharp contrast. Jonson demands keen critical judgment, stressing the absurdity of the vision, exposing it as immoral, antisocial, and a perversion of creative energy. Shakespeare is more tolerant of the vision itself. Without ignoring its moral, ethical, or political hazards, he nevertheless reveals and seems even to relish its promised satisfactions. Here the two artists offer complementary views of the same landscape. And yet the two attitudes are closer than might be expected, for each is complicated and balanced by the intimations of an opposing view.

Shakespeare is preeminent among playwrights when it comes to matters of revaluation and qualification and balance. Whether we call it "negative capability" or "complementarity" or "indefinition," we feel the pull of conflicting viewpoints as we experience any of Shakespeare's major plays.[51] The tragic power of *Othello* or *King Lear* is generated by the collision of two truths: that the ideal world is supremely beautiful and valuable, and that the ideal world is impossible to realize and sustain. Shakespeare's depiction of his characters' visions of perfection differs from Jonson's, of course, in that the imaginative speculations of the tragic heroes are given a more complete and straightforward hearing. We are conscious of the unreality, to be sure, for the context guarantees it.

> *Bra.* Look to her, Moor, if thou hast eyes to see:
> She has deceived her father, and may thee.
> (*Exeunt* [*Duke, Senators, Officers, &c.*])
>
> *Oth.* My life upon her faith!—Honest Iago,
> My Desdemona must I leave to thee;
> (*Othello*, 1.iii.292–95 [Pelican text])

Nevertheless, Shakespeare does insist upon the desirability of the vision, actively encouraging his audience to wish for Hamlet's realm of truth, for a state in which Coriolanus need not demean himself, for a world encompassing Egypt and Rome where Antony might love and govern. Within the passages devoted to such ideals there is far less exaggeration and irony than in the equivalent Jonsonian fantasies. In short, it is hardly surprising that Shakespeare's treatment of his heroes' visions is ambivalent.

What is surprising, however, is the brutality with which Shakespeare obliterates the visions he has invited us to contemplate.[52] The juxtaposition of the beautiful dream with its immediate destruction is a fearsome spectacle which, because this is tragedy, is unmatched by anything in Jonson. But that ruthless disillusionment is the Shakespearean version of the ironies that undermine the Jonsonian visions, and both methods serve to distance the romantic view, to expose its unreality, and to generate a grave pessimism about human possibility. It is frightening to witness the transformation of imaginative talent into the dementia that afflicts the tragic heroes. As Maynard Mack has shown, "the hero tends to become his own antithesis. . . . Othello the unshakable, whose original composure under the most trying insults and misrepresentations almost takes the breath away, breaks into furies, grovels on the floor in a trance, strikes his wife publicly. King Lear, 'the great image of authority' both by temperament and position, becomes a helpless crazed old man crying in a storm, destitute of everything but one servant and his Fool."[53] The fury with which the world attacks the idealistic hero is a measure of Shakespeare's consciousness of the perils of the imagination.

Shakespeare's unparalleled talent for achieving balance and suggesting ambivalence should not blind us, as it sometimes has in the past, to Jonson's sensitivity to other points of view. The orthodox characterization of Ben Jonson as the stern and dogmatic moralist needs to be amended. Aldous Huxley perceived the complexity of the playwright's mature vision when he proposed that Jonson "might have been a great romantic, one of the sublime inebriates,"[54] and his suggestion is consistent with Swinburne's view: "There is in *Volpone* a touch of something like imagination, a savour of something like romance which gives a higher tone to the style and a deeper interest to the action. The chief agents are indeed what Mr. Carlyle would have called 'unspeakably unexemplary mortals': but the serious fervour and passionate intensity of their resolute and resourceful wickedness give somewhat of a lurid and distorted dignity to the display of their doings and sufferings."[55] What these commentators are able to hear—and surely it is significant that both are themselves artists—is the sound of the opposing voice chanting the beauties and pleasures of romantic desire. This counterpoint is especially audible in the comic masterpieces, but Jonson's willingness to let it be heard is one of the artistic decisions that distinguish these great works from the journeyman efforts. In the comical satires the targets—social, political, moral, and aesthetic vices and their dramatic embodiments—are so large and easy to demolish that the sense of challenge or conflict is limited. In these mature dramas, however, the ironies cannot utterly overwhelm or efface the appeals of the dreams, ridiculous as the dreamers may be.

Many of Jonson's dreamers make compelling claims, and the dramatist allows the audience, if only temporarily, to feel the attraction of the visions.[56] Hiram Haydn anticipates the work of Stephen Greenblatt and other recent critics when, in discussing the complexity of an attempt to chart the literary and intellectual history of any period, he emphasizes the paradoxical place of evil in the work of one of the most moral of great poets: "For all of Spenser's avowed ethical purposes in composing the cantos [of *The Faerie Queene*], he is never so much the poet, never so passionate and compelling an artist as when—in the Bower of Bliss or Garden of Adonis passages, for example—he is dealing with sensuous and even voluptuous material."[57] The most imposing figures in Jonsonian drama are the magnificent perverts, Sejanus, Volpone, Morose, Sir Epicure, Catiline, Busy; and the most memorable passages are their expressions of desire, their dreams of expectation. Alexander Leggatt, who examines such passages under the rubric of "false creations," argues that Jonson gives to Volpone "an energy that compels attention. Against our better judgment, he appeals to us, and his appeal is undeniable. No one who has ever felt like breakfast in bed can watch Volpone in the first act without a touch of envy. No one who enjoys the game of dressing up can feel that a purely moral reading of the speeches to Celia . . . tells the whole story."[58] The creator has endowed his creations with his own abundant creativity, and surely the attractions of these dreams are evidence of immense artistic range. It would be a mistake to deny the absurdity or even the potential horror in the fantasies of a Morose or a Mammon. But the greatness of the mature comedies owes much to the tension, the artful balance, between Jonson's firm opposition to romantic speculation and his willingness to confess the lure of such visions. Jonson's plays are moral acts, but their profound morality is a function of the great risks the artist has allowed himself to take.[59]

§ V

Human aspiration, like most activity, may be noble or may be ludicrous, depending on the standpoint of the viewer. The categories of comedy and tragedy are useful guides to point of view, for they help the playwright to organize and the audience to evaluate the actions dramatized. Although the interpretation of man's visionary impulses in the Shakespearean texts I have been considering is essentially tragic and in the Jonsonian plays essentially comic, each artist qualifies and complicates his presentation so thoroughly that he stretches the conventional limits of the genres, revealing the fundamental relation between ridiculous and heroic forms of endeavor. Bernard Shaw perceived the complexity of the issue when he called *Coriolanus* Shakespeare's greatest comedy.[60] The resemblance between the richly suggestive visions of the two playwrights ought to indicate that firm generic distinctions may be a hindrance as well as an aid to understanding. We tend to forget that the rigid modern division between comedy and tragedy was not maintained so faithfully in the Renaissance, that great tragedies were always followed by merry songs and bits of foolery, and that the age accepted the Socratic view that the arts of comedy and tragedy are one.[61] Removal of this generic barrier for purposes of comparison reveals important similarities of method, purpose, and achievement in the work of these playwrights and opens territory that might be explored more extensively. The common ground occupied by Shakespeare and Jonson in these mature plays, the territory I have been surveying in this chapter, is characterized by Salingar's phrase, "the sternest moral realism," a description which brings to mind Joseph Conrad's dictum that the purpose of great art is "to make you see." Here at least Jonson and Shakespeare seek to promote moral realism in much the same way, by dramatizing the experience of characters who lack or disregard or misapply it. The destruction of the specious dramatic visions leads to moral artistic visions.

Even more important is that the artistic visions proceeding from these tragic and comic actions are similarly skeptical and negative. The characters' initial visions promise great opportunity, universal order, limitless pleasure, correspondence between word and deed, unblemished love, transcendence, the conquest of nature. The creators' visions emphasize failure. To observe this stress is not to indulge in the easy nihilism that has afflicted a number of modern interpretations and damaged too many recent stage productions. As I have tried to establish, the balances achieved by both Jonson and Shakespeare forbid such a label.[62] These plays do exhibit actions suggesting vitality, creativity, the awareness of error, great heroism, and wit. But they also stimulate a sense of limitation, foster a climate of doubt, and illustrate what man is and what he can never be.

Such pessimism is accompanied by a countervailing force, the implicit affirmation suggested by the work of art itself. The paradox of these authors' skepticism is that the plays that embody it, works like *Hamlet* or *The Alchemist,* add new dimensions to our understanding of the human subject. We know that we ought not to endorse Volpone's attempts on Celia's chastity, that we must abhor Macbeth's dream of glory. But the work of the playwright allows us to participate in such guilty pleasures, and his success at embodying them relieves the pain depicted. The fools' paradises are ephemeral; the artists' visions are permanent, unlikely to vanish in fume. And we must remember, finally, that these several texts constitute only a phase, only a segment of each artist's career. For both of them, there is a world elsewhere.

CHAPTER 5

Ideal Realms

Jonson's Masques and Shakespeare's Late Plays

Jonson and Shakespeare themselves become the dreamers when they turn to the creation of the masques and romances. In the satiric comedies and the tragedies, contemplation of an ideal world is the province of fools and doomed heroes, and the conceived perfection must remain illusory, overwhelmed by harsh reality. At the end of *The Alchemist* or *Coriolanus*, all that survives of Mammon's "Novo Orbe" or Martius's state of merit is its splendid poetic embodiment. Shakespeare and Jonson are themselves responsible for the invention of their characters' fantasies; and if we detect some authorial sympathy for even the most ludicrous or quixotic of these dreams, then it is hardly surprising that the two poets themselves should pursue such visions and give themselves over to the imagining of harmony. The masques and romances may be regarded as artistic realizations of the glorious realms that these characters can only wish for, and I want to examine these texts as related theatrical expressions of an ideal vision of human experience. Within a very few years of each other, Shakespeare and Jonson sought relief from the concentration on human failure and error informing *Volpone* and *King Lear*, turned to forms that allowed speculation on the possible, and indulged themselves and their audiences in the contemplation of triumph.

The idealism and affirmative emphasis of the masque are so inconsistent with Jonson's usual dramatic practice that the normal critical response has been to quarantine it, to stress its formal differences from drama and thus to preserve a consistently satiric image of Jonsonian theatre.[1] Jonson himself, however, appears to have taken his masques as seriously as his plays: according to Herford and Simpson, he "lays down the theory of 'these devices' in the same terms which Aristotle applies to the drama,"[2] and Jonson himself, in describing his choice of a subject for *The Masque of Queenes,* declares that he is "observing that rule of the best *Artist,* to suffer no object of delight to passe w^{t}hout his mixture of profit, & example" (lines 7–9). Similarly, the introduction to *Hymenaei,* with its well-known metaphor of full tables (Jonson's) and empty trenchers (his competitors'), sounds very much like the polemical preface to one of the comedies. The problem that always absorbed Jonson, man's inherent tendency to deceive himself, to misuse his gifts, to fail, is approached obliquely in the masques. The greatest of his plays are marked by the fervency with which he imagined this kind of lapse, and the source of this fervor is his positive understanding of what man ought to be. Here is the passageway to the masquing chamber. In his early courtly entertainments Jonson represents the virtues from which the rogues and fools of his plays so extravagantly depart. He imagines an alternative to failure. The patent unreality of the masques, their fairy-tale quality, actually constitutes a link, not a barrier, with the more conventional dramatic work. Just as *Volpone* is a fable about greed, *Oberon* is a fable about munificence.

No one would assert that the range of Shakespeare's dramatic achievement has gone unrecognized, and the criticism published in the past two decades records a particular fascination with the romances. Two points, however, ask for emphasis. The first is that in his last phase Shakespeare considers from a reverse angle the issues that dominated his thinking when he wrote the great tragedies. Infidelity of personal, familial, and political kinds, the confusing search for truth, the capacity of love, the powers and threats of the imagination are all reexamined, seen from a new perspective, given a fresh emphasis, analyzed not with a dropping but with an auspicious eye. Where the tragedies examine good in a context of evil, the romances consider evil in a context of good. This shift in viewpoint is equivalent to that which occurs in Jonson's career: the romances are to the tragedies as the masques are to the satiric comedies. Second, Shakespeare's turn to romance was not merely an innate change in direction, the woodnotes wild offered in a major key. It is vital to recognize that Shakespeare's late idealism has its parallels in other careers of the period, notably Jonson's, that his submission to the call of romance must have been to some extent a response to the stimulus of contemporary fashion, and that his imaginative scope, while perhaps singular in degree, is not unique in kind.

Shakespeare's exchange of perspective was more or less linear or sequential, the positive presentation of good and evil succeeding the negative, at least as far as we can discern from the current evidence about dating.[3] Jonson, on the other hand, was able to treat the negative and positive strains of experience simultaneously: *The Masque of Blacknesse* appeared about the same time as *Volpone;* the noble ladies who represent virtue in *The Masque of Queenes* are coeval with the swarm of Collegiates in *Epicoene;* and the golden splendors of *Oberon* sprang from the same imagination that had recently produced the tawdry world of *The Alchemist.* The simultaneity of Jonson's base and beauteous visions is, I suspect, partly responsible for the familiar charges of flattery and opportunism. Had the masques followed the great satiric comedies chronologically, they might have received greater attention from critics, who could have descried a progress towards transcendence, as they have with Shakespeare's late works. The romances constitute a discrete and unified group. But it strikes me that, for both playwrights, the impulse to imagine an ideal is comparable, regardless of when it occurs. An implicit idea of *The Alchemist* is that the poet's imagination can accomplish what the fakery of Subtle and Face cannot, transmuting the baseness of nature into perfect form. This is what Shakespeare and Jonson themselves achieve in these works.

Occasionally critics have addressed themselves to connections between the court masques and Shakespeare's late plays, but such investigations have usually lost their way in a thicket of supposed cases of influence or have failed by overstating drastically Shakespeare's response to the vogue of courtly entertainments.[4] The narrow approach is much less productive than a broad comparison of purpose, form, and idea. The masque is a theatrical form, and its essentially dramatic properties will manifest themselves as my analysis proceeds and will justify the comparison with Shakespearean romance. It may be that the masque's differences from orthodox drama—its occasional nature, its extreme degree of stylization, its courtly performers, and its lack of a conventional narrative—were the very features that prompted Jonson to set forth a vision of harmony at all. With a modern, nonclassical form, in other words, he may have felt at liberty to develop positively the ideas that he mocks in the plays. We must not underestimate the differences between the Jonsonian masque and the drama, just as we must not forget that *The Tempest* is a play, not a Shakespearean version of a masque. But different or not, the masque and the dramatic romance represent related artistic vehicles in the service of similar artistic ends.

The scope of my inquiry will be limited mainly to the masques that Jonson wrote from 1605 (*The Masque of Blacknesse*) to 1611 (*Oberon*), and to *Pericles, Cymbeline, The Winter's Tale,* and *The Tempest.* In Jonson's case such limitation is unnecessary: since this is not a study of particular influences, virtually any of the masques would serve to illustrate the argument. But the early examples make the point as well, and there is some advantage in concentrating on works of chronological propinquity. With Shakespeare I have mostly neglected *Henry VIII* and *The Two Noble Kinsmen* (although I refer occasionally to the former) on the grounds that their collaborative nature makes them different enough from the four principal texts to cloud the discussion. Coleridge's reference to *Henry VIII* as "a sort of historical masque or show-play" indicates its links to the style described here; but its overriding concern with historiography suggests that by the time he wrote it Shakespeare was moving in yet another direction without having abandoned his romantic style completely.[5] Likewise, *The Two Noble Kinsmen* probably differs from the four principal romances more than it resembles them, and the authorship problem in particular creates more difficulties than study of the play in this context offers rewards. I have confined myself to the major and more or less typical texts.

The assumption with which I have begun—that Jonson and Shakespeare in these works share a common purpose, the expression of an ideal vision of experience—will prove itself as the main argument unfolds. It is, simply, that the two artists have embodied comparable visions into related forms and that they have conveyed those visions by means of comparable dramatic strategies. Those that I have elected to examine include theatrical machinery and spectacle, binary structures, symbolic representation, a spirit of mystery or magic, uncommon self-consciousness (even for these authors), and a host of common ideas. The masques are by definition spectacular affairs, and one of the hallmarks of the romances is their extraordinary theatricality. The dependence upon spectacle creates a sense of self-consciousness about both forms: we see the "art, which deliberately displays its art" that Granville-Barker noticed in *Cymbeline*.[6] Such a self-conscious style tends to distance the audience, at least temporarily, and this disengagement makes the masques and romances seem more remote, more exalted than most of their authors' other works. Such an atmosphere of mystery is appropriate to the consideration of ideals, and another chief cause of this magical spirit is the symbolism at the heart of these pieces. Reliance upon a symbolic mode in exploring the problem of transcendence is characteristic of authors at least as far back as Plato, and if one had to identify a single feature that most obviously links these romances and masques it would be that their characters and actions deliberately suggest something beyond themselves. Also, the shapes of the chosen forms further reflect a common purpose: the complementary structure of antimasque and masque that Jonson developed in these years has its counterpart in the tragicomic movement of a play like *The Winter's Tale*. My general conclusion is that Shakespeare and Jonson in their maturity turned to similar modes of expression unlike anything either had produced before, did so in order to express comparable visions of order and beauty, and created texts that give to their careers a depth and range unmatched by that of any other contemporary playwrights.

Earlier in their careers both playwrights had occasionally included in their plays masquerades and skits drawn from the model of courtly entertainments, usually for the amusement of courtly characters. One thinks of the masque of Muscovites in *Love's Labor's Lost*, the mechanicals' play in *A Midsummer Night's Dream*, the masque of Hymen in *As You Like It*, and, on the other side, the masque that concludes *Cynthia's Revels*. After the ascension of James the masque became a central feature of cultural and social life at court, and Jonson became the chief purveyor: in 1605 he wrote *The Masque of Blacknesse* at the request of Queen Anne, having already furnished speeches and entertainments for royal occasions, and in the following years he developed and varied the form in *Hymenaei, The Masque of Beauty, The Haddington Masque, The Masque of Queenes, The Speeches at Prince Henry's Barriers,* and *Oberon*. Spectacular episodes begin to appear more abundantly in Shakespeare's plays at the same period, notably the masque of Amazons in *Timon* and the pageant of kings in *Macbeth*. From *Pericles* forward these masquelike properties of music, dancing, pageants, transformations, and theophanies become so prominent that they fundamentally alter the nature of the works containing them.

The elements that suggest Shakespeare's acquaintance with the masque are well-known and have been documented in detail by a variety of writers interested in influence, but a short review of the major cases is in order. In *Pericles* the entrance of the knights at Pentapolis (II.ii) is conducted as a symbolic processional and leads to the competition for Thaisa's hand, which takes the form of the barriers popular at court (although the tournament takes place off-stage). The apparition of Diana to Pericles is brief but introduces a magical quality, and even though the quarto designates that the play was performed at the Globe, some spectacular effects must have accompanied the arrival of the goddess. Shakespeare elaborates the theophany considerably in *Cymbeline*, beginning with the entrance of Posthumus's dead father and mother, introducing his two brothers *"with wounds as they died in the wars,"* and allowing these figures to encircle the sleeping Posthumus and to pray for Jupiter's mercy upon their beleaguered son. In immediate reply, *"Jupiter descends in thunder and lightning, sitting upon an eagle: he throws a thunderbolt. The Ghosts fall on their knees"* (v.iv.92s.d.); after his speech justifying heaven's treatment of mortals, he *"ascends,"* leaving the spirits open-mouthed and convinced.[7] This dream sequence runs nearly a hundred lines, and the spectacular effects indicated in the stage directions, even if they were not set down by Shakespeare's own pen, must reflect the circumstances of early performances. The staging must have made the interlude seem rather like a masque: emblematically dressed figures and a deity participate in a two-part *scena* culminating in a transformation and vision of universal order. Although little of the rest of *Cymbeline* can be directly connected to the masque, it must be said— and will be said later in this chapter—that the self-conscious virtuosity of the plot and the theme of transformation give the play a sophistication that would have satisfied the extravagant taste of a Jacobean courtly audience.

Most of the evidence for Shakespeare's interest in the masque comes from *The Winter's Tale* and *The Tempest*. Although no actual deities appear in *The Winter's Tale*, the introduction of personified Time as the presiding spirit brings to mind the tutelary gods of the masques, as do the Apollonian judgment and prophecy. The costumes, music, dance, and seasonal merriment of the sheep-shearing suggest a rural counterpart to a courtly celebration of itself, and it is worth remembering that three of the participants are royal masqueraders: Florizel is got up as a shepherd, Perdita (ignorant of her status as a princess) as the goddess Flora, and Polixenes as an old stranger. A group of rustics who "call themselves saltiers" join the throng, and it is announced that "One three of them, by their own report, sir, hath danced before the King" (IV.iv.337–38). *The Winter's Tale* was performed at the Globe on May 15, 1611, and these lines probably allude to *Oberon*, performed at court January 6 of the same year, which contains an antimasque of satyrs who perform "an antique dance; full of gesture and swift motion." It is not certain that the King's Men were the actors who played the satyrs in *Oberon*, but they sometimes performed such duties, and Shakespeare may have imported their wild dance and then commented on it as a kind of in-joke. Oberon is drawn onto the stage by a pair of white bears, perhaps the figurative parents of the notorious bear that exits in pursuit of, and then dines upon, Antigonus. Finally, the statue scene, depending as it does upon formal presentation, music, and mystery, surely reminded some spectators of the magical transformation they had seen in the masques.

With *The Tempest* it is not necessary to go as far as one recent commentator, who claims that after the first scene the play "becomes a masque,"[8] to observe its affinities with the kind of spectacle into which the masque had developed by 1611. Its masquelike qualities are so prominent that to review them is practically to touch upon every important figure and episode in the work; this preliminary discussion must be limited to a very few. Prospero's wedding masque becomes the centerpiece when one regards *The Tempest* in a courtly context, and Geoffrey Bullough, whose conservatism in such matters is well known, goes so far as to print the text of *Hymenaei*, Jonson's wedding masque of 1606, as a "Possible Source." He also notes the popularity of island settings at court and mentions the two "sea-masques," *Blacknesse* and *Beauty*, as relevant texts.[9] Enid Welsford devotes much of a chapter in *The Court Masque* to the proposition that *The Tempest* was influenced "not only by the masque in general, but by certain masques in particular,"[10] focusing upon the parallels I have mentioned and a few others as well.

Recently Gary Schmidgall in his study of *The Tempest* has taken up these suggestions and introduced a host of others.[11] Clearly, if one wishes to argue that Shakespeare's late efforts owe something of their being to the court masque, *The Tempest* is the place to begin. But these beginnings have not proved very satisfactory.

What is needed is a persuasive way of discussing Shakespeare and contemporary theatrical fashion. Gerald Eades Bentley in a famous essay attributes the style of the last plays to the acquisition by the King's Men of the theater at Blackfriars, arguing that Shakespeare "turned from his old and tested methods and produced a new kind of play for the new theatre and audience."[12] Glynne Wickham sees the romances as specialized entertainments devised for particular occasions at court, and Frances Yates's work likewise finds topical meanings in all these texts.[13] Schmidgall, quoting Prospero's announced intention to "court" "a most auspicious star," sees the turn to romantic spectacle as an effort at commercial survival: "We can imagine Shakespeare observing the revitalization at court, the increasing profitability of preferment there, the decidedly romantic and pastoral tastes of the new queen, the ravishing enticements of Inigo Jones's new scenic inventions, regarding himself as a dramatist with yet a few more plays in him, and deciding to change his dramatic style."[14]

None of these suggestions, however, has pleased many or pleased long. In fact, most admissions of Shakespeare's sensitivity to theatrical trends have been accompanied by depreciation of their importance for his work. Bentley's contention about theatrical facilities has been attacked as being based on circumstantial evidence and rhetorical questions.[15] Wickham's and Yates's theories lack solid proof, and reaction to Schmidgall's work has not been favorable, at least as far as Shakespeare is concerned: Barbara Mowat objects that "the masses of scholarly data so carefully collected and quoted have little to do with *The Tempest*."[16] This position is typical of many who have addressed themselves to the problem of what the last plays owe to the masque. Even as thorough and objective an editor as Frank Kermode refuses to allow the masque a very important role in Shakespeare's development, as his remarks on the structure of *The Tempest* indicate: "No one would deny a general influence from the court masque, but it should not be allowed to obscure the fact that Shakespeare in this play resorts to something like the formal structure which he used with varying degrees of success in his earlier attempts at romantic comedy."[17] This conclusion represents a consensus on the matter, subordinating as it does the evidence for contemporary influence to the playwright's own inclinations and experience. It evades the question I posed earlier: should we not attempt to establish as precisely as possible the connections between the masques and the plays?

One of the most judicious treatments of Shakespeare's response to contemporary theatrical taste is Arthur C. Kirsch's essay, "*Cymbeline* and Coterie Dramaturgy." His analysis is concerned mainly with the relation of Shakespearean romance to the form of Fletcherian tragicomedy, but the basis of his argument will serve equally well for my remarks about the masque. "It is no doubt a species of folly peculiar to theatre historians to assume that once you explain the conditions of performance and the class of audience you explain the play, but it is surely just as foolish to assume that these things do not count at all, especially since there is so much evidence in Shakespeare's case not only that he was thoroughly professional, but that he was profoundly stirred by the idea and conventions of the theatre itself."[18] This strikes me as the right approach: we cannot keep from speculating on why Shakespeare made certain artistic choices, and as long as we are moderate about it, such consideration may be productive. Kirsch demonstrates parallels in structure and tone between *Cymbeline* and certain plays of dramatists working in the private theaters, notably Marston and Beaumont and Fletcher, and the conclusion he draws from this evidence seems indisputable: "That Shakespeare should have been affected by the dramatic developments in the private theatre is not only possible but probable."[19]

I believe that Shakespeare's need for a means of expressing an idealized vision of life led him to exploit the form that Jonson had recently devised for a similar purpose. The tracing of particular parallels and allusions can be instructive, but there is greater value in a comparison of common visions and parallel forms. Support for such an inquiry comes from John Bender, who argued in 1974 that "scholars and critics could profitably turn a fresh glance toward . . . the analysis of structural affinities between masques and plays—that is, as opposed to the study of masques in plays, which has been well gone through."[20] Bender thus echoes Allardyce Nicoll's recommendation that "we should look in these last plays, not for dramatic or theatrical devices taken from what may be called the body of the masque, but rather for imaginative vistas inspired by its soul."[21] These, then, are my two fields of concentration, "imaginative vistas" and "structural affinities," and since the latter are easier to identify, I begin with forms.

§ I

The structure of the masque is binary, consisting of antimasque and masque proper, a picture of evil and disorder succeeded by a vision of beauty and harmony. This duality is inherent even in the earliest courtly entertainments: the honored monarch's capacity for ordering and per-fecting nature assumed the existence of negative forces. But the purpose of the first masques was the celebration of the sovereign's virtues and powers, so the weight naturally fell upon the conquest of unruly nature: in Sidney's *The Lady of May*, for instance, the masque began in the park with the arrival of the queen, whose presence determined the shape of the entertainment from its commencement. Since Jonson concentrated his imaginative energies upon the depiction of chaos as well as upon the positive forces that vanquish it, he expanded and fortified the portrait of error as a foil to this revelation of good, which he then also magnified and enriched to give balance and definition to the entire portrait. The main result of this expansion of the negative side was the growth of the antimasque. Stephen Orgel has shown that "even in the early disguis-ings, the antic masque was controlled by a larger structure, super-seded—physically, if not always logically—by the court dances. This ordering of misrule was to become the central action of the masque in Ben Jonson's hands."[22] A useful way of studying Jonson's development of the form from 1605 to, say, 1612 is to trace his strategies for exposing the manifestations of error and confusion and then to notice his elabora-tion of the masque itself to accommodate this greater scope of evil.

Jonson's identification and exploitation of this dual structure are apparent in the contrast between *Hymenaei* (1606) and *The Masque of Queenes* (1609). In the wedding masque, after the entrance, all in or-derly fashion, of pages, Hymen, "a *youth,* attyred in white," attendant pages, "a personated *Bride,*" the auspices (the bridal pair's sponsors), and musicians, the company sings a general hymn to marriage and

Hymen orates in wonder at the glory of King James and Queen Anne. But then the order is disrupted:

Here out of a Microcosme, *or* Globe, *(figuring Man) with a kind of contentious Musique, issued forth the first* Masque, *of eight men.*

These represented the foure Humors, *and foure* Affections, *all gloriously attired, distinguisht only by their severall* Ensigns *and* Colours; *and, dancing out on the Stage, in their returne, at the end of their daunce, drew all their swords, offered to encompasse the* Altar, *and disturbe the* Ceremonies. (Lines 109–16)

It takes very little to subdue them. Hymen briefly defends the virgins whom these wild men have come to threaten, when Reason appears dressed emblematically and *"figur'd in a venerable personage"* to deliver a speech beginning "Forbeare your rude attempt." After only twenty lines the intruders are vanquished: *"At this, the* Humors *and* Affections *sheathed their swords, and retired amazed to the sides of the stage, while* HYMEN *began to ranke the* Persons, *and order the* Ceremonies" (lines 157–59). As the evening proceeds, the humours and affections are integrated into the main masque as Order unites them with representatives of marital harmony. Clearly these threats to virtue and equilibrium are refugees from Jonsonian comedy—abstractions, to be sure, but transparent symbols of the dangerous impulses and weaknesses with which the poet was constantly concerned. Their function is to give the virtues of reason and order stuff with which to work. What the epithalamion says about marriage is true for the dramatic quality of the masque as well: "Joyes, got with strife, increase" (line 519). This is the principle of contrast which the duality of antimasque and masque is designed to serve. But in this early celebration of marital harmony and bliss, Jonson has given such threats of strife little attention and no chance of triumph. Recognizing the dramatic and symbolic value of such contrary forces, however, Jonson invents another such episode for *The Haddington Masque*, where Cupid *"attended with twelve* boyes, *most antickly attyr'd, that represented the sports, and prettie lightnesses, that accompanie* Love" (lines 158–60) all perform *"a subtle* capriccious Daunce" until they are subdued by Venus and put in their place.

The antic dances of the Humours and Affections and of Cupid and his boys are intimations of the fully articulated antimasque first seen in

The Masque of Queenes. In the prose introduction to that work Jonson himself surveys the development I am tracing:

And because her Matie (best knowing, that a principall part of life in these *Spectacles* lay in they^r variety) had commaunded mee to think on some *Daunce,* or shew, that might praecede hers, and have the place of a foyle, or false-*Masque;* I was careful to decline not only from others, but mine owne stepps in that kind, since the last yeare I had an *Anti-Masque* of Boyes: and therefore, now, devis'd that twelve Women, in the habite of *Haggs* or Witches, sustayning the persons of *Ignorance, Suspicion, Credulity,* &c. the opposites to good *Fame,* should fill that part; not as a *Masque,* but a spectacle of strangenesse, producing multiplicity of Gesture, and not unaptly sorting wth the current, and whole fall of the Devise. (Lines 10–22)

These hags and their Dame take up over half the printed text of *Queenes,* and Jonson has lavished some of his most inventive and colorful verse upon their charms and incantations.

I have bene gathering Wolves hayres,
The mad Doggs foame, and the Adders eares;
The spurging of a dead mans eyes,
And all, since the Evening Starre did rise.
(lines 159–62)

I had a dagger, what did I wth that?
Kill'd an infant, to have his fat.
A Piper it got, at a Church-ale,
I bad him, agayne blow wind i'the tayle.
(lines 175–78)

Jonson here relies on his comic gift for the perverse, the disgusting, the excessive; but freed from the demands of comic verisimilitude that guide him in conventional drama, he is able to amuse himself and his audience at great length and with imaginative freedom.

This demonic fantasia is the "foil, or false masque," as Jonson says, to the real thing—the spectacle of the eleven mythic or legendary queens, led by Bel-Anna, enshrined in the House of Fame. At the sound of a blast of music, "not only the *Hagges* themselves, but they^r *Hell,* into wch they ranne, quite vanished" (lines 356–57), the scene is given over to the gorgeous edifice of Fame, and the witches are supplanted by the figures of Heroique Virtue, his daughter Fame, and the twelve queens. Orgel, in his acute analysis of this work's antithetical structure, argues that "the world of *Queenes* is one of moral absolutes" and that the witches "must, therefore, totally disappear before the masquing can begin."[23] But it strikes me that Jonson has made an effort to employ the antimasquers in the final tableau. Fame instructs that "those Hagges be led, as Captives, bound" before the queens' chariots in the noble procession, and this is a valuable symbolic event. Enslaved and stripped of their power, the witches continue to furnish pictorial and moral color. Evil is vanquished but not destroyed, even in Jonson's ideal vision of beauty and order. One must suppose that the hags might break loose. *Oberon* seems even more meaningful than *Queenes,* since the satyrs are won over by the glories of the Prince and the mention of James, but in both masques the principle is similar. As Barish puts it, "The antimasque thus articulates dramatically the dualism already implicit in the masque form. . . . To the degree that the antimasque distorts or parodies the theme of the masque, it functions, as E. K. Chambers has pointed out, like the subplot of an Elizabethan play. As in Shakespeare's 'ideal comedies,' whose affinities with the masque are close, the subplot of the antimasque decrees that the good society enshrined at the end shall not triumph without at least a token protest from the forces of disorder."[24]

The fully developed masque approximates most nearly the tragicomic structure of a play like *Cymbeline* or *The Winter's Tale. Cymbeline* is a problematic case, owing to its complex plot and technical experiments,[25] but it nonetheless exhibits two distinct worlds representing opposing varieties of human behavior and corresponding to the settings of antimasque and masque. The constricted, shifty, potentially tragic realm of the court is balanced by the honest, fresh, potentially comic realm of Wales to which Imogen, who belongs there spiritually, retreats. The poisonous Queen and her ludicrous son Cloten are like Jonson's Humours, satyrs, and hags, forces of darkness, anarchy, and absurdity. The parallel is given greater point by the attitude which Shakespeare stimulates toward these figures: just as the form of the masque protects the spectator from taking the threats of the antimasque too seriously, so the asides of Cornelius (about the Queen) and the Lords (about Cloten) keep the villains from troubling the audience and prefigure the failure of their schemes. Iachimo is dangerous, to be sure, but his threats are counterbalanced by the integrity of Imogen and the faithful ministrations of Pisanio, and he is kept offstage after the second act, only to repent in the last. In other words, Shakespeare has used tragicomic distance and shape to contain the forces of evil just as Jonson has insulated them in his antimasques. Ultimately the comic values associated with Wales are triumphant. Malice, confusion, separation, error, false assumption, blindness, and strife dominate the first four acts; repentance, clarification, reunion, love, and peace win through in the final scenes. The Queen and Cloten are eliminated, and Iachimo is converted to good and then forgiven. The complexities of the plot create several moments that might be called turning points—Posthumus's chastened reappearance is one—but the most likely, particularly in light of the comparison with the masque, is the apparition of Jupiter in v.iv. The god establishes the same relation between joy and strife as that set forth in the end of *Hymenaei:* "Whom best I love I cross; to make my gift, / The more delay'd, delighted" (v.iv.101–2). For the moment of transformation in the masque, the designer arranges a drastic change in visual perspective to correspond with the poetic shift from evil to good. And this is Shakespeare's method at this crucial moment in *Cymbeline.* In Daniel Seltzer's words, the theophanies of Diana and Jupiter may be seen as "experiments toward joining visual and moral wonder."[26]

This pattern of tragedy followed by comedy, of error by correction, is even more striking in *The Winter's Tale.* Few critics can resist the temptation to speak of the play's two parts, and with good reason. Despite occasional protests against this scheme of division,[27] the audience is invited—by the change of place, the shift in tone, the gap in time, and the entrance of Time himself—to regard the work as a diptych. The figure of Time supplies the audience with the kind of assurance that Jupiter and Diana offer, a change in perspective from the hothouse of Leontes' court to the rural world of fertility, youth, and merriment. The two halves modify each other: the joys of Bohemia cannot efface the memory of pain carried over from Sicilia, yet the comic spirit of the festival also qualifies that memory.[28] Moreover, a network of parallels and contrasts links the two halves; it resembles the system of antitheses that supports the meaning of *The Masque of Queenes.*[29]

The relation of these two parts is equivalent to that of antimasque and masque. The first three acts of *The Winter's Tale* represent a vision of anarchy arising from Leontes' diseased imagination, while the fourth and fifth move toward a cure for his evil and finally establish a harmonious unity. This harmony proceeds from the constructive imaginations of Camillo (in guiding the lovers to Sicilia), of Autolycus (in offering to act as an advocate for the rubes), of Paulina (in preserving Hermione), and of Leontes (in bringing the statue to life). If we look more closely, we perceive countermovements and contradictions that argue against a neat pattern: the first half is not all tragedy nor the second all comedy. Polixenes' disruption of the fourth-act festivities would seem to fit with the forces of disorder. But this is one basic distinction between the dramatic method of Shakespearean plays, which permits variegation and internal contrast, and the essentially pictorial style of the Jonsonian masque. This difference, however, does not invalidate the structural parallel apparent in Shakespeare's conversion of tragic beginnings into comic endings by means of magic or providential agency. And the unity of parts achieved at the end of *The Winter's Tale*, with Leontes and Polixenes reunited, Florizel replacing Mamillius, and Hermione restored, is equivalent to the integration of anarchy into order in the final moments of *Oberon*. Finally, this way of describing the organization of the play is reinforced by the spectacle and joy of the ending.[30]

To move from *The Winter's Tale* to *The Tempest* is to discover that in the later play Shakespeare has lopped off the usual first half and condensed it into Prospero's expository narrative in 1.ii. The structure thus resembles that of a masque with a narrated antimasque or, putting it another way, an antimasque in the process of being integrated into or subordinated to the main masque. The well-known complaint that *The Tempest* lacks conflict because Prospero's white magic makes him virtually invulnerable, which has led to a host of fanciful defenses, most of them psychological, is founded upon a structural truth: Shakespeare has thrown the emphasis upon the late phase of the action. The potential tragedy that matters, Prospero's neglect of his dukedom and Antonio's perfidy, is in the past; the plot to kill Alonso is a late manifestation of wicked impulses already intercepted by positive forces. In other words, the process of transformation is in progress: the opening storm is the equivalent of the blast of sound that traditionally sent the antimasquers confusedly scurrying for cover. Prospero, like the eponymous god in *Hymenaei*, has begun "*to ranke the Persons, and order the Ceremonies*" (line 159).

The ceremonies that Prospero orders, the spectacular effects that set this play apart from the rest of the canon, reinforce the suggestion that

Shakespeare found certain properties of the courtly entertainment useful in staging his idealized conception of sin and redemption. Although the transformation has begun, it is incomplete, and we witness the final manifestations of the process. If the court party can be considered the antimasquers, then we see the efforts of wisdom and virtue to control the forces of chaos and self-interest so that order and hierarchy may be restored to the state. Although the presence of Gonzalo makes the event less schematic than it might be, the conversion happens as it would in a genuine masque. Alonso, Sebastian, and Antonio, tempted by and deprived of the banquet, are "amazed," driven into a frenzy both physical and unmistakably moral:

> Gon. All three of them are desperate: their great guilt,
> Like poison given to work a great time after,
> Now 'gins to bite the spirits.
> (III.iii.104—6)

The means used to generate this ecstasy would have been appropriate at Whitehall, where the play was in fact performed: "*thunder and lightning;*" "ARIEL *like a Harpy;*" "*with a quaint device, the banquet vanishes;*" "*to soft music, enter the Shapes again, and dance.*" Even Ferdinand experiences an abbreviated version of this transformation, by which he discovers his own insignificance: "*He draws, and is charmed from moving.*" The satyrs and lower figures of the antimasque are here represented by Stephano, Trinculo, and Caliban, who meet a defeat worthy of such a paltry threat. They are tempted by the trappings of majesty, a load of "*glistering apparel,*" and the two aliens, Caliban's warning notwithstanding, celebrate their expected triumph in a momentary masque: "O King Stephano! O peer! O worthy Stephano!" (IV.i.222). As Caliban tells them, although he does not put it in these Jonsonian terms, it is the body of a masque without a soul.

An interpretation of *The Tempest* that sees Shakespeare playing with the conventions of the masque, using and commenting on the process of idealization at the heart of the form, helps to account for the play's liberal ironies. Ernest Gilman writes perceptively that the episode of the foolish conspirators with the frippery constitutes a kind of antimasque that interrupts Prospero's wedding masque. According to this view, Shakespeare's inversion of the familiar order "deflates Ferdinand's edenic quivering (now exposed, gently, as a naive and infatuated audience response to the masque)" and challenges the very premises of the form.[31] Gilman thus describes one function of the several elements that Shakespeare has borrowed from the masquers' trunk. They work straightforwardly, as aids in the idealization of experience, and ironically as well, as a means of questioning the transcendent vision. This dual purpose is soon apparent: Prospero's recreation of order is a very rough transformation. The forces of evil cannot be thoroughly accommodated and may not even be subjugated. Antonio's menacing silence in the final moments, which everyone has noticed, is surely a Shakespearean caveat to the final harmony. The structural affinities between *The Tempest* and the masque are so numerous and so striking that it would be perverse to deny that recognition of them can augment our appreciation of the play.

§ II

The [late] plays were written at a time when masques had developed into a sophisticated and complex art under the genius of Ben Jonson and Inigo Jones, and courtly audiences were accustomed to symbolism in these, in which all the scenery and all the characters were likely to be emblematic. Possibly in this wholesale use of symbolism, rather than in the increase of scenic effects and pageantry, may lie the most crucial influence of this new development in courtly entertainments on Shakespeare.[32]

R. A. Foakes, in this passage about *Henry VIII* and the late plays, deflects attention from the superficial and towards the fundamental resemblances between masque and romance, the use of symbolic representation. Shakespeare and Jonson found the symbol especially useful in communicating an ideal vision because it is the medium uniting action and idea in the play, or body and soul in the masque. It may be that Shakespeare, attracted by the suggestive possibilities of the masque's symbolic design, began to exploit the representative potentiality of the stories he chose to dramatize. In any case, the abundance of symbolic imagery is largely responsible for making both the masques and romances what they are.

The terms *symbol* and *allegory* have become so vexed that they are rarely dependable referents, but anyone seeking to describe the effect of these works is hamstrung without them. In fact, modern skittishness about their use is probably a handicap in understanding how action, dialogue, and other theatrical machinery convey meaning. Renaissance poets and theorists often used the terms elastically and even interchangeably, a freedom that is probably a function of the cultural tendency to think symbolically.[33] Jonson is careful to show that his symbolism is not mindlessly simple, not merely a matter of A for B, as in his annotations to his *Part of the Kings entertainment, in passing to his Coronation:* "The *Symboles* used, are not, neither ought to be, simply *Hieroglyphickes, Emblemes,* or *Impreses,* but a mixed character, partaking somewhat of all, and peculiarly apted to these more magnificent Inventions: wherein, the garments and ensignes deliver the nature of the person, and the word the present office" (lines 253–59). The character who functions symbolically in this pageant, Theosophia, represents a general idea (of divine wisdom), but her role is also adapted to the specific circumstances and purposes of this occasion. Along with Agrypnia (vigilance), Agape (loving affection), Omothymia (unanimity), and others, Theosophia contributes to the representation of those qualities that constitute good government as an idea and, just as important, good government of Britain in 1603.

If these symbols are not too simple, neither are they too complicated. In *Hymenaei,* although Jonson provides some explanation for the eight men who issue from the "Microcosme, *or* Globe," he contends that the audience should have apprehended their significance without aid:

> And, for the *Allegorie,* though here it be very cleare, and such as might well escape a candle, yet because there are some, must complaine of darknesse, that have but thicke eyes, I am contented to hold them this Light. First, as in *naturall bodies,* so likewise in *minds,* there is no disease, or distemperature, but is caused either by some abounding *humor,* or perverse *affection;* after the same manner, in *politick bodies* (where *Order, Ceremony, State, Reverence, Devotion,* are parts of the *Mind*) by the difference, or praedominant will of what we (*metaphorically*) call *Humors,* and *Affections,* all things are troubled and confused. These, therefore, were *tropically* brought in, before Marriage, as disturbers of that *mysticall bodie,* and the *rites,* which were *soule* unto it; that afterwards, in *Marriage,* being dutifully tempted by her *power,* they might more fully celebrate the happinesse of such as live in that sweet *union,* to the harmonious lawes of Nature and Reason. (1.112a)

In addition to glossing the meaning of this group of characters, these notes express Jonson's own understanding of the figurative method of the masque. Jonson is not precisian about the difference between symbol and allegory: although he uses *"Allegorie"* to designate the interpretation presented here, he clearly does not limit his figures to the simple significance that we associate with naive allegory. Instead, he elucidates the multiple meanings of his figures of disorder: affections or humours (themselves metaphors) influence individual bodies and minds, two bodies and minds united in marriage, many bodies and minds joined in a state, all connected in nature. The point is that his use of symbolism is flexible and clear.

The masque is an inherently symbolic structure, a spectacle in which event, character, dance, music, scenery, poetry, and even the audience combine to celebrate, on one level, King James, the Stuart court, and the realm of Britain; on a second, the principles of kingship, court, and country; on another, the ideas of authority, patriotism, and political organization; and on yet another, divine rule, human obedience, and natural order. When Prince Henry, in the transformation that is the climax of *Oberon,* appears in his chariot *"drawne by two white beares, and on either side guarded by three* Sylvanes," the audience readily perceives the various layers of signification: the English prince represents a fairy ruler who represents the idea of a Prince who represents divine sovereignty. The connection between literal scene and figurative meaning is pressed, moreover, in the verse celebrating Oberon's arrival. The fairy prince's entrance is described as an act of homage to King James, and whether or not we believe that Jonson did not solve the problem of how to include James in a masque in which the king could not actively participate,[34] the attempt to involve the monarch symbolically is transparent. The Sylvans and Silenus describe the prince and his followers—indeed, the entire assembly of masquers—in relation to the monarch, and the praise is developed in terms that clarify the symbolism I have been discussing. The evening constitutes "A night of homage to the *British* court, / And ceremony, due to ARTHURS chaire"; all glory is placed before "this only great, / True majestie, restored in this seate"; "He is the matter of vertue, and placed high"; "He is a god, o're Kings" (lines 322–44). From James to Arthur to kingship to divine authority, this figurative pattern associated with the sovereign applies to virtually every other important feature of the masque.

The symbolism could hardly have escaped the merrymakers at

Whitehall as they observed celebrated members of the court impersonating celebrated figures of mythology. The presentation of Queen Anne and her ladies as legendary persons surpasses mere analogy, since the masquers who embody great women are themselves great women. So it is with Prince Henry as ruler of nature in *Oberon*. This dual perspective, in which the audience is simultaneously made conscious of the literal and figurative levels of representation, is an essential instrument of Jonson's didactic purpose. The masques "educate by praising, by creating heroic roles for the leaders of society to fill," as Orgel puts it,[35] and this was the conventional aim of the form which Jonson adapted with skill and wit. But the literal and figurative meanings modify each other, and Jonson sees to it that the larger ideas are not obscured by the presence of the actual persons. He provides a universal context for the court, clothes the familiar in the raiment of the legendary, and thus urges the audience to look through the particular to the general. This conception of masquer and symbolic figure corresponds to Shakespeare's use of a stage character, who becomes familiar through the course of the drama, to suggest something beyond himself.

In the romances the literal characters are more significant than the characters in any of Jonson's masques, but their figurative capacity is also vital. Drama is by its nature more literal, more verisimilar than the masque; yet any dramatist, depending on his purposes, is free to adjust the balance between the specific and the abstract, the particular and the typical. Shakespeare, in looking beyond the miseries of a specific conflict and imagining a world in which tragic failure forms only part of a larger, harmonious pattern, has chosen to shift his emphasis from the individual character toward the world at large and to focus not on the unique properties but on the universal qualities of characters and actions. This adjustment in favor of the symbolic would seem to be one of the chief characteristics of these late plays.[36] The romances evince Shakespeare's late tendency to generalize, to expand the implications of the actions portrayed, to illuminate the typical qualities of the characters, and to depend in play after play upon a series of symbols implying the complex harmony of nature and the stern benevolence of Providence. This direction of the audience beyond the particular and toward the universal, this extraordinary suggestiveness, is a property the romances share with the masques.

The Tempest is the obvious place to test such conclusions, and

Stanley Wells has demonstrated how "Shakespeare makes his romance story a carrier of what might be regarded as a scheme of ideas on a philosophic topic."[37] Few would want to endorse such an interpretation of Shakespeare's earlier works, but for the late plays, and for *The Tempest* most noticeably, it seems inescapable. The numerous allegorical readings (many of them misguided) are responses to this text's unusually representative qualities, which are shared to a lesser extent by the other plays in this group. *Pericles* seems especially rich in archetypal imagery and persons; the religious texture of *The Winter's Tale* is a commonplace; and if we keep ourselves from being dazzled by the virtuosity of plotting in *Cymbeline,* we will find many of the same universal patterns there. Even *Henry VIII,* rooted though it is in the actual, conveys to its audience a sense of deeper meanings and historical patterns in ways that the earlier histories do not attempt.

The characters with which Shakespeare has peopled these late plays differ from their comic (and tragic) ancestors in being less individualized, more nearly representative of qualities or traits or ideas. The heroines of the romances, although they do what the plays require of them, are less memorable than Portia, Rosalind, or Viola. The comic heroines display what we might anachronistically call personality; the later figures lack it because they do not need it. More explicitly than their predecessors, the young women in the romances embody values that will triumph at the last—beauty, youth, innocence, fertility, renewal, continuity. Shakespeare has given them all except Imogen symbolic names consistent with the romantic imagery (and if Imogen is a slip for Innogen, the historical wife of King Kymbeline, then the principle applies to her as well).[38] Visually, the symbolic function of these heroines is not lost on directors: in performances of *The Winter's Tale* Perdita usually seems to have been cast solely for her beauty.[39] The symbolic function is supplemented with individualizing touches: Imogen is generous (in offering aid to Iachimo), Perdita spunky (in debating Polixenes), and Miranda delightfully sympathetic (in all things). But these women are more than characters.

Concentration on the typical governs Shakespeare's portraiture in general. Florizel and Ferdinand are the male counterparts of Perdita and Miranda in representing youth and hope for the future, and they offer the masculine virtues of courage (even rashness) and vigor. When Miranda first meets Ferdinand she recognizes the moral beauty his attractive person represents: "I might call him / A thing divine; for nothing natural / I ever saw so noble" (1.ii.420–22). Even though the judgment is admittedly naive, the play endorses it. At the opposite end of the scale, Cymbeline's Queen is the type of the wicked stepmother, Cloten that of the stupid son or foolish pretender. Hermione, in responding to her husband's deranged outbursts, enacts the pattern of all patience, her stoicism making her a relative of Griselda. Leontes' experience virtually demands archetypal interpretation: he undergoes a pattern of sin, repentance, purgation, and redemption that Shakespeare presents as an intensified version of everyman's experience and that calls up inescapable Christian connotations. The dramatist's penchant for concentration and figuration seems to increase from play to play, exerting the strongest effect in *The Tempest,* where the principal characters divide neatly into groups of good and evil. Some have seen the influence of the morality plays in this schematic approach to characterization, and while the theory has much to recommend it, even more pertinent are the familiar conventions of romance—wicked brothers, virtuous daughters, slandered wives, witches, monsters, gods. (In fact, morality and romance are closely related, as Howard Felperin and others have demonstrated.)[40] Clearly these dramas are fairy tales, and the characters of fairy tales, created to teach lessons of good and evil, are not individualized but representative.

As with character, so with action. Drama makes certain literal demands in both areas, of course, but much of the action is best understood as representing something beyond what is portrayed on the stage. Stanley Wells comments helpfully on this connection between persons and events: since the characters of romance "are comparatively little distinguished by variety of style," he says, "actions the more easily take on symbolical value. It is not necessary to go outside the play to see Ferdinand's log-carrying as an expression of a theme that crops up at many points. On a realistic level it is no hardship for a healthy young man to spend a few hours carrying firewood; but any hint of this attitude in performance is ruinous."[41] The theme to which Wells refers is the idea of control, control of nature, of other men, of passion, of the self. The symbolic action radiates into other parts of the play, and in this respect Ferdinand's stint at the woodpile is a touchstone for much of the action of the other romances. The revival of Thaisa by Cerimon—who takes her from the sea, frees her from a coffin filled with precious spices and jewels, and gives her life again by means of fire and music—creates the same kind of resonance in the rest of the play, but also avails itself of the familiar imagery of Christianity. Thaisa herself is a kind of jewel, the sea's casting her up is consistent with nature's destructive and reconstructive forces, and her resurrection is one of the many important physical and metaphysical revivals which give the romances their miraculous overtones.

Wells's cautionary statement that "it is not necessary to go outside the play" to apprehend the symbolic value of certain actions, while properly intended as a corrective to the rash of "critical excesses" *The Tempest* has provoked, strikes me as perhaps too restrictive. With actions such as Ferdinand's log-bearing and Thaisa's resuscitation, the plays virtually compel us to look not only into other parts of the internal pattern but also outward toward the natural design, the divine pattern of which these episodes represent a part. Even the least symbolic of the romances, *Cymbeline,* insists that we extend our understanding of its action beyond the confines of the play itself. When Imogen awakens over the body of Cloten, for example, an intricate and profound set of associations comes into play. The awakening signifies first the revival of Imogen's good fortune; the disguised torso implies the death of the old Posthumus and prepares for the arrival of the altered, penitent man; the death of Cloten and the benign effects of the Queen's drugs expose the self-destructiveness of the malign forces at Cymbeline's court; and the heroine's joining the Roman forces dressed as Fidele prepares for the peace between Britain and Rome. Emrys Jones, noting that the event lying in the background of *Cymbeline* is the birth of Christ, points out that Shakespeare transferred the historical events of Guiderius's reign to the uneventful years of Cymbeline's so as to take advantage of this date and to end on a "note of transcendental peace."[42] Each character must endure a period of strife concluding in peace, a pattern repeated in the historical movement towards international, even cosmic harmony. As for *The Winter's Tale,* its solstitial rhythms and mythological implications have been so thoroughly discussed by Northrop Frye and others that it would be redundant to do more than mention them. One minor instance will serve, Mamillius's death in act 3, of which Patrick Crutwell writes: "The death of Mamillius is not the death of a small boy; it is the death of innocence."[43] It is the death of innocence in Leontes, in the world of the Sicilian court, in the world of the play, in every life. And one might apply this simply stated distinction to all the play's actions: the marriage of Florizel and Perdita is the mending of personal, familial, and political wounds; the restoration of Hermione is an outpouring of grace on penitent man. "In these plays one feels that the meaning which Shakespeare is striving to express lies almost beyond the capacity of a drama filled only with human characters."[44]

This striving for resonance helps to explain Shakespeare's reaching out toward the spectacle of the masque. Recognition of the symbolic quality of the masques and romances supplies a context for appreciating the theatrical effects which have too often dominated discussion. Music, dance, magic, exotic settings, visions—all these provide theatrical support for the symbolic communication of ideas and must be understood as functional, not merely decorative, properties. In Jonsonian terms we might say that they pertain to the body of the work and should be regarded—Platonically, if you will—as means by which one apprehends the soul they represent. This symbolic unification of all parts of the masque is probably Jonson's chief contribution to its development, and Shakespeare's interest in spectacle, likewise, is most important as a strategy for enriching the meaning of his actions, images, and ideas. It is not enough to notice that songs and visions function dramatically as they have not in earlier comedies;[45] such effects must also be connected with the poetic meaning, the symbolic texture of the piece.

Jonson's symbolic expression of a vision of beauty and order depends upon a feature of the masque that the reader can only imagine: dance. The masque originated in courtly dancing as well as in disguising, and even at the Stuart court the revels were for many the highlight of the evening. In *The Masque of Queenes,* for example, the famous ladies "tooke out the Men, and dauncd the *Measures*; entertayning the time, almost to the space of an hower, w^{t}h singular variety" (lines 736–38). To neglect the dancing was to commit a serious blunder, as the king's famous outburst at *Pleasure Reconciled to Virtue* attests: "Why don't they dance? What did you make me come here for? Devil take you all, dance." Although Jonson was naturally less interested in choreography than in poetry, he employed the convention to furnish general support for the theme of the evening. And as he gained experience he used dancing more variously, as in *The Gypsies Metamorphosed,* where dances are spaced throughout the proceedings, and more specifically, as in *News from the New World,* where King James is explicitly identified as the mover of the graceful spectacle (lines 334–45).

In every masque, however, the revels constitute a central symbolic image. Jonson envisages a realm of balance, grace, and beauty, of which the measured motion supplies a concluding visual symbol. Men and women join in harmonious action and thus represent the concordant operation of society, nations, and planets. In *Queenes,* following the hour of dancing mentioned above, there occurs a "third *Daunce;* then w^{c}h a more numerous composition could not be seene: *graphically* dispos'd into *letters,* and honoring the Name of the most sweete, and ingenious *Prince, Charles, Duke* of *York* Wherin, beside that principall grace of perspicuity, the motions were so even, & apt, and they^r expression so just; as if *Mathematicians* had lost *proportion,* they might there have found it" (lines 749–56). The gorgeous spectacle in this case illustrates the idea of virtuous celebrity, as the next song explains: "Who, *Virtue,* can thy powr forget, / That sees these live, and triumph yet?" (lines 764–65). The traditional dances provide thematic color and beauty for its own sake, but their more important function is to dissolve the distinction between masquer and spectator. "In terms of the action of the masque, the point made by the revels is that the masquers are capable of moving from the stage into the world of the court. . . . it was the *idea* of the revels that was significant."[46] When courtiers dance with Penthesilea and Camilla, they are "taken out" of their ordinary places and drawn into a nobler sphere. They become, if only temporarily, the perfect beings Jonson has imagined humans to be. They achieve the illusion of transcendence. And in these works, as we shall see, illusion is very nearly all.

The centrality of dancing in the masque is one of the chief distinctions between it and the drama. Whereas Jonson shapes his subject so as to accommodate dancing, Shakespeare seems to work in reverse, calling for dances when his narrative requires them and tailoring them to fit that narrative. Alan Brissenden, in *Shakespeare and the Dance,* has demonstrated that dancing becomes significantly more frequent and prominent in the plays written after 1607.[47] In *Pericles* several episodes are choreographically heightened: the royal tournament at Pentapolis, certainly, and perhaps the various dumb shows and the final assembly at the temple of Diana. (Ron Daniels's 1979 Stratford production used movement often and to great effect, notably in the opening scene with Antiochus and his daughter, whose incest was suggested in a dance.) *Cymbeline* offers fewer such opportunities, but it is likely that in Posthumus's dream vision the Leonati are intended to move rhythmically when "*They circle Posthumus round as he lies sleeping*" (v.iv.29s.d.). The dancing in *The Winter's Tale* occurs mostly at the Bohemian festival and includes the performance of the Saltiers probably imported from *Oberon*: much of this dancing is of the wilder sort associated with the antimasque, and Brissenden makes the intriguing argument that the scene upends the traditional order of the masque, with the king as the figure of disruption, not concord.[48] This may be so, but surely the rustics' dances underscore the sense of merriment and freedom absent from the court of Sicilia. In *The Tempest* dancing proper is confined mainly to the inhabitants of the spirit world (there is only one female mortal in the cast); as they gracefully offer the banquet and enact the wedding masque, the supernatural creatures perform dances that fulfill precisely the same functions that they do in Jonson's masques: the representation of harmony between the upper and lower worlds.

Actual dancing, however, contributes less to the romances than the symbolic connotations of patterned movement. Explicit images of the dance are not even especially prominent, although there are a couple of striking instances. Interestingly, these are negative: references to dancing in the last plays are apt to be to the abandoned, uncontrolled motion of the antimasque,[49] such as Pericles' reference to the "dancing boat" on which Marina is born and Thaisa "dies," and Leontes' lament that his "heart dances, / But not for joy, not joy" (1.ii.110–11). But much more valuable than these specific images is the general attention given to such properties as order, measure, grace, and harmony, which are characteristic of dancing but not limited to it. In other words, human conflict and resolution are represented symbolically as part of a larger pattern of movement and countermovement, and this natural design may be seen as a form of divine choreography. The sea is often described in such a fashion. Its ebb and flow, the alternation of turbulence and calm, here call to mind not the still, sad music of humanity but a benevolent rhythm that ultimately produces concord and fertility: in a sense, therefore, Pericles' description of the "dancing boat" is ironically positive, for the sea yields up Thaisa alive and finally reunites father, daughter, and mother. Relevant also is Florizel's praise of Perdita:

> when you do dance, I wish you
> A wave o'th'sea, that you might ever do
> Nothing but that, move still, still so,
> And own no other function.
>
> (1v.iv.140–43)

The rhythm of these lines suggests perpetual motion, and at various points in the last plays Shakespeare insists that all elements of nature—not only the waves of the sea but the seasons of the year, flora and fauna, the heavenly bodies—participate in a graceful pattern of motion best described as a dance. So it is with the characters: partners separate and reunite, weary revelers retire and fresh ones replace them, groups divide and reassemble. And in "The Vision" in *Henry VIII* Shakespeare includes in this measured system the heavenly beings themselves, whose graceful dance Queen Katherine yearns, and is soon allowed, to join.

Surely symbolic texture is the most important similarity between masque and romance. Shakespeare's passage from tragedy to romance, according to Derek Traversi, is marked by "the deliberate abandonment of realism"; Traversi sees "a tendency . . . towards a conception of the art of the theatre in which character and action alike are real in relation to the poetic unity to which they belong, and finally to that alone." To make such observations, he argues, is not to deny a certain quotient of concreteness. "It is simply to say that the characters and situation of Shakespeare's final comedies are more exclusively conditioned than ever before by the poetic emotion, that the plays themselves are to be regarded accordingly as expanded images, and that these images in turn attain their full expression by moulding to their purpose the conventions of the stage."[50] This description of the romances as "expanded images," diminishing as it does the role of narrative, clarifies the relation of romance and masque, for in a general way Traversi's analysis applies also to the masque as Jonson developed it. Shakespeare educes his suggestive imagery from a literal story, Jonson from the literal Presence. Jonson's symbolic expansion of this doubleness—king and King—may have stimulated Shakespeare's movement towards the universal. Shakespeare hardly needed Jonson to show him that music could offer more than pleasing sounds, that dancing could signify order and beauty and even divinity. But it may be that Jonson's having extracted complex poetic meanings from the traditions of the masque suggested to Shakespeare new uses for familiar materials. Whether or not one artist taught the other is less important than the congruence of their methods.

§ III

Description of these dramatists' ideal worlds is not an easy task—Milton too had trouble writing about heaven—but is made somewhat easier by the idealist's natural tendency to simplify. Northrop Frye points out that "in romances heroes are brave, heroines beautiful, villains villainous, and the frustrations, ambiguities, and embarrassments of ordinary life are made little of."[51] Shakespeare's and Jonson's presentations of the conditions of life in their ideal realms are guided by the same interest in the typical that governs their depiction of character and action, an emphasis which permits a general approach to the content of these visions. The most fruitful way to begin is to notice that the world of the masques and romances is a mirror image of that examined in Chapter 4. Or, more precisely, the relation between worlds within these works is reversed: in the tragedies and satiric comedies, romantic illusion is shattered by the harshness of a fallen world; in the ideal works, the penalties of the fall are suspended and the beauteous illusion becomes the reality.

Each work is founded upon a contrast between two worlds, a competition corresponding to the structural contrast between antimasque and masque or between tragic and comic conclusions. In imagining and representing experience as it might be, Shakespeare and Jonson begin with the romantic dreams rejected in their skeptical works and reshape them into balanced versions. The adjective is crucial: these are not paradises where a dreamer may walk naked among his succubae. But the worlds that emerge from the final scenes of the romances and last tableaux of the masques are generalized versions of those conceived by Shakespeare's tragic heroes and even, in their more altruistic moments, by Jonson's comic dreamers. The claims of the sublunary world are certainly not forgotten, and the contribution of irony to the final vision is palpable; but the drag of mortality makes the leap beyond it all the more exhilarating. In the masques and romances we discover a world of order and clarity such as Hamlet seeks, a state of justice that could satisfy Coriolanus or Adam Overdo, a realm in which Dapper might find himself chosen by the Queen of Faery, a place of familial unity dreamt of by Lear, "nature, naturiz'd 'gainst all infections" (11.i.64). It is a world redeemed.

The geography of these ideal worlds differs radically from the enclosed urban spaces of Jonsonian comedy or the perilous landscapes of Lear's Britain or Coriolanus's Rome. Jonson relies heavily upon Inigo Jones's scenic splendors, which provide a visual equivalent of the charmed worlds that Shakespeare draws with words.[52] There are threats to Jonson's lovely and orderly locales, but they are vanquished by the magnificence of the principal settings: there is Britania, "*A world, divided from the world*" in *Blacknesse* and *Beauty;* Albion, with its unifying pun (*All be one*), in *Love Freed from Ignorance;* the "Artificial Sphere of Silver" with its "Zodiac of Gold" in *The Haddington Masque;* the House of Fame in *Queenes;* and the translucent palace replacing the conventional rock and trees in *Oberon.* As symbolic showplaces for the representation of virtue and harmony, these landscapes are suffused with the light of understanding and majesty.[53] It is more difficult, however, to classify the settings of the romances, since *Pericles* moves all over the map and *The Tempest* is celebrated for its unity of place. Either there are contrasting locations or the dominant setting is subject to conflicting interpretations by the inhabitants (the grass on Prospero's island being "lush and lusty" to Gonzalo, "tawny" to Antonio). But always the truly memorable settings—Wales and Bohemia, for example—are those associated with the triumphant values of freedom and honesty, and in the sea plays the natural realm surrounding the characters, although potentially destructive, is finally shown to be benevolent. In both the masques and the romances, the beauties of the pastoral landscapes and crystal palaces are magnified by the forces of disorder and corruption that threaten them. But Providence banishes or subdues the powers of natural chaos, as at the end of *The Masque of Beautie:*

VULTURNUS

Rise, aged *Thames,* and by the hand
Receive these *Nymphes,* within the land:
And, in those curious *Squares,* and *Rounds,*
Wherewith thou flow'st betwixt the grounds
Of fruitfull *Kent,* and *Essex* faire,
That lend thee gyrlands for thy hayre;
Instruct their silver feete to tread,
Whilst we, againe to sea, are fled.

With which the *Windes* departed; . . . (lines 300–308)

In the idealized view that we are shown, divine artistry insures the benevolent cooperation of all nature's forces.

These beauteous realms are governed by benevolent deities. "The fingers of the powers above do tune / The harmony of this peace," declares the Soothsayer at the end of *Cymbeline* (v.v.467–68). This providential interpretation of the rapprochement between Britain and Rome—as well as the rhetoric that expresses it—is typical of the teleology that informs masque and romance and constitutes a major link between them. In Shakespeare's early comedies the shape of events implies providential direction, but the favorable powers for the most part remain offstage.[54] Jonson in his satiric comedies and Shakespeare in his tragedies stress man's responsibility for his condition. It may be that God or the gods have arranged the universe so that an Edmund or Cornwall comes to a bad end or so that the greed of a Volpone will get the better of him, but the source of this implied order is not of overriding interest to either dramatist. In the works considered here, however, both artists seek to make their visions intelligible and credible by indicating the origins of order and meaning. We hear the harmonious music and at times are even allowed to see the divine musicians in performance.

Gods and goddesses were conventional characters when Jonson took up the masque, but he made unique use of their symbolic potentialities. Mythology and legend supplied him not only with familiar figures but also with a wealth of associations to elucidate the virtues (or vices) with which each masque was particularly concerned. Moreover, such beings and their connotations help to create artistic coherence, a principle demonstrated especially in *Hymenaei,* the celebration of unity in marriage prepared for the Essex-Howard wedding. Although it is called the masque of Hymen, its presiding deity and dedicatee is " I U N O, whose great name / Is U N I O in the *anagram*" (lines 232–33), and the decisive moment is the discovery of the goddess enthroned amid clouds at *"the upper part of the* Scene." The traditional iconography associated with Juno (peacocks, lilies, a lionskin) is carried through in the visual decoration, and Jonson draws upon his classical learning to amplify the meaning of the vision. For example, he assigns to each of her eight attendants *"surnames of Iuno,* ascribed to her for some peculiar property in marriage," such as Iuga, signifying the yoking of equal partners in wedlock.[55] Reason, seconded by his servant Order, attends to the details of ranking and introducing the participants, and the songs and dances extend the idea of harmony that the presence of Juno and Hymen guarantees.

Jonson employs mythology to extend the theme of union beyond marriage.[56] The joining of individuals in marriage reflects the cooperation of families (the houses of Essex and Howard were on poor terms), of nations, and of natural forces:

> And as, in *circle*, you depart
> Link'd *hand in hand;* So, *heart in heart,*
> May all those *bodies* still remayne
> Whom he (with so much sacred payne)
> No lesse hath bound within his realmes
> Then they are with the O C E A N S streames.
> Long may his U N I O N find increase
> As he, to ours, hath deign'd his peace.
> (lines 423–30)

Jonson's comedies and epigrams indicate that what was soon to happen to the bride and groom would have come as no surprise to him, but the masques suggest what might be, so in each Jonson constructs similar analogies between monarch and god. Although classical figures such as Venus and Cupid appear, Jonson also draws upon native legend in *Oberon,* plays once with Arthurian material in *Prince Henry's Barriers,* and even invents a goddess when necessary, as with *"Bel-Anna,* Royall *Queene* of the *Ocean"* in *Queenes.* Deity provides a kind of shorthand: the visual power of the masque means that the poetry must be used economically, and the introduction of known figures establishes immediately a hierarchy from which the poet can draw his own particular and universal meanings. The example of *Hymenaei* is typical, as John C. Meagher argues: "Jonson contrives, with the aid of the devices of the scene and in the poetical presentation, to present Juno not as an abstraction or as a mere figure for marriage but as an authentic deity, with all the glory appropriate to a goddess—with all the glory bequeathed by Neoplatonic mythography."[57]

Events in the world of the romances are clearly directed from above, whether or not a divine representative enters to say so. Such a being does descend in *Pericles,* where "Celestial Dian, goddess argentine" instructs the hero to go to Ephesus with his lamentable tale of the lost Thaisa, offering happiness if he complies and misery if not, and in *Cymbeline,* where Jupiter declares his responsibility for the happy arrangement of mortal affairs. Gods and goddesses *per se* are absent from *The Winter's Tale* and *The Tempest,* which contain instead the Delphic oracle of

Apollo, Time personified, and Ariel and other attendant spirits (who represent goddesses in a masque). Shakespeare's altered practice constitutes a retreat from specificity: in the first two plays we see the watchful divinity, in *The Winter's Tale* Apollo issues a judgment and prophecy from offstage, but in *The Tempest* the divine power with which Prospero communicates is not even named. Paradoxically, the decision to eschew concrete presentation increases the sense of divine potency.

The Tempest seems by far the most religious of the romances precisely because the source of heavenly influence remains nebulous. Shakespeare's depiction in Prospero of a mage, a medium with access to divine power but still human, attests to the existence of supernatural protection but avoids the problems attending the literal presentation of a stage god. Likewise, the playwright takes advantage of the spectacular effects of theophany but prevents heaven from seeming mundane in allowing Prospero to present the masque of Ceres. A "creaking throne comes down, the boyes to please," but it is not the real thing; instead, it is a dramatic representation of theophany performed by spirits under the control of a human with supernatural help. The magic of which Prospero is master gives him power over Ariel and his "meaner fellows," but there is a sense in which all the spirits and even Prospero himself are agents of a greater force. The supernatural world is kept at a distance, its full power never completely revealed. The strategy here would seem to magnify the power of the gods, and in one sense it does, but Shakespeare is able to use this mystery ambiguously. A crucial feature of *The Tempest* is that Shakespeare will not specify exactly where divine care ends and human effort begins. When Gonzalo praises the "gods" for having "chalk'd forth the way / Which brought us hither" (v.i.203–4), an interpretation to which Alonso assents, neither is aware of Prospero's hand in arranging the fortunate shipwreck. Yet there is truth in the old counselor's providential view, for Prospero has accepted divine aid by intercepting the party on their return from Tunis. In other words, the harmonies that emerge at the end of *The Tempest* are a function both of divine grace and human virtue, and the impossibility of assigning exact responsibility makes Shakespeare's ideal vision all the more credible and all the more attractive.

The conditions of life for humans in the graceful worlds of Shakespeare and Jonson are much the same, but rather than seek out every close parallel and correspondence, I shall instead consider the particular qualities that each artist has chosen to emphasize. Jonson's presentation of the ideal society has a distinctly political focus owing to the circumstances of performance. His visions direct attention to the structure of the ideal cosmos, the organization of elements, of spirits, and of men and women. Since the very arrangement of the audience in the Banqueting House at Whitehall encourages this attention to hierarchy, Jonson capitalizes on this feature of the event, associating the monarch with divinity, the courtiers with divine "faculties," and the world of the court with the heavens. The masque begins with the macrocosm, with the ideas presented first in their universal forms: the audience perceives the ideal of marriage, for instance, and is then invited to make the local applications. Shakespeare's practice, on the other hand, is to concentrate on the particular case and to develop universal significance from it. It might be said that Jonson works deductively, Shakespeare inductively. Or to return for a moment to the symbolic method, Jonson devotes primary attention to the vehicle in his symbolic scheme, Shakespeare to the tenor. And where Jonson seems especially concerned with the outlines or structures of his ideal state, Shakespeare shows greater interest in the content, what we might call the color of his vision.

Jonson's idealized world creates above all an impression of pleasing order. The luminous atmosphere reveals that this world has been rearranged—arrangement is the key to the meaning of the masques. Throughout the comedies Jonson addresses the problem of self-government, and in the masques the conditions of performance prompt him to consider that issue on a larger scale. In masque after masque Jonson contends that the foundation of the ideal state is an efficient and unbroken hierarchy. The mythological atmosphere transports the spectator to what seems a prelapsarian state where quarreling among the gods is unknown, where all things work together for good. "O then! what *deities* will dare / With HYMEN, or with IUNO to compare?" (*Hym.*, lines 338–39). Lower beings cooperate with the deity and are rewarded for doing so, a truth that receives direct expression in *Oberon*:

To [his] sole power, and magick they doe give
The honor of their being; that they live
Sustayn'd in forme, fame, and felicitie,
From rage of fortune, or the fear to die.
(lines 331–34)

Unity in all things—in the heavens, in nature, among nations, among the peoples of a nation, in the family—is one of the great themes of the masques, *Hymenaei* being its supreme expression. The integrity of each member of society is an implicit idea, although Jonson gives relatively little attention to individuals. The rampaging egos that animate the comedies are relegated to the antimasque and ultimately ejected or integrated into the whole. Such an ordered, unified world is the opposite of that found in the plays, where the action is motivated by the divisive forces in human nature, impulses that separate men from men (or men from their money). Here is real justice, not the bogus and hypocritical variety practiced in Venice; this is a true commonwealth, not the spurious kind rigged up by Subtle, Face, and Dol for the sake of convenience and then exploded by pride; the governor here, unlike the monstrous Tiberius, is wise, generous, and frank.

Jonson frequently identifies his brilliant realm with Renaissance notions of the golden age. The cooperation of men with men and of men with nature produces material abundance as well as social order. Labor, that penalty of the fall, is replaced with rewarding stewardship, for nature gives of herself willingly. This is a version of the classical trope *sponte sua*,[58] seen most prominently in "To Penshurst" and repeated in *The Golden Age Restor'd*:

> Then earth unplough'd shall yeeld her crop,
> Pure honey from the oake shall drop,
>   The fountains shall runne milke:
> The thistle shall the lilly beare,
> And every bramble roses weare,
>   And every worme make silke.
> (lines 163–68)

The verse, marked by a combination of fluid meter and forceful rhyme, suggests the ease and order of perfected nature. Moreover, such abundance, as with all things in the ideal state, is not subject to decay, and the classical texture of the work creates a sense of immortality. Time is summoned only to be exiled. In the fallen world, time

> Is eating every piece of houre
>   Some object of the rarest worth.
> Yet this is rescued from his rage,
> As not to die by time, or age.

> For beautie hath a living name,
> And will to heaven, from whence it came.
> (*Love Freed*, lines 364–69)

This conclusion, immediately preceding "the going out," informs the assembly that the evening must end, but it also reminds them that by their participation in these solemnities they have conquered time, have assisted in the creation of an immutable world.

Jonson's emphasis on permanence leads to the awareness that the world of the masques is essentially Neoplatonic.[59] In *Love Freed*, shortly before the passage just cited, one of the priests delivers a speech beginning "How neere to good is what is faire!" (line 348) and continuing with the notion that our senses respond naturally to the beautiful and lead us to emulate the good. To suggest, as some have done, that Jonson is catering to shallow philosophical fashion is no more relevant than the old view that the masques constitute little more than flattery. This sphere of light and music exerts an irresistible attraction upon the nobler side of human nature, so that progress toward the good is inevitable. The clarity of the atmosphere dissipates the problems of perception of which fallen man is usually the victim. The "Barriers" performed the night after *Hymenaei* represent a contest between "two *Ladies*, the one representing *Truth*, the other *Opinion;* but both so like attired, as they could by no note be distinguish'd" (lines 683–86). But this state of confusion is only temporary, for the struggle ends abruptly when "*a striking light seem[s] to fill all the hall,* and *out of it an* angell *or* messenger of glory" comes forth to identify and honor the figure of Truth. For once, appearance and reality do not conflict. In this state the claims of Reason (in *Hymenaei* an imposing figure carrying a sword and lamp) are easily understood and readily obeyed. She delivers but one speech, and "*At this,* Humors *and* Affections *sheathed their swords, and retired amazed to the sides of the stage*" (lines 157–58). Ease of recognition leads naturally to right action, personated in *Queenes* by Heroique Virtue. This resplendent figure, dressed as Perseus, silences the hags and summons his daughter Fame to introduce the celebrated women of the past and present. The light that fosters understanding and virtue also permits the world to observe and applaud such action and to honor the poets who celebrate it. This poet celebrates the Platonic doctrine that love of beauty impels man's soul toward the good. Love of persons is a recurrent theme, even sexual love in the wedding masques, and Cupid is treated much less frivolously than he might be. Jonson concentrates on love's power to inspire, to move, to prompt the soul toward the ideal, to elicit responses to beauty, to create beauty. In the finale of *Love Restor'd*, the dances are generated by love:

Have men beheld the Graces daunce,
    Or seene the upper Orbes to move?
So these did turne, returne, advance,
    Drawne backe by doubt, put on by love.
(lines 280–83)

The chief differences between the Jonsonian and Shakespearean versions of an ideal society are attributable to the formal and circumstantial differences between masque and play. Certain distinctions are a function of the basic difference I have already pointed out, that the masque implies the particular in its presentation of the general, while the play reveals the general in its depiction of the particular. As playwright, Shakespeare is concerned first with the specific case, in particular human problems, a focus which means that his field of vision is more limited than Jonson's. Whereas the masques address immediately the great structures of kingdom and cosmos, the romances are concerned with smaller units, notably the family. The difference between the pictorial masque and the narrative play naturally influences both authors' consideration of an ideal realm. The masque celebrates the arrival of a harmonious state; the play is mostly given over to reaching it. And finally, Jonson follows tradition by depicting his vision in pagan terms, whereas the happy state of Shakespearean romance, even though it may be represented in a pagan world, is implicitly, and sometimes explicitly, Christian.

The ideal society as Shakespeare imagines it does not become fully visible until the final scene and can be understood only in relation to what has gone before. The language chosen by critics to describe the nature of such a world demonstrates its intimate connection to the fallen state from which it emerges. Reconciliation, reunion, restoration, regeneration—the list of similar nouns might be extended endlessly. The point is that the realm of concord to which the romances move is a reconstructed state, a new Jerusalem built from the ruins of the old, and Shakespeare never neglects the contrast between the two. The events constituting the happy ending are especially joyful because they correct errors or heal wounds. Rather than rehearse the names of reunited couples or families, I shall mention the telling case of Posthumus and Imogen because it illustrates Shakespeare's departure from his earlier comic practice: here he depicts a couple already married. Virtually all the marriages in the romances are more than weddings of individuals. Florizel and Perdita and Ferdinand and Miranda strengthen by their unions the reunions of their parents and the states they govern, and the marriage of Camillo and Paulina adds support to the theme that no beginning is wholly new. Of course every artist who imagines a better world erects it with materials taken from this one, arranges them into a more pleasing shape, and points to the differences between old and new. But Shakespeare seems to dwell on the origins of the new in the old, a practice creating a paradoxical effect: it serves both to intensify the loveliness of the new creation and to adumbrate its fragility. To notice this mixed effect is to admit the great component of irony in Shakespeare's late vision, a topic to be taken up shortly. For now, it is enough to say that Jonson's ideal realm appears more independent of reality, more fantastic, more nearly chaste than Shakespeare's, whose Eden never seems completely safe from the serpent's tooth.

The Shakespearean romantic universe breeds and is sustained by many of the same virtues with which Jonson is concerned, but here they are examined in smaller units. Love is a *sine qua non* of both realms, but Shakespeare's dramatization of the idea appears in the love of a woman for a man, a husband for a wife, a parent for a child, a master for a servant, a friend for a friend, and from these instances we are encouraged to extrapolate, to recognize the universal force of love. In *Pericles* and *Cymbeline* Shakespeare depicts the love of a god for a man, and the larger significance of this case is unmistakable, but even here Shakespeare has confined himself to particular situations, symbolic though they be. Never is his practice as expansive as Jonson's. This distinction appears likewise in the two writers' treatments of government, that great subject of many of the masques. Stephen Orgel's remarks on *Oberon* illuminate the Jonsonian method: "England becomes great through the imposition of classical order upon British nature; the rough native strength of the castle is remade according to the best models, civilized by arts of design, by learning and taste. In the same way the Prince of Faery, the new Prince of Wales, comes out of the woods, tames the rough satyrs, and descends to salute his father, the real King James, in the Palladian architecture of the Whitehall Banqueting House."⁶⁰ Through the universal scene we glimpse the individual embodiments of the idea. The process in *The Tempest* works in reverse. From the conflict of Prospero with his enemies, particularly with Caliban, and most importantly with himself, we are exposed to the principles of enlightenment, moderation, forgiveness, and self-control that not only insure personal and political harmony but also govern the universe itself. Numerous other virtues— loyalty in Pisanio and Camillo, courage and hope in Marina, perseverance in Pericles, self-understanding in Posthumus, Leontes, and Prospero, chastity in Miranda, reputation in Imogen—might be summoned to illustrate that the Jonsonian and Shakespearean paradises look very much alike, however differently we are made to perceive them.

Although the Platonic principles of experience evident in the masques apply almost as well here, Shakespeare's conception is more frankly Christian. Shakespeare does not attribute the happy endings to the influence of God, but he represents him in surrogates such as Diana, Jupiter, Apollo, and the "gods" to whom Gonzalo gives thanks. Howard Felperin is surely right in asserting that "by employing pagan deities from conventional romance in *Pericles,* and by surrounding them with Christian-providential associations, Shakespeare has the best of both worlds: a timeless romantic action with unmistakably Christian relevance."⁶¹ The unmistakability of such relevance is heard in the vocabulary associated with the happy issues of the dramatic conflicts. It is a "great miracle" that Thaisa has been saved, that "this queen relives." Her resurrection establishes a pattern repeated with the mariners in *The Tempest,* with Hermione, and with Imogen when she recovers from the drug and again when she rises from the scornful blow delivered by Posthumus in the final scene. Posthumus refuses revenge on Iachimo ("The pow'r that I have on you is to spare you; / The malice towards you to forgive you"), and Cymbeline follows his son-in-law's example with "Pardon's the word to all" (v.v.419–20, 423). Imogen rejoices that she has lived "To see this gracious season" (v.v.402). Everyone is familiar with the religious imagery of *The Tempest,* the references to guilt, sin, repentance, baptism, rebirth, salvation, fresh garments, and the benevolent Father. The "resurrection" scene in *The Winter's Tale* makes as strong an impression as it does partly because the language is charged: "grace," "graces," "faith," "hope," "transported," "redeems," "holy," "blessing," "exaltation," "I'll fill your grave up," "stol'n from the dead."

These are the terms of the New Covenant, the chief expositor of which is represented by his namesake, Paulina. The First Gentleman's forecast of the scene uses Pauline vocabulary in claiming that "Every wink of an eye, some new grace will be born" (v.ii.110–11).

Such language reveals the world of the romances to be at last a state of grace. If men and women cannot escape the mistakes that ought to damn them, heaven grants unwarranted happiness. Ironies work constructively, accidents incline toward the positive, second chances are the rule, the normally devastating effects of time are converted into a process of fruition, and the harsh rules of cause and consequence are suspended.[62] These conditions apply even though characters such as Posthumus, Leontes, and Alonso, and the audience too, for that matter, know that they should not. "The tragic heroes, and we along with them, persist in expecting romance and get tragedy; the romantic protagonists are disabused of all romantic expectations and get romance."[63] The romance that they get, too good to be true, is received with childlike wonder. These protagonists forget what they know, believe the unbelievable, become as little children, and thus they are able to enter Shakespeare's version of a terrestrial kingdom of heaven.

§IV

It remains to observe some similar ways in which the masques and romances work upon an audience. Shakespeare and Jonson, having imagined a world in which disorder can be converted to harmony, wounds healed, failure transformed into victory, and suffering understood as a prelude to joy, are careful to stress both terms, the suffering as well as the joy. Thus one of their main instruments is irony. The introduction of irony serves, in the first place, to make the glorious visions credible. As Stanley Wells says, "*The Tempest* is a romance containing a built-in criticism of romance; not a rejection of it, but an appreciation both of its glories and its limitations."[64] The dual structure of both kinds of works contributes to such an effect, but perhaps even more significant is what Wells calls "the alternation and balance between the palpably unreal and the illusion of reality" so that "romance is toughened by a strain of anti-romance."[65] The correspondences between this world and that emphasize the unstable nature of reality and the limits of human perception, and this theme in turn gives reality to the unreal, suggests

175

the possibility of the impossible. It would be surprising if two of the world's masters of irony should abandon this tool in creating some of their most sophisticated works. Even in presenting a world where there may be no discrepancy between appearance and fact, they use it to their advantage.

Whatever we choose to call this basic form of human weakness—shortsightedness, the partial view, taking the part for the whole, the illusion of permanence, solipsism—the masques and romances are organized so as to expose and mend it. Characters who succumb to despair or who triumph in their success may expect a change in fortune. So it is with the satyrs in *Oberon* as they exult over the drowsing sylvans guarding the gates of the prince's palace:

SATYRE 3
Would we'had *Boreas* here, to blow
Off their leavie coats, and strip 'hem.

SATYRE 4
I,I,I; that we might whip 'hem.

SATYRE 3
Or, that we had a waspe, or two
For their nostrills.

SATYRE 1
Hayres will doe
Even as well: Take my tayle.

SATYRE 2
What do'you say to'a good nayle
Through their temples.

SATYRE 3
Or an eele,
In their guts, to make 'hem feele?
(lines 174–89)

Their petty tricks and mischievous jealousies are soon exploded when the sylvans awaken and the gates of the palace are opened. Caliban and his conspirators experience a similar reversal.

The pattern works in reverse too, as in Alonso's desperate lament for the loss of Ferdinand:

Even here I will put off my hope, and keep it
No longer for my flatterer: he is drown'd
Whom thus we stray to find; and the sea mocks
Our frustrate search on land. Well, let him go.
(III.iii.7–10)

These disconsolate words are succeeded almost immediately by the apparition of the banquet which appears to be a magical gift but turns out to be an illusion; and yet the disappointment of the mirage is merely a stop on the way to satisfaction, the genuine vision of Ferdinand and Miranda playing at chess. Numerous other instances suggest themselves: the unhappy daughters of Niger in *The Masque of Blacknesse;* the desperate Pericles of act 5; the unhappy Perdita who resolves to "queen it no inch farther"; the demonically jubilant hags in *Queenes;* the Leonati in the last act of *Cymbeline,* uttering imprecations against what they believe to be divine caprice. All these figures come to find their conditions altered and their limited understanding expanded: satisfaction is miraculously forthcoming, hopes are defeated, and Perdita will queen it indeed.

The simplest way of putting it is to say that characters in both kinds of works experience a shift in perspective, and the audience enjoys a comparable shift in vision. Even though our point of view is usually more inclusive than that of the characters, we still find that our knowledge is incomplete and our confidence in our perception unfounded. Jones's settings gave Jonson a physical embodiment of this metaphysical shift, of course, and apparently the speed and power of the transformation bewildered the audience into accepting the "reality" of the new vision and even doubting the existence of the old one altogether.[66] The courtly audience, acquainted with the conventions of the form and surely expecting something like this flash of light and order, was not often taken by surprise. In developing the antimasque, however, Jonson found ways to delay the sense of illumination and to challenge the audience's confidence in its own apprehension. The momentary confusion with which *Love Restored* opens reveals Jonson's exploitation of irony in a form not normally regarded as ironic. An entering masquer frets that there will be no masque; he is greeted by Plutus disguised as Cupid, who confirms that the masque is cancelled and then, revealing himself, rails against the excesses of the entire enterprise; and Plutus is followed by Robin Goodfellow, who, in an extended recitation of his difficulties entering the hall, further confounds identity, fiction, and truth. The dodge that Robin has used in seeking entry announces the main issue in this comic antimasque: "We are all *masquers* sometimes" (line 103). This episode is like the induction to one of the satiric comedies, where Jonson plays with the boundaries of the real and the illusory. As Stephen Orgel puts it, "We have been led with remarkable ease from the world of the court to the world of fable. Beneath the actor's disguise and the theatrical illusion lies not everyday life, but the realm of the antimasque. Plutus' revelation at once renders the fiction of the masque as real as the realities of Whitehall."[67]

Shakespeare also adjusts the dramatic perspective to guide our response to the events of the romances, particularly the sense of potential tragedy. The most obvious cases are the removal to Wales in *Cymbeline* and to Bohemia in *The Winter's Tale*. The audience escapes the perversions and errors of the courts of Cymbeline and Leontes, and in *The Winter's Tale* the figure of Time explicitly announces the removal as a shift in spatial and temporal perspective. But there are more complex cases. The descent of Jupiter is as surprising to the audience as it is to the shades of the Leonati, who are themselves a shock to Posthumus and the audience. We have witnessed, as the characters have not, the turning awry of wicked schemes, have seen Imogen escape attempted murder, have been aware that the decapitated body belongs not to Posthumus but to Cloten. But until Jupiter enters to explain the divine system of teleology in the play-world, we have no certainty of a happy ending. This challenge to human comprehension is compounded in *The Winter's Tale* with the restoration of Hermione. Shakespeare has purposefully misled us, encouraging us to believe Paulina's announcement of her lady's death and reinforcing that impression with Antigonus's dream. Thus, when the statue comes to life, we are confronted with the problems of epistemology.

The first two scenes of *The Tempest* issue a similar challenge to the spectator's understanding. For the audience at the first performance—as for every audience unfamiliar with the play—the tempest that opened

The Tempest was a tempest, a natural disaster like that from which Viola has escaped in the second scene of Twelfth Night. Shortly, however, that original audience perceived that it had been tricked, that the storm was not natural but an artificial creation of Prospero's magic. As in a masque, a discordant setting yields to an ordered one, replacing the audience's limited comprehension with more complete vision. Throughout the play Prospero and Shakespeare repeatedly disorient the characters and the spectators with shifting definitions of the real. The apotheosis of this strategy is the wedding masque; as E. M. W. Tillyard memorably puts it, "On the actual stage the masque is executed by players pretending to be spirits, pretending to be real actors, pretending to be supposed goddesses and rustics."[68] Even though we in the audience are able to penetrate these levels of reality, thanks to a point of view continuous with that of the dramatic artificer, Prospero, we are still at the mercy of the artificer of The Tempest. So at the end of the work the world of the play dissolves into the real world and the spectator finds himself transported from illusion to truth, but the boundary between the two is less certain at the end than it was at the beginning.[69]

Shakespeare's manipulation of characters and audience into entering what Tillyard calls "planes of reality" and then exchanging these planes for others is more complex than Jonson's method in the masques, but the techniques are analogous. Jonson transforms the world of the antimasque into that of the masque and then, with the compliments to King James and the commencement of the revels, transforms the world of the masque into the world of Whitehall. In both Shakespeare's romances and Jonson's masques the fiction is shown to be not merely a version of reality but a part of reality: the art itself is nature. Orgel's description of the movement from antimasque to masque and how that movement came to change in Jonson's work helps to illustrate the point: "After 1609, Jonson begins to conceive of the antimasque not as a simple antithesis to the world of the revels, but essentially as another aspect of it, a world that can therefore ultimately be accommodated to and even included in the ideals of the main masque. The productions of the second decade, starting with Oberon (1611), begin to represent the transition less as a single moment of transformation than as a gradual process of refinement. This process, for the courtly audience, is an education in the meaning of the revels."[70] We might go on to say, moreover, that the revels are an education in the meaning of Whitehall and of the world outside, as are the final scenes of the romances. *Henry VIII* announces this point explicitly in its prophetic glances toward the future which, for the first audiences, was the comparatively recent past. Both artists insist upon the evanescence of all experience, the unstable, tragicomic composition of human life, and the unreliability of all judgments. In each of these works we move from the theater or the banqueting room into yet another scene, and having reached the end of the visible artistic pattern, we would be foolish to assume that we have witnessed the finale.

The manipulation of illusion so important to these works is part of a larger design: these artists suggest the uncertainty of mortal experience by insisting on the fragility of their fictional worlds. The positive and negative properties of time in Shakespeare's romances are well established. With one hand time can offer clarification and comfort, while with the other it may destroy or withdraw its pleasures, and this bivalence gives these plays their tragicomic shape. Throughout each of the romances Shakespeare dwells upon the impermanence of the play itself, using its brevity and unreality to indicate the insubstantiality of the world it symbolizes. Personified Time offers the most explicit statement of this crucial theme:

> I witness to
> The times that brought them in; so shall I do
> To th'freshest things now reigning, and make stale
> The glistering of this present, as my tale
> Now seems to it.
> (*Winter's Tale*, IV.i.11–15)

As Inga-Stina Ewbank puts it, Time is here "anticipating Prospero in his use of the very form of the work of art of which he himself is a part, as an image of transience,"[1] and her glance at *The Tempest*, with its symbolic structure of masque, play, and world, indicates the prevalence and importance of the theme of impermanence. A less celebrated but no less instructive case is *Henry VIII*. Shakespeare's treatment of rather recent history depends to a great extent upon familiarity with the events dramatized: the falls of Buckingham, Katherine, and Wolsey with which the play is concerned, and the impending falls of Cromwell, Cranmer, and

Anne Bullen with which the future was to deal.[72] We are asked to admit the transience of earthly glory and the shakiness of what seems firm:

> Think ye see
> The very persons of our noble story
> As they were living: think you see them great,
> And follow'd with the general throng, and sweat
> Of thousand friends; then, in a moment, see
> How soon this mightiness meets misery.
> (Prologue, lines 25–30)

The glistering past will be exposed to scrutiny, and the historical resolution will be made the cause for rejoicing (in the birth of Elizabeth) and for lamenting (in the falls of the principal survivors). This is an alternate means of developing the theme of mutability. Whereas in *The Winter's Tale* and *The Tempest* Shakespeare shows the illusory quality of life by emphasizing that quality in the form that represents it, in *Henry VIII* he employs a more immediate story with well-known results to underscore the insecurity in the lives represented.

In the masques, despite their idealization of king and court, Jonson nevertheless manages to remind the royal audience that the image of perfection is only an image and that its evanescence is as much a part of its meaning as its representation of perfection. That the masques were designed for a single evening's performance must have contributed to a sense of their unreality. As Jonson himself puts it at the end of *Hymenaei,* in summarizing what the reader has not seen, "Onely the envie was, that it lasted not still, or (now it is past) cannot by imagination, much less description, be recovered to a part of that *spirit* it had in the gliding by" (lines 576–79). This consciousness of impermanence is not limited to Jonson's appended reflections on the splendors of the evening, however. The last lines of the masque itself remind the audience that such perfection as the masquers embody is rare and passing:

> Shut fast the dore: And, as they soone
> To their *perfection* hast,
> So may their ardors last.
> So eithers strength out-live

All losse that *Age* can give:
And, though full yeares be told,
Their formes grow slowly old.
(lines 558–64)

Awareness of the subsequent fortunes of the celebrated couple perhaps gives unwarranted point to the theme of mutability, but the Stuart audience must have sensed the poignance of these lines. The destructive power of time is inescapable; the best that can be hoped for is that its effects can be delayed. The masque ends with a wish, but equally important is the implication that fulfillment of it is impossible.

This preoccupation with mutability amidst ideals creates a paradoxical effect, just as in Shakespeare's romantic vision. The end of *Oberon* explicitly addresses the problem of coming to an end, of the inevitable transience of the masque. Phosphorus arrives to declare that the night must end: "Then, doe I give way, / As the night hath done, and so must you, to day" (lines 442–43). And in the final song the sun is said to be alarmed "Lest, taken with the brightnesse of this night, / The world should wish it last, and never misse his light" (lines 454–55). These conclusions are so apparently antithetical to the spirit of the entertainment that Jonson must have had good reason for including them, and we do well, when faced with contradiction, to look for paradox. Alexander Leggatt's explanation of Jonson's frequent reference to the masque's unreality is pertinent: "The masques that—like *Oberon* and *The Vision of Delight*—admit their own transience can, paradoxically, claim a more solid basis in reality, since this final honesty places the vision of beauty in the context of a normal world. . . . Through time things are ended; but through time they are also ordered, measured and fulfilled. The awareness of reality appears first to destroy the masque, but ends by confirming it."[73] This is the same principle that accounts for Hermione's wrinkles in the last scene of *The Winter's Tale*. For both the writer of plays and the writer of masques, the ironies and complexities and doubts that impinge upon the vision of perfection do not invalidate that vision but serve instead to make it more readily available to the audience. The ideal is grounded in the real; illusion is connected with reality; fantasy is not a hopeless dream.[74]

Thus staged, the masques and romances are new creations, temporary alternative realities in which the audience may participate as a respite from the stale realm of the actual. The identification of the play world with the physical world is the most persistent and significant kind of self-consciousness evident in these texts: "The confusions between actors and audience, illusion and reality which *The Tempest* promulgates is . . . the fundamental principle of the masque."[75] By demolishing the barrier between fiction and truth, both artists seek to persuade the spectator of the value of illusion. If the world created in the theater is no more evanescent and uncertain than the world outside, then the satisfactions and joys of fiction may be considered legitimate and meaningful substitutes for what the world too rarely supplies. The participant in the theatrical event is invited to choose his illusions, provided that he knows them to be illusions.

The dreamers in the tragedies and satiric comedies make the mistake of trying to inhabit an illusory world without recognizing its unreality. Capable of imagining a more nearly perfect world, they are without the artistic means of realizing their visions. The creators succeed where their characters fail by incorporating that transcendent vision into play and masque. The vision is given permanence and reality—as much as is possible in an impermanent and unreal world—and the artist mediates between audience and vision, allowing the spectator to inhabit an ideal state without suffering the consequences of approaching it directly. The strategies of including the audience in the fiction and of calling attention to the artifice of the work emphasize the artist and his control of the theatrical experience. The heroes of these works are not Prospero and King James but Shakespeare and Jonson themselves.

Epilogue

Those hostile to the argument of this book will not be convinced by reiteration of my claims, and those hospitable to the analysis will not need it. But in a study that covers two such formidable authors and as many disparate texts as this one does, a brief coda is appropriate.

There is much more work to do in comparing these two dramatists. I have said little about the Roman plays as Roman plays, about Jonson's and Shakespeare's complex and shifting views on all things Roman, from their Latin literary predecessors to the problems of historiography. Feminist critics have not addressed themselves to Jonson as zealously as to Shakespeare, but Jonson's apparent unsuitability for such analysis should not be a deterrent, and the results might be illuminating. The question of representation—addressed directly by Jonson, obliquely by Shakespeare, and pursued at some length by earlier critics, who called it verisimilitude—will probably never be exhausted. And there is still much to say about both authors' politics. My purpose has been to open the floor for discussion, and I have concentrated on two main areas, external and internal connections.

The subject of influence—of little interest to criticism for the past few decades—has attained respectability again under the rubrics of "the new biography" and "intertextuality," and perhaps this new freedom will encourage awareness of the importance of my subjects' external literary relations. We must keep in mind that Shakespeare and Jonson were acquainted with each other, wrote for the same actors, had (enjoyed?) a professional connection. Any treatment of Jonson's artistic beginnings must take account of Shakespeare's inescapable presence, not only Jonson's rebellion against it but his attempts to conform to it and to adjust his own impulses to it. The middle of Shakespeare's career, specifically his progression from comedy to tragedy, is imperfectly understood without attention to the satiric model that Jonson loudly presented at the turn of the century. Worry about terms—*satire, problem comedies*—has diverted attention from the extent to which Jonson's satiric fulminations must have been helpful to an ideologically and formally unsettled Shakespeare. And the masques must have profited from Jonson's consciousness of Shakespeare's romantic temper, just as Jonson's strategies for mediating the ideal world to an audience at Whitehall are pertinent to Shakespeare's theatrical surrender to the satisfactions of the romantic ideal. Although a formalist bias has shaped much of my analysis, I am convinced that an appreciation of such personal connections can enhance understanding and evaluation.

I have used a good deal of space lamenting the power of prejudice, insisting that inflexible conceptions of either author or canon are inaccurate and demanding that the well-known boxes into which we tend to put their work be dismantled. Obviously Shakespeare and Jonson were fascinated by some of the same topics: imagination, language, self-delusion, obsession, evil, theatricality, power. They were capable of taking similar attitudes toward such topics. Occasionally, they even developed their concerns by means of some of the same dramatic strategies. Both were capable of imagining an ideal, both of scourging its opposite. Their very greatest works proceed from similar antiromantic impulses. The manifest differences should not obscure the areas of genuine mutual interest.

Neither, however, should the familiar antitheses of form and idea be ignored. The conventional oppositions are useful, and not only because they are more or less accurate. What makes them especially revealing is that for artists as sensitive and self-conscious as these two, the mature vision includes a critique of its own limitations. Thus the vigorous "realism" for which Jonson is celebrated (and for which he celebrated himself) depends upon his awareness of the appeals of romance. Conversely, the comic idealism that informs Shakespeare's romantic comedies is given weight and conviction because the dramatist seriously entertains the point of view of a Jaques or a Malvolio. To read either artist sensitively, even Jonson, whose monomaniacal tendencies are well known, is to admit the interdependence of comedy and tragedy, epideixis and satire, idealism and disgust. Moreover, the operation of such balances within each artistic vision implies a larger complementarity between the two *oeuvres*. In searching for new dramatic forms, shifting back and forth from one kind to another, stretching the conventional formal boundaries, in refusing, in general, to remain content with any single theatrical mode, both playwrights were struggling to do justice to visions more capacious and complex than, even in the case of Shakespeare, criticism has been willing to admit. With both Shakespeare and Jonson, there is something of the other in each.

Notes

INTRODUCTION

1   Jonas A. Barish, "Introduction" to *Ben Jonson: A Collection of Critical Essays* (Englewood Cliffs, N.J.: Prentice-Hall, 1963), p. 1.

2   Ibid.

3   Robert Ornstein, "Shakespearian and Jonsonian Comedy," *SS* 22 (1969): 43.

4   A typical example of this approach is found in David L. Frost's *The School of Shakespeare: The Influence of Shakespeare on English Drama, 1600–1642* (Cambridge: Cambridge University Press, 1968). Frost attacks Gerald Eades Bentley's argument, derived from contemporary allusion, that Jonson was the more highly regarded playwright in the seventeenth century. Bentley's work is *Shakespeare and Jonson: Their Reputations in the Seventeenth Century Compared,* 2 vols. (Chicago: University of Chicago Press, 1945). In general, Bentley's thesis has met with vigorous objection; whether it is true or not, the negative response to it indicates the firmness of modern taste.

Frost goes on to dismiss Jonson from his analysis of Shakespearean influence with the remark that "their activities were not parallel" (p. 20). Similarly, Peter G. Phialas insists that Shakespeare and Jonson adopted different methods to "dramatize two different responses to the human situation." See "Comic Truth in Shakespeare and Jonson," *SAQ* 62 (1963): 80. Virtually all such phrases are euphemisms for a manifest preference.

5   For a statement of this point of view, see George Parfitt, who asserts that Jonson is surely Shakespeare's greatest contemporary but "the most consistently unlike Shakespeare in dramatic method." *Ben Jonson: Public Poet and Private Man* (London: J. M. Dent, 1976), p. 132. Similarly, Gabriele Bernhard Jackson's fine book on Jonson contains only two references to Shakespeare, one proclaiming the impropriety of comparison: "Jonson has had much to bear from critics irresistibly tempted to set him against his greatest contemporary. . . . Apart

from date, however, there is very little similarity in the intention or achievements of their work to make such comparisons fruitful." *Vision and Judgment in Ben Jonson's Drama,* Yale Studies in English, 166 (New Haven: Yale University Press, 1968), p. 93.

6   An early dissenter from the prevailing wisdom was E. E. Stoll, who recognized that too much attention was being paid to the doctrine of the humours, that the simplicity of Jonson's style of characterization was often exaggerated, and that simultaneous study often produced distortion. See his sensible and careful chapter entitled "Shakespeare and Jonson" in *Shakespeare and Other Masters* (Cambridge: Harvard University Press, 1940), pp. 85–120. This essay has received less notice than it deserves.

A stimulating comparison of themes is offered by S. Musgrove in the second of three lectures, "Tragical Mirth: *King Lear* and *Volpone,*" collected under the title *Shakespeare and Jonson,* Auckland University College Bulletin no. 51, English Series, no. 9 (1957). Musgrove's method in this lecture is, to my way of thinking, sensible: "In comparing these two plays I am not, in the main, looking for literary borrowings of a direct kind, nor for verbal indebtedness: but for larger likenesses of theme and imaginative invention" (p. 21). The volume begins promisingly, with a desire "to see [Jonson and Shakespeare] not as 'classicist' set against 'Elizabethan,' but as two men working within the same dramatic kinds and with similar dramatic intentions" (pp. 3–4); but too often the argument descends into speculation about echoed lines and possible cases of influence. For treatment of parallel themes, see Harry Levin's brilliant essay, "Two Magian Comedies: *The Tempest* and *The Alchemist,*" SS 22 (1969): 47–58.

Maurice Charney contributes some extremely sensible remarks on the impropriety of segregating Shakespeare from his contemporaries in "Shakespeare—and the Others," SQ 30 (1979): 325–42.

Critics who have attempted to describe the relationship more precisely include Anne Barton and Ian Donaldson. See, in addition to Barton's *Ben Jonson, Dramatist* (Cambridge: Cambridge University Press, 1984), the paper she delivered before the Second Congress of the International Shakespeare Association at Stratford in August of 1981: "Jonson and Shakespeare," in *Shakespeare, Man of the Theater,* ed. Kenneth Muir, Jay L. Halio, and D. J. Palmer (Newark: University of Delaware Press, 1983), pp. 155–72. Donaldson has edited a collection of essays entitled *Jonson and Shakespeare* (Totowa, N.J.: Barnes and Noble, 1983). Few of the papers contained therein are as fresh as one might wish—some concern themselves only with Shakespeare or with Jonson—but the idea of the collection is laudable. See Donaldson's admirable introduction; D. H. Craig's "The Idea of the Play in *A Midsummer Night's Dream* and *Bartholomew Fair*," pp. 89–100; F. H. Mares's "Comic Procedures in Shakespeare and Jonson: *Much Ado About Nothing* and *The Alchemist*," pp. 101–118; Ann Blake's "Sportful Malice: Duping in the Comedies of Jonson and Shakespeare," pp. 119–34; and Anthony Miller's "The Roman State in *Julius Caesar* and *Sejanus*," pp. 179–201.

Two studies that would seem pertinent but which I have not found very helpful are Nicholas Grene's *Shakespeare, Jonson, Molière: The Comic Contract* (Totowa, N.J.: Barnes and Noble, 1980), and Zvi Jagendorf, *The Happy End of Comedy: Jonson, Molière, and Shakespeare* (Newark: University of Delaware Press, 1984).

7   The most important of such studies is probably Jonathan Goldberg's *James I and the Politics of Literature* (Baltimore: Johns Hopkins University Press, 1983), esp. chs. 3 ("The Theater of Conscience") and 4 ("The Roman Actor: *Julius Caesar, Sejanus, Coriolanus, Catiline*, and *The Roman Actor*"). Goldberg's role in developing the new historical criticism means that he is interested less in particular texts and authors than in broad theoretical questions, as the argument of his book indicates: "The underlying thesis of this study is that language and politics—broadly construed—are mutually constitutive, that society shapes and is shaped by the possibilities in its language and discursive practices" (p. xi). Such criticism is certainly not limited by the stereotypes I have deplored—indeed, it breaks down categories with a vengeance—but concentration on the linguistic medium and its relation to political authority makes it less useful than it might be to one interested in literary forms and the treatment of them by individual artists. Much the same may be said of some of the new linguistic studies: for example, see Patricia Parker, "Deferral, Dilation, Différance: Shakespeare, Cervantes, Jonson," in *Literary Theory / Renaissance Texts*, ed. Patricia Parker and David Quint (Baltimore: Johns Hopkins University Press, 1986), pp. 182–209.

8   Alexander Leggatt has identified many of the contradictions between Jonsonian theory and practice: *Ben Jonson: His Vision and His Art* (London: Methuen, 1981). See especially pp. xv–xvi and ch. 6, "The Poet as Character," pp. 199–232.

9   In 1601 Jonson pilloried Marston in *Poetaster*, portraying him as Crispinus, the title character whose barbarous vocabulary attests to his artistic incompetence; yet four years later Jonson collaborated with Marston and Chapman in composing *Eastward Ho!* Likewise, Marston ridiculed Jonson harshly and repeatedly at

the turn of the century, and then in 1603 dedicated *The Malcontent* to him. Such curious patterns of censure followed by collaboration should teach us how to interpret Jonson's legendary blasts at Shakespeare.

10   Ivor Brown, "Not So Big Ben," *Drama* 99 (1970): 44. Brown here alludes to Thomas Fuller's famous account of the "wit-combates" between the two dramatists. See E. K. Chambers, *William Shakespeare: A Study of Facts and Problems,* 2 vols. (Oxford: Clarendon Press, 1930), 2:245.

11   This addition to Drummond's *Conversations* was inserted into an edition of Theophilus Cibber's *The Lives of the Poets of Great Britain and Ireland* (London, 1753), 1:241. Barish quotes it in his "Introduction," p. 3.

12   The question of when Shakespeare and Jonson became acquainted with each other, while it does not affect our understanding of their work, is a fascinating one. Certainly they were known to each other by 1598. It is at least possible that they were working in the same theatrical troupe in 1592, possible that they toured together during the plague year of 1593, possible that they acted in each other's very earliest works. The validity of this argument depends on whether Shakespeare was ever associated with Pembroke's Men and whether the "Mr. Johnson" who was a hireling member of the company was actually Ben Jonson. For the most cogent discussion of what is known and how it might be interpreted, see Mary Edmond, "Pembroke's Men," *RES*, n.s., 25 (1974): 129–36. David George doubts Edmond's conclusions in his own complicated, and at times highly speculative, essay concerning the development of the major troupes: "Shakespeare and Pembroke's Men," *SQ* 32 (1981): 305–23. Scott McMillin also doubts the identity of this Mr. Johnson: see "Simon Jewell and the Queen's Men," *RES*, n.s., 27 (1976): 176, a rejoinder to Edmond's article.

13   In his *Life* of Shakespeare (1709), Nicholas Rowe claims that *Every Man in His Humour* had been rejected by the Lord Chamberlain's Men, but that Shakespeare came across the script, recognized its merit, and recommended its production.

14   Summary and discussion of these references are provided by E.A.J. Honigmann, *Shakespeare's Impact on His Contemporaries* (Totowa, N.J.: Barnes and Noble, 1982), pp. 100–103. The text containing the greatest concentration of allusions is *Every Man out of His Humour:* there are glances at Shakespearean characters (notably Falstaff), lines (two from *Julius Caesar*), and plots (Mitis's famous gripe that Jonson's play contains no "crosse-wooing" and no clown). The quarto text of *Every Man Out* (1600) contains "more than hath been publickely Spoken or Acted," and it may be that Jonson's break with the Lord Chamberlain's Men— perhaps he blamed the company for the play's failure—prompted him to supple-

ment his text with swipes at his former fellows and their chief writer. Whether the Elizabethan theatergoers heard or read these statements, they would have been struck by Jonson's newfound confidence and independence of mind.

15   Jonson's jealousy of Shakespeare's popularity is accompanied by envy at the speed with which his colleague composed. The famous opinion that Shakespeare, who "never blotted out line," ought to have "blotted a thousand" (*Discoveries*, lines 649–50) should be read in this light. Honigmann points out that this charge reflects the sentiment found in the prefatory letter to *The Alchemist*, where Jonson distinguishes "between those, that (to gain the opinion of Copie) utter all they can, how ever unfitly; and those that use election, and a meane" (lines 27–29). See *Shakespeare's Impact*, pp. 98–100.

16   For commentary on these allusions, see Herford and Simpson, 1:333–35, 9:343–46; and Gabriele Bernhard Jackson's edition of *Every Man In* (New Haven: Yale University Press, 1969), pp. 186–88. Jackson presents a list of plays by other authors in which even more flagrant violations of the stated principles appear, and she cites similar statements of disapproval from Sidney, Whetstone, and Cervantes. Jonas A. Barish cautions against reading these references too specifically, complaining that from the eighteenth century onwards "the prologue to *Every Man in His Humour* was read not as a critical manifesto but as a savage diatribe (an 'insolent invective') against Shakespeare, wherein every rift was loaded with rancorous ore" ("Introduction," p. 2).

17   For example, an amusing reference to *Julius Caesar* is clarified by an awareness of this difference in point of view. At the denouement of *Every Man Out*, when Puntarvolo turns on Carlo Buffone and begins to seal his lips to silence his teasing, Carlo turns to Macilente, his comrade in raillery, and cries "*Et tu Brute!*" (v.vi.79). More than a gratuitous or envious dig at a momentous episode in a popular tragedy, this is probably a parodic comment on Shakespeare's tragic style, which Jonson regarded as morally indefinite and which he would seek to improve in *Sejanus*. For an extensive discussion of Jonson's opinion of *Julius Caesar*, see J. Dover Wilson, "Ben Jonson and *Julius Caesar*," *SS* 2 (1949): 36–43.

18   See the Longer Note in Harold Jenkins's Arden edition of *Hamlet* (London: Methuen, 1982), pp. 470–73.

19   Elton notes the following parallels: Jonson was known early in his career as a braggart, and the friendly Drummond (among others less charitable) so describes him; Ajax's fame was as a soldier, and Jonson often made much of his military experience; Ajax's stupidity may be an ironic inversion of Jonson's self-proclaimed learning; Cressida's servant describes Ajax as "valiant as the lion,

churlish as the bear, slow as the elephant, a man into whom nature hath so crowded humours that his valour is crushed into folly, his folly sauced with discretion" (1.ii.20–24), all traits associated with Jonson's public image; and the envy that Ajax cannot restrain is implicit throughout Jonson's comments on his peers. William Elton, "Shakespeare's Portrait of Ajax in *Troilus and Cressida*," *PMLA* 63 (1948): 744–48. Elton reflects the view of Roscoe Small, who attempts at length to show that Ajax is a detailed portrait of Jonson and that the purge is *Troilus and Cressida*. See *The Stage-Quarrel between Ben Jonson and the So-Called Poetasters* (Breslau, 1899), p. 170.

20   For the various points of view in this controversy, see J. B. Leishman's edition of *The Three Parnassus Plays* (London: Ivor Nicholson & Watson, 1949), pp. 59–60 and 370–71; E. K. Chambers, *The Elizabethan Stage*, 4 vols. (Oxford: Clarendon Press, 1923), 4:40; and Cyrus Hoy, *Introduction, Notes, and Commentaries to Texts in "The Dramatic Works of Thomas Dekker,"* 4 vols. (Cambridge: Cambridge University Press, 1980), 1:195–97.

21   See Kenneth Palmer's Introduction to his Arden edition of *Troilus* (London: Methuen, 1982), pp. 17–22.

22   One of the best commentaries on Jonson's use of the unities for the creation of meaning is R. L. Smallwood's " 'Here, in the Friars': Immediacy and Theatricality in *The Alchemist*," *RES* 32 (1981): 142–60. See also Robert N. Watson, "*The Alchemist* and Jonson's Conversion of City Comedy," in *Renaissance Genres: Essays on Theory, History, and Interpretation*, ed. Barbara Kiefer Lewalski, Harvard English Studies, 14 (Cambridge: Harvard University Press, 1986), esp. pp. 338–39.

23   Ekbert Faas, in his recent *Shakespeare's Poetics* (Cambridge: Cambridge University Press, 1986), discusses Shakespeare's disregard for the unities in light of Jonson's professed commitment to them. Despite what seems to me a slightly condescending attitude toward Jonson, he makes some valuable remarks about the inconsistencies in Jonson's practice. See esp. pp. 58–60.

24   *Samuel Johnson: Rasselas, Poems, and Selected Prose*, ed. Bertrand H. Bronson (New York: Holt, Rinehart and Winston, rpt. 1971), p. 276.

25   Anne Barton speculates reasonably and informatively on Jonson's lost tragedies—*Page of Plymouth; Robert II, King of Scots;* and *Richard Crookback*—in *Ben Jonson, Dramatist*, pp. 9–13.

26   Nevill Coghill, "The Basis of Shakespearian Comedy," *E&S* 1 (1950): 15.

27   Ibid.

28   Madeleine Doran places these two different styles of comedy in their contempo-

rary context: "The essential difference between the two modes of English comedy is one of attitude and tone. The emphasis is on a different set of human motives—on the one hand, on poetic longings for love and adventure; on the other, on the grosser appetites for women, money, or power. The defining difference of tone is the difference between lyrical sentiment sympathetically expressed and critical satire." *Endeavors of Art: A Study of Form in Elizabethan Drama* (Madison: University of Wisconsin Press, 1954), pp. 148–49.

29 The scope of my title is such that I owe the reader some explanation for covering only a fraction of the announced territory. I have not treated the Roman plays of either playwright as Roman plays, first because I concentrate for the most part on forms, and second because the breadth of the topic deterred me. A thorough comparison of Shakespeare's and Jonson's attitudes toward "Rome" in all its senses, attitudes reflected in their Roman tragedies and in other texts, could fill a volume on its own. Goldberg's chapter "The Roman Actor" is suggestive on this topic.

I have said less than I might have about *Bartholomew Fair,* thanks chiefly to Thomas Cartelli's "*Bartholomew Fair* as Urban Arcadia: Jonson Responds to Shakespeare," *Ren D,* n.s., 14 (1983): 151–72. This essay takes up Anne Barton's point that Jonson came to terms with his animus toward Shakespearean comedy, but modifies her argument by suggesting that this accommodation occurred not at the end of the 1620s, but rather as early as 1614, in his composition of *Bartholomew Fair.* "What has not been noted is that the play's comparative benevolence is closely bound up with Jonson's ongoing attempt to 'break through' and move beyond the 'aberrations' that conventionally characterize the relations between social classes in purely satiric comedy; that the method employed by Jonson to effect this breakthrough into saturnalian clarification owes much to the methods employed by Shakespeare in his pastoral comedies (e.g., *A Midsummer Night's Dream* and *As You Like It*) and romances (especially *The Tempest*) to structure and organize his own breakthroughs; and that the play as a whole dramatizes Jonson's efforts at coming to terms with Shakespearean influence and his Shakespearean inheritance" (p. 155). John Gordon Sweeney III, in his recent *Jonson and the Psychology of Public Theater* (Princeton: Princeton University Press, 1985), disputes the familiar axioms about Jonson and his rival in his discussion of Jonson's achieving "freedom from his anxieties about the nature of commercial theater" (p. 157); like Cartelli, Sweeney sees *Dream* as the relevant Shakespearean text: "The fact is that *Bartholomew Fair* is very Shakespearean in Frye's terms, almost to the point of parodying a play like *A Midsummer Night's Dream*. Instead of the world of the fairies we have the fair, but the energies swirling around in both are remarkably similar" (p. 164).

Although I comment here and there on the problem of representation and the two dramatists' disagreements about the issue of verisimilitude—in a sense it is the basis for all their differences—this is a problem that can bear further exploration.

My analysis might have been extended to include a chapter on Jonson's last plays, the "dotages" which have been unjustly reviled since Dryden's day; but Anne Barton has recently explored these texts and written persuasively on the aging Jonson's interest in Shakespeare. See the last chapters of *Ben Jonson, Dramatist*. Katharine Eisaman Maus, *Ben Jonson and the Roman Frame of Mind* (Princeton: Princeton University Press, 1984), and Sweeney, *Public Theater*, both treat the late plays, though less extensively than Barton.

CHAPTER 1: A PLEASANT COMEDY

1   *Conversations* with Drummond, Herford and Simpson, 1:143.

2   For example, L. A. Beaurline's *Jonson and Elizabethan Comedy* (San Marino: Huntington Library, 1978), despite its promising title, contains only two references to *The Case Is Altered* in over three hundred pages of text. Douglas Duncan, in *Ben Jonson and the Lucianic Tradition* (Cambridge: Cambridge University Press, 1979), does not mention the play. J. B. Bamborough argues that *The Case Is Altered* "is very unlike the kind of play we expect from Jonson, and indeed it is a good deal nearer to Shakespearean comedy than he ever came again." *Ben Jonson* (London: Hutchinson University Library, 1970), pp. 20–21; on these grounds Bamborough devotes one paragraph to it. Some critics who are interested in particular features of Jonson's work do treat the play, but their analyses tend to stress resemblances to later plays: see especially Jonas A. Barish's *Ben Jonson and the Language of Prose Comedy* (New York: Norton rpt., 1970), pp. 93–97, and Gabriele Bernhard Jackson, *Vision and Judgment in Ben Jonson's Drama*, pp. 99–102. J. M. Nosworthy, *"The Case Is Altered,"* *JEGP* 51 (1952): 195–214, is interested mainly in the problem of authorship. Those who distort the play in attempting to make it "satiric" include John J. Enck, whose *"The Case Is Altered:* Initial Comedy of Humours," *SP* 50 (1953): 195–214, is substantially reprinted in *Jonson and the Comic Truth* (Madison: University of Wisconsin Press, 1957); Robert E. Knoll, *Ben Jonson's Plays: An Introduction* (Lincoln: University of Nebraska Press, 1964), pp. 25–31; and

Stephen Hannaford, "Gold Is But Muck: Jonson's *The Case Is Altered*," *Studies in the Humanities* 8 (1980): 11–16.

3   C. H. Herford, in his Introduction, (1:305–27), does treat the general connection with Shakespeare and the milieu, but he does so without much enthusiasm for the topic. An excellent, fair-minded consideration of this issue is C. R. Baskervill's *English Elements in Jonson's Early Comedy*, rpt. University of Texas Bulletin, no. 178 (Austin, 1911), p. 105. Anne Barton provides an extremely useful analysis of *The Case Is Altered* (*Ben Jonson, Dramatist*, pp. 29–44). Her focus is the connection between Jonson's play and Shakespeare's most direct adaptation of Plautus, *The Comedy of Errors*. Although our conclusions are similar, she seems to think of the youthful Jonson as a little more sure of himself than I do.

4   I hold to the relatively recent view that *A Tale of A Tub* is a Caroline play and that Herford and Simpson were wrong to put it first in the Oxford edition. See Barton, *Ben Jonson, Dramatist*, pp. 321–23, and Sir W. W. Greg, "Some Notes on Ben Jonson's Works," *RES* 2 (1926): 129–45.

5   T. S. Eliot, "Ben Jonson," rpt. in Barish's *Ben Jonson: A Collection of Critical Essays*, p. 20.

6   Katharine Eisaman Maus, in her recent study *Ben Jonson and the Roman Frame of Mind*, presents a Jonson whose Latin ancestors are serious figures such as Seneca, Horace, and Juvenal, and who has little interest in lighter ones such as Plautus and Ovid. She notes that in *Discoveries* Jonson endorses "Horace's low opinion of Plautus" (p. 150).

7   Herford and Simpson, 1:309. In comparing *The Case Is Altered* with its sources, I have used the Loeb edition of *Plautus*, with an English translation by Paul Nixon, 4 vols. (New York: G. P. Putnam's Sons, 1917). The most helpful discussions of Jonson's treatment of these sources are those of Herford and Simpson, 1:307–17, and John J. Enck, *Jonson and the Comic Truth*, pp. 21–33.

8   Shakespeare's habitual dependence on twins, shipwrecks, divided families, clever servants, and irate fathers makes it too easy to regard his taking up of Plautus for *The Comedy of Errors* as the most natural thing in the world. Plautus was known and appreciated in the sixteenth century. His comedies had been a staple of the theatrical repertory at court, in the universities, and in the schools since early in the century; one of his plays was probably the first classical comedy performed in England, at court in 1519; and even some of the popular moralities and interludes of the middle years of the century show traces of Plautine influence. See David Bevington, *From Mankind to Marlowe* (Cambridge: Harvard University Press, 1962), pp. 31 and 64.

Nevertheless, Plautus's comedies were not obvious models for a young playwright in 1590, as Leo G. Salingar argues: "The living theatre [Shakespeare] must have known when he became an actor himself was still medieval in many essentials, while performances of classical comedies were still rare in England and were mostly confined to academic audiences when he began writing about 1590. It is true, and deserves emphasis, that Shakespeare was probably the first English dramatist, and certainly one of the first, to adapt classical and renaissance comedy for the public playhouses in England, and also true (as far as we can tell) that he applied the principles of classical comedy much more thoroughly than any English writer before him. He has received less than his due as a classical innovator in this respect, largely because Ben Jonson and the critics who followed him were classicists of a more theoretical cast." Salingar, *Shakespeare and the Traditions of Comedy* (Cambridge: Cambridge University Press, 1974), p. 59. Likewise, G. R. Elliott asserts that "the budding dramatist [Shakespeare], more or less influenced by the ancient classical sense of form, was reacting from the slipshod construction of contemporary romantic comedy." "Weirdness in *The Comedy of Errors*," rpt. in *Shakespeare's Comedies*, ed. Laurence Lerner (Harmondsworth: Penguin, 1967), p. 20.

9   Plautus's Phaedria, the model for Rachel, never appears in the *Aulularia;* her voice sounds from inside the house as she is delivered of Lyconides' child. Although Philopolemus, the original for Paulo, finally does enter in the last act of *I Captivi,* for the reunification of the family, his absence is the crucial fact. In other words, Plautus uses these two figures as invisible forces determining the action from outside the play: Phaedria attracts suitors who nettle Euclio, and Philopolemus's captivity generates Hegio's irrational behavior.

10   The best account of these complementary effects is found in Wayne C. Booth's *The Rhetoric of Fiction* (Chicago: University of Chicago Press, 1961), pp. 254–56.

11   Bertrand Evans, *Shakespeare's Comedies* (Oxford: Clarendon Press, 1960).

12   One of the courtiers, speaking of the supposed Chamont (actually Camillo-Gasper), remarks that "had Camillo liv'd / He had been about his yeares" (IV.i.14–15), with which comment Ferneze concurs. Shortly thereafter, Phoenixella suggests that "this young Lord *Chamont* / Favours my mother" (IV.ii.47–48). The actual Chamont tosses out an even more tempting piece of bait in his soliloquy describing Gasper's arrival:

How I blesse the time wherein *Chamont*
My honor'd father did surprise *Vicenza*,
Where this my friend (knowen by no name) was found,
Being then a child and scarce of power to speake,

198

> To whom my father gave this name of Gasper.
> (IV.iv.23–27)

13 See Barton, *Ben Jonson, Dramatist*, ch. 14, "Harking Back to Elizabeth: Jonson and Caroline Nostalgia," pp. 300–320; also see Maus, *Ben Jonson and the Roman Frame of Mind*, p. 149.

14 Although Jonsonian comedy is usually considered "masculine" and Shakespearean comedy "feminine," and justly so, it is worth noting that the numbers of women in both authors' plays are not significantly different. *Two Gentlemen*, *Shrew* (assuming that the hostess in the Induction returns as, probably, the widow), *Merchant*, and *Twelfth Night* all contain three women; *Errors*, *Dream*, *As You Like It*, *Much Ado*, *All's Well*, and *Measure* all contain four; *Labor's* has five.

15 Herford's discussion of Rachel's function, which emphasizes inordinately her role in the intrigue and depreciates the importance of her feelings for Paulo, suffers from his general reluctance to admit the romantic qualities of the drama.

16 The end of the *Aulularia* is lost, and the two Arguments that introduce the comedy offer conflicting testimony on whether Euclio is permitted to keep the pot of gold. See Nixon's edition of the play, 1:232–33.

17 The Oxford editors seem uncomfortable with the "unclassical" style of *The Case Is Altered*. Herford dismisses the play's temporal and spatial range by emphasizing that all the action takes place in and around Milan and that the events could transpire in no more than a few weeks. Insisting that "no child new swaddled in the first act becomes a graybeard in the fifth" and playing with other phrases from the celebrated Prologue to *Every Man In*, he tries to show that *The Case Is Altered* is not characterized by Elizabethan romantic extravagance and so implicitly to suggest that Jonson's inchoate classical restraint is operating here. He virtually admits the problematic nature of his argument about unity of action, however: "That the writer had achieved a real unity of action is less certain, although he clearly exerted much resource in the effort" (1:312).

18 Jonson might have learned such "Elizabethan" conventions from someone other than Shakespeare, say from Peele or from Lyly (from whom Shakespeare himself learned); but by 1597 the most available source was Shakespeare's recent work.

19 Barton, *Ben Jonson, Dramatist*, pp. 35–36.

20 C. R. Baskervill notices these numerous parallels and develops them at length: see *English Elements*, pp. 103–4. Later commentators have not taken up his suggestions, however.

21 This point is made by Baskervill, *English Elements*, p. 104, and by Herford and Simpson, 9:319.

22   There is the chance that Shakespeare and Jonson both found the tale in the same work, perhaps the lost English play from which the German *Julio and Hyppolita* derived. The initial scenes between Angelo and Paulo bear a resemblance to those in *Julio and Hyppolita*, but most of Jonson's action is closer to *Two Gentlemen*; furthermore, the date of the lost play is unknown and may be later than *Two Gentlemen* or later than both. See Geoffrey Bullough, *Narrative and Dramatic Sources of Shakespeare*, 8 vols. (New York: Columbia University Press, 1957–75), 1:208–9; and Clifford Leech's exhaustive Introduction to his New Arden edition of *The Two Gentlemen of Verona* (London: Methuen, 1969), pp. xxxix–xli. If *Two Gentlemen* is a major source for *The Case Is Altered*, then Jonson either saw the play performed or read a manuscript; it was first printed in the Folio. There is no record of an Elizabethan production, although Meres's reference suggests that one must have occurred. Since the date of composition cannot be ascertained, we can only guess at when Jonson might have seen a performance. The likelihood of his having done so increases if the later datings, 1593 or 1594, are accepted; or possibly the play was revived, as seems to have been the case with the 1594 Christmas production of *Errors*. Still another alternative, if Jonson and Shakespeare were personally acquainted in 1597, is that Jonson might have read the comedy.

23   Here I find myself slightly at odds with Barton, who contends that already Jonson was guying this sort of ending even as he presented it. "Although the revelations and miraculous reunions of this ending have been implicit in the plot structure of *The Case Is Altered* from the start, Jonson seems to have felt when it came to the point of the fifth act that material of this kind ought not to con adults into belief." *Ben Jonson, Dramatist*, p. 43. I would argue that if this were the case, the ending would be less flat than it is, would have more of an identifiably ironic edge.

24   For a thorough discussion of this important Jonsonian strategy, see Ray L. Heffner, "Unifying Symbols in the Comedy of Ben Jonson," rpt. in Barish, *Ben Jonson: A Collection of Critical Essays*, pp. 133–46.

25   Barton, *Ben Jonson, Dramatist*, p. 39.

CHAPTER 2: FIE ON SINFUL FANTASY

1   For speculation and fact concerning Jonson's first association with the Lord Chamberlain's Men, such as Rowe's claim that Shakespeare recommended *Every Man In* after its having been rejected by the company, see Herford and Simpson, 1:331 ff.

2 Gabriele Bernhard Jackson's analysis of this incompatibility of technique and vision is to me the most helpful discussion of *Every Man In* and one of the best pieces of writing on Jonson. See the Introduction to her edition of *Every Man in His Humour*, pp. 1–3 and 20–25.

3 Anne Barton describes with admirable precision the tensions apparent in the Quarto text of *Every Man In*, showing just how Jonson cautions the audience about the possibility for change. It will become clear that I consider her view of the ending a little dark, particularly her contrast between the conclusion of this play and that of *The Merry Wives*. See *Ben Jonson, Dramatist*, pp. 48–49.

4 See H. J. Oliver's persuasive analysis in the New Arden edition (London: Methuen, 1971), pp. liv–lvii; Jeanne Addison Roberts, *Shakespeare's English Comedy* (Lincoln: University of Nebraska Press, 1979), pp. 41–50; and William Green, *Shakespeare's Merry Wives of Windsor* (Princeton: Princeton University Press, 1962), pp. 21–49. The first proponent of the early date was Leslie Hotson, *Shakespeare versus Shallow* (Boston: Heath, 1931), whose suggestions were refined by Green.

   The matter is not absolutely settled, but as Charles Forker wrote in his review of the New Arden edition, "If Oliver cannot precisely be said to have settled the dating problem beyond dispute, he has at least shifted the burden of proof—a heavy burden—to the shoulders of the opposition." *Shakespeare Studies* 8 (1975): 423.

5 Fredson Bowers, in his Introduction to *The Merry Wives* in *The Complete Pelican Shakespeare*, gen. ed. Alfred Harbage (Baltimore: Penguin Books, 1969), speaks of the gallery of fools "with their parodies of the serious Jonsonian humours" and adds that Shakespeare, in creating the main plot, was "not a little aided by Jonson's portrait of the jealous husband Kitely in *Every Man in His Humour*" (p. 335). Sallie Sewell, "The Relation between *The Merry Wives of Windsor* and Jonson's *Every Man in His Humour*," *Shakespeare Association Bulletin* 16 (1941): 175–89, contends that Jonson's portrait of Bobadilla led Shakespeare to create Falstaff as he did, particularly in the quality of vanity. Baskervill, *English Elements*, p. 127, sensibly demurs from making too much of the parallels he notes.

6 I should point out that some critics still doubt the validity of the new date. See, for example, G. R. Hibbard's New Penguin edition (Harmondsworth, 1973), pp. 48–50.

7 Sir Francis Bacon, *The Advancement of Learning and The New Atlantis*, ed. Arthur Johnston (Oxford: Clarendon Press, 1974), p. 140.

8 Concentration on the doctrine of the humours has hampered rather than aided

the understanding of Jonson's comic theory and practice. According to Calvin Thayer, "Medical theory lies back of the comic theory of the humours, to be sure, but scholars have . . . exaggerated its importance as a prerequisite for understanding the plays of Ben Jonson." *Ben Jonson: Studies in the Plays* (Norman: University of Oklahoma Press, 1963), p. 26. Some sensible correctives to the strict view of the humours are found in Henry L. Snuggs, "The Comic Humours: A New Interpretation," *PMLA* 62 (1947): 118, and James D. Redwine, Jr., "Beyond Psychology: The Moral Basis of Jonson's Theory of Humour Characterization," *ELH* 28 (1961): 316–34.

William Bracy, *The Merry Wives of Windsor: The History and Transmission of Shakespeare's Text,* University of Missouri Studies, 25, no. 1 (Columbia: University of Missouri, 1952), devotes a chapter to the relation between *The Merry Wives* and *Every Man In* as regards the subject of the humours. Although I find him a little too eager to clear Shakespeare of the charge (and the accompanying opprobrium) of imitating Jonson, Bracy offers a clear statement of the uses of the humour concept in Chapman, Shakespeare, and Jonson. Many of his data and conclusions derive from Baskervill, and many of mine from them both.

9   The *OED* defines *imagination,* in addition to the senses already explored, as "scheming or devising; a device, contrivance, plan, scheme, plot; a fanciful project."

10   Many have noticed the resemblance between this scene and the interview between the king and Hubert in *King John* (111.ii in the Arden text). C. R. Baskervill believes that Jonson had his eye on Shakespeare's exchange in creating his own comic version of it: *English Elements,* pp. 42–62. Herford and Simpson, ever vigilant to rescue Jonson from the shadow of Shakespeare, dismiss the importance of the parallel: "Even if he owed anything to this suggestion, Jonson's treatment is entirely his own, and he added at least one happy touch—Kitely's final pretense, after disclosing his mind, that the real secret is still untold, followed by a solemn adjuration to the clerk not to disclose it to his mistress" (1:348).

11   Ford and Thorello deliver the most passionate soliloquies; Ford addresses a quarter of his part directly to the audience, in asides and soliloquies, until his awakening in act 4; and Thorello speaks mostly to the audience or to servants or minor figures like Giuliano, those remote from the central group of characters. Jackson has shown that the tendency towards privacy or social separation is one of the marks of Jonson's comedy of "noninteraction," and she persuasively applies the principles to other characters as well, obvious cases such as Lorenzo Senior and even persons who do not appear alone but who are isolated by

temperament or stupidity, like Stephano (Introduction to *Every Man in His Humour*, p. 1).

12   Barton, *Ben Jonson, Dramatist*, p. 49.

13   William Carroll, " 'A Received Belief': Imagination in *The Merry Wives of Windsor*," *SP* 74 (1977): 187. More recently Carroll has expanded upon the argument put forward in this essay and developed his treatment of Falstaff in *The Metamorphoses of Shakespearean Comedy* (Princeton: Princeton University Press, 1985), pp. 178–202.

14   Ibid., p. 188.

15   Ibid., pp. 191–92.

16   Another piece of business, the gulling of the Host by the "Germans," is harder to account for. If the text as we have it is an accurate record of what Shakespeare expected his audience to see, then the episode fits as follows: Evans and Caius, humiliated by the Host's contrivance of the false duel, determine not to allow his pride to go unpunished and thus invent a canard to discomfit him. This is consistent with the revenge theme as well as with the theme of imagination and self-delusion. See G. R. Hibbard's Introduction to his edition of *The Merry Wives of Windsor* (Harmondsworth: Penguin, 1973), pp. 26–28, and Evans, *Shakespeare's Comedies*, p. 111.

17   *Shakespeare and the Traditions of Comedy*, p. 231.

18   Roberts, *Shakespeare's English Comedy*, pp. 52–53, suggests that the Latin lesson may have been included to amuse the original aristocratic audience.

19   Mark Rose has written what I consider the most illuminating study of the Francis episode: see *Shakespearean Design* (Cambridge: Harvard University Press, 1972), pp. 50–59.

20   Of this remarkable passage, Hibbard offers an especially valuable analysis: "It is Falstaff's use of poetic images that makes this speech. Simile follows simile in an inexhaustible stream, transforming both what we have seen—the conveying out of Falstaff in the buck-basket—and what we have not seen—his being thrown into the Thames—from incident into art" (Introduction to *The Merry Wives of Windsor*, p. 33).

21   For thoughtful treatment of these figures' language, see Oliver, ed., *The Merry Wives of Windsor*, pp. lxxii–lxxv, and Carroll, " 'A Received Belief,' " 200–205.

22   Carroll attaches much significance to this point: "The energy of imagination— the power to animate (Quickly's errors), to transform (Ford's mania), to deceive (the wives' plots)—is perhaps the deepest concern of the play, and this underlying seriousness should help us to understand how *The Merry Wives* is related to the plays that surround it in the canon" (" 'A Received Belief,' " p. 209).

23   Martin Seymour-Smith, for one, contends that *"Every Man in His Humour* is in
      one sense a weak play because neither in Q nor F does it really ever begin to show
      how poetry is in fact, or can be, a serious matter," and in analyzing the dif-
      ferences between the two versions he suggests that Jonson recognized the weak-
      ness and did his best to correct it: "Seeing that the poetry theme was not properly
      followed through, and realizing that it could not be without serious damage to
      the play, Jonson makes it incidental." Introduction to *Every Man in His
      Humour,* ed. Martin Seymour-Smith (London: Ernest Benn, 1966), pp. xxvii–
      xxviii.
            The same critical narrowness mars Jackson's otherwise sensitive analysis.
      She believes that Jonson's critique of humanity is fragmented into several dis-
      crete sections, of which poetry is one. "Jonson here strings the characters to-
      gether like beads, on thematic threads which hold a few at a time" (Introduction
      to *Every Man in His Humour,* p. 12). She concludes (rightly) that the poetry
      thread is too short to accommodate all the characters and incidents. I am con-
      vinced that there is greater unity in *Every Man In* than these and most other
      critics have been willing to allow.
24   Critics have been hard on Jonson for making his comic hero a poet who writes
      no poetry: see, for example, Joseph Allen Bryant, "Jonson's Revision of *Every
      Man in His Humour,"* SP 59 (1962): 646. It might be pointed out, however, that
      they have been equally severe on the hero who does so (Horace, in *Poetaster*).
25   See Alan Dessen, *Jonson's Moral Comedy* (Evanston: Northwestern University
      Press, 1971), p. 47.
26   Barish, *Ben Jonson and the Language of Prose Comedy,* pp. 101–3, 90. In a
      characteristically perceptive analysis of Bobadilla's verbal patterns, Barish notes
      the "rich, fruity diction," outlandish oaths, obsessive use of "I," the incantatory
      quality of some speeches, and the "affected singularity" of the style in general
      (pp. 101–3).
27   J. W. Lever provides some valuable comments on Bobadilla's language as a self-
      protective device: "Behind this verbiage he seeks to defend himself against the
      many slights and humiliations inflicted by life." Introduction to *Every Man in
      His Humour: A Parallel-Text Edition of the 1601 Quarto and the 1616 Folio,*
      ed. J. W. Lever (Lincoln: University of Nebraska Press, 1971), p. xviii. Also
      relevant is Robert E. Knoll's argument that Bobadilla "must live in a flamboyant
      world." *Ben Jonson's Plays,* p. 40.
28   As Jackson slyly remarks about the Genoan exploit, "There appears to have
      been no such battle." Notes to her edition of *Every Man In,* p. 100.
29   An interesting connection between imagination, artistry, and military strategy

appears in *The Arte of English Poesie*, where George Puttenham asserts that for proper artistic composition, imagination must be conjoined with judgment, and one of the analogies he furnishes is military: without this combination, "no man could devise any new or rare thing: and when it is not excellent in his kind, there could be no politique Captaine, nor any witty enginer or cunning artificer." See the edition of Gladys Doidge Willcock and Alice Walker (Cambridge: Cambridge University Press, rpt. 1970), p. 19.

30 Barish shows that when Bobadilla later explains his behavior to Matheo (IV.iv.11–17), he loses "himself in a forest of asyndetic clauses, stiffened by anaphora, that suggest the extent to which he can 'bewitch' himself with his own rhetoric." *Prose Comedy*, p. 102.

31 Anne Barton disagrees, concluding that "his excuses for the cowardice so shamingly revealed . . . are too feeble for even Bobadilla to sustain. Unlike Falstaff, this braggart soldier has no talent for the monstrous and witty lie that ingeniously wrenches a true cause the false way." *Ben Jonson, Dramatist*, p. 50.

32 For another perspective on this comparison, see Leonard F. Dean, "Three Notes on Comic Morality: Celia, Bobadill, and Falstaff," *SEL* 16 (1976): 263–71.

33 Douglas Duncan has noticed a meaningful juxtaposition in this entrance. After pointing out that the cue for Musco to enter is Thorello's final couplet in I.iv about resolving to be himself despite his fantasy, Duncan writes: "Thorello's anguished struggle to realize the self is contrasted with the light-hearted evasion of the self by the rogue-disguiser. Both are intelligent enough to know themselves, but the latter declines the task of self-improvement imposed on all human 'creatures', preferring to manipulate the delusions of others and so become the 'creator' of Jonson's plot." *Ben Jonson and the Lucianic Tradition*, pp. 126–27.

34 As John J. Enck notes, Giuliano never appears on stage for long because he gets so angry so quickly that the dramatist can do nothing else with him. *Jonson and the Comic Truth*, p. 40. When Giuliano does speak in complete sentences, to Thorello about Prospero and friends, he singlemindedly repeats himself in perfect Bergsonian fashion. He is disgusted at Matheo's efforts to woo Hesperida, not because the poetry is execrable but simply because it is poetry: "Oh heares no foppery, sblood it freates me to the galle to thinke on it. *Exit*" (III.iv.37–38).

35 See Jackson, *Vision and Judgment*, pp. 19 ff., in addition to her Introduction to the Yale edition of *EMIH*, for clear statements on the problem of representing virtue and common sense dramatically.

36 See Bertrand Evans's discussion of discrepant awareness and its contribution to tone in *Shakespeare's Comedies*, pp. 99–103.

37 Roberts is probably accurate in her conclusion that "this is not the random

world of farce," that we see "cause and effect, human interaction and rational principle." *Shakespeare's English Comedy,* pp. 69–70. Still, I would argue that the effect of its action upon an audience is similar to that of farce: we tend to respond with scornful laughter.

38 Again, see Rose, *Shakespearean Design,* pp. 50–59. For a comprehensive discussion of the intriguing notion that Shakespeare wrote *The Merry Wives* while in the midst of composing 2 *Henry IV,* see Roberts, *Shakespeare's English Comedy* pp. 42–50, and Oliver, ed., *The Merry Wives of Windsor,* pp. lv–lvi.

39 See Ruth Nevo, *Comic Transformations in Shakespeare* (London: Methuen, 1980), pp. 142–61. Nevo seems to accept 1597 as the proper date for *The Merry Wives*—indeed, her argument would seem to depend upon it—but she never specifically says so.

40 Nancy Leonard has argued that "the use of the terms 'romantic' and 'satiric' to distinguish Shakespeare's comedies from Jonson's implies a mutual exclusiveness which there is good reason to distrust." See "Shakespeare and Jonson Again: The Comic Forms," *RenD,* n.s., 10 (1979): 45. This revisionist proposition arises from her study of *Twelfth Night* and *Volpone,* plays much more nearly representative of Shakespeare's and Jonson's normal comic styles than the texts I have considered here. If the labels are problematic in treating the typical, they can seriously hamper analysis of any plays slightly off center.

CHAPTER 3: UNSTABLE FORMS

1 Studies of self-consciousness and the idea of metadrama are numerous. The best studies of Shakespeare's use of the *theatrum mundi* metaphor are those of Anne Righter (Barton), *Shakespeare and the Idea of the Play* (Harmondsworth: Penguin, 1967), esp. chs. 6 and 7; and of James L. Calderwood, *Shakespearean Metadrama* (Minneapolis: University of Minnesota Press, 1971), as well as Calderwood's later works. For Jonson's ambivalent views on the theater and the contribution of these views to the plays, see Edward B. Partridge, "Ben Jonson: The Makings of the Dramatist (1597–1602)," in *Elizabethan Theatre,* ed. John Russell Brown and Bernard Harris, Stratford-upon-Avon Studies, 9 (London: Edward Arnold, 1966), pp. 221–44; Jonas A. Barish, "Jonson and the Loathed Stage," in *A Celebration of Ben Jonson,* ed. William Blissett, Julian Patrick, and R. W. van Fossen (Toronto: University of Toronto Press, 1973), pp. 27–53; and Jackson I. Cope, *The Theatre and the Dream: From Metaphor to Form in Renaissance Drama* (Baltimore: Johns Hopkins University Press, 1973), pp. 211–44, which also contains some discussion of Shakespeare.

2   The remarks of Dieter Mehl, although concerned specifically with the play within the play, are helpful in this context: "It is hardly surprising to see that the convention of the play within a play is to be found mainly in periods when not only dramatic literature but also theatrical practice were flourishing, when dramatists experimented with established forms, and—perhaps most important of all—when the purpose and function of drama and its illusionary character were subjects for searching discussion." "Forms and Functions of the Play within a Play," *RenD* 8 (1965): 42.

3   Partridge argues—justly, I think—that "nothing that Jonson had written up to this time, nothing, indeed, in the history of Elizabethan drama, quite prepares one for *Every Man Out*." "The Makings of the Dramatist," p. 229. See also W. David Kay, "The Shaping of Ben Jonson's Career: A Reexamination of Facts and Problems," *MP* 67 (1969–70): 224–37.

4   Partridge calls these various levels "experiments in perspective." "The Makings of the Dramatist," p. 231.

5   According to George Parfitt, "The moral teaching of the play is less overt than is often assumed (which is not to claim that it is particularly arcane) and the choric figures of Cordatus and Mitis are not primarily moral teachers: their main function is to explain and assess the aesthetic quality of the play." *Ben Jonson: Public Poet and Private Man*, p. 47. As Douglas Duncan puts it, "Devices such as prologues, inductions, and chorus, and the use of authorial spokesmen, were meant to train the audience's critical sense as well as to tell it what to think." *Ben Jonson and the Lucianic Tradition*, p. 134. See also Calvin Thayer, *Ben Jonson: Studies in the Plays*, p. 31: "*Every Man Out of his Humour* appears to be a comical satire on the subject of comical satire."

6   On the importance of Jonson's change from a public to a private company, see Kay, "The Shaping of Ben Jonson's Career," and Beaurline, *Jonson and Elizabethan Comedy*, pp. 11–18.

7   Alexander Leggatt thinks that this final couplet "may well be Jonson's considered estimate of his play; but it is presented as the climax of a self-portrait whose main effect is comic. Jonson knows, and virtually admits, that this is an odd way for a play attacking self-love to end; but that in itself is part of the joke." *Ben Jonson*, p. 204.

8   For details about this skirmish in the War of the Theaters, see Hoy's Introduction to *Satiromastix* in *Introductions, Notes, and Commentaries*, 1:179–98.

9   An excellent treatment of the complexities of this topic is Robert C. Jones's "The Satirist's Retirement in Jonson's 'Apologeticall Dialogue,'" *ELH* 34 (1967): 447–67.

10   See Righter, *Shakespeare and the Idea of the Play,* esp. ch. 7, "The Cheapening of the Stage."

11   Joseph Summers treats the issue of affectation brilliantly in "The Masks of *Twelfth Night,*" rpt. in *Shakespeare: Modern Essays in Criticism,* ed. Leonard F. Dean (Oxford: Oxford University Press, 1967), pp. 134–43.

12   R. A. Foakes comments helpfully on such matters, especially on the way that Troilus "acts" the part of romantic lover; see *Shakespeare: The Dark Comedies to the Last Plays* (Charlottesville: University of Virginia Press, 1971), p. 51.

13   "Shakespeare had often, in the plays he wrote before *Hamlet,* considered the nature of poetry, the imagination, and the actor's art. . . . *Hamlet,* however, is unique in the density and pervasiveness of its theatrical self-reference. The glaringly topical and, in some ways, uncharacteristic passage about the 'little eyases' and the 1601 War of the Theatres which embroiled the adult companies with the children's troupes (11.2.338-61) is acceptable in this play as it would not be in another precisely because *Hamlet* as a whole is so concerned to question and cross the boundaries which normally separate dramatic representation from real life." Anne Barton, Introduction to *Hamlet,* ed. T.J.B. Spencer (Harmondsworth: Penguin, 1980), pp. 27–28.

Northrop Frye makes much the same point: "*Measure for Measure,* then, is a comedy about comedy, as *Hamlet* is a tragedy about tragedy." *The Myth of Deliverance: Reflections on Shakespeare's Problem Comedies* (Toronto: University of Toronto Press, 1983), p. 25.

The centrality of Shakespeare's concentration on the theater in *Hamlet* may be judged by the number of theatrical works generated by the play that make use of the same theme. Tom Stoppard's *Rosencrantz and Guildenstern Are Dead* is probably the most famous instance, and Ernst Lubitsch's *To Be or Not To Be* is almost as densely layered.

14   Northrop Frye writes that "at the end of *Hamlet* we get a strong feeling that the play we are watching is, in a sense, Horatio's story." *Fools of Time* (Toronto: University of Toronto Press, 1967), p. 31. On this point see also Lawrence Danson, *Tragic Alphabet* (New Haven: Yale University Press, 1974), pp. 48–49.

15   Jackson, Introduction to *Every Man In,* p. 20.

16   G. K. Hunter, Introduction to the Arden edition of *All's Well* (London: Methuen, 1959), p. xxxv.

17   Arrigo Boito captures the mechanistic viewpoint in the "Credo" he devised for Iago in Verdi's *Otello:*

        And I believe man to be the jest of an unjust fate,
        from the germ of the crib

to the worm of the grave.
And after so much mockery comes Death. [My translation]

18   A. P. Rossiter discusses this matter sensitively in his treatment of the "problem comedies"; see *Angel with Horns,* ed. Graham Storey (London: Longmans Green, 1961), p. 116. Also, for a fascinating treatment of Desdemona's conscious and unconscious sexuality, see Stephen Greenblatt, *Renaissance Self-Fashioning* (Chicago: University of Chicago Press, 1980), pp. 247–52.

19   Philip Edwards contends that these two figures are "trapped by their own kind of ethical idealism." *Shakespeare and the Confines of Art* (London: Methuen, 1968), p. 117.

20   Clifford Leech, "The Meaning of *Measure for Measure,*" *SS* 3 (1950): 66–73.

21   For valuable distinctions between Jonson and Asper and Macilente, see Herford, Introduction to *Every Man Out,* 1:386–88; Alvin Kernan, *The Cankered Muse* (New Haven: Yale University Press, 1959), pp. 158–61; Jackson, *Vision and Judgment,* pp. 43–47; and Leggatt, *Ben Jonson,* pp. 186–87.

22   I would suggest that T. S. Eliot is guilty of this misplaced emphasis, and his famous essay has set the tone for much subsequent interpretation. "Ben Jonson," rpt. in Barish, *Ben Jonson: A Collection of Critical Essays,* pp. 14–23.

23   For a lucid account of this progression, see R. B. Parker, "The Problem of Tone in Jonson's 'Comicall Satyres,'" *Humanities Association Review* 28 (1977): 43–64: "In the first lines of *Every Man Out* Asper shrugs off the caution of Mitis and Cordatus with a Juvenalian outburst directed at human folly in general. . . . Crites, the satirist figure of *Cynthia's Revels* (or 'Criticus' as he was named in the quarto), has a distinguishably different rhetoric, less Juvenalian and more melancholy stoic. . . . The fierceness is further internalized and diminished in Horace" (pp. 47–48).

24   Ibid., p. 44.

25   See Kernan, *The Cankered Muse,* pp. 184 ff., and Jackson, Introduction to *Every Man In,* pp. 16–21.

26   O. B. Hardison has demonstrated that praise and blame were almost inseparably linked in Renaissance poetic theory: see *The Enduring Monument* (Chapel Hill: University of North Carolina Press, 1962), pp. 102–6. More recently, W. H. Herendeen and Alexander Leggatt have proved the impropriety of dividing Jonson's work into censorious and epideictic categories, arguing instead that these two effects are part of the same artistic aim and vision: see Herendeen, "'Like a Circle Bounded in Itself': Jonson, Camden, and the Strategies of Praise," *JMRS* 11 (1981): 137–67, and Leggatt, *Ben Jonson,* esp. ch. 3, "Images of Society," pp. 74–118.

27   Jones, "The Satirist's Retirement," pp. 464–66.

28   I have treated this ideological and formal development in my essay "Jonsonian Comedy and the Value of *Sejanus*," *SEL* 21 (1981): 287–305.

29   The combination of tones is so artfully arranged that a director can easily distort the work by emphasizing one at the expense of others. The 1979 Stratford production by Terry Hands dressed all the characters in gray and made Sir Toby into a detestable reprobate; romance was virtually banished, and the final effect was unsatisfactory largely because it was monotonous. The strongest productions are those, like the 1969 version by John Barton, which manage to capture many flickers of darkness and light at once. G. R. Hibbard effectively describes Judi Dench's performance as Viola in the latter production and relates it to the problem of tone: see "Between a Sob and a Giggle," in Muir, Halio, and Palmer, *Shakespeare, Man of the Theatre*, pp. 121–23.

30   This same principle of tonal multiplicity can be applied to the histories and tragedies as well. In the first tetralogy, the novice playwright attends mostly to the perils of political division and the social and national consequences of private evil. The effects he seeks are essentially simple and, relatively speaking, didactic. By the time he writes *Richard II*, however, Shakespeare's view of history is considerably more complex, and the second tetralogy is thus marked by a more expansive and subtle presentation of personal and political problems and their interplay. Complexity of character adds much to the tonal variety, and Bolingbroke, Falstaff, Hotspur, and the Prince contribute to the immense range of tone and meaning in *1 Henry IV*. *Henry V* illustrates the proposition that tonal balance signifies full exploitation of a mode's potentialities. In the first place, the play is composed of scenes depicting heroic patriotism, military slaughter, political fraud, petty self-interest, royal romance, coarse buffoonery, lament for the death of Falstaff, and regional jokes. Moreover, the unifying figure is himself problematic, at one moment a Christian king, at the next an unscrupulous seeker after power and fame. Norman Rabkin's by-now celebrated discussion of rabbits and ducks, in which he isolates the tension between praise and blame for Henry, attests to my point about the complexities of tone in Shakespeare's development of a mode. Rabkin, "Rabbits, Ducks, and *Henry V*," *SQ* 28 (1977): 279–96; rpt. in *Shakespeare and the Problem of Meaning* (Chicago: University of Chicago Press, 1981), pp. 33–62.

     The counterpart to *Henry V* among the tragedies is surely *Antony and Cleopatra*. Does the play celebrate the greatness of lovers who have transcended the mutable world, or does it attack the pride of egoists who only think they have done so? The balance here is so exquisite that critics regularly take opposite sides. In his earliest tragedies, *Titus, Romeo,* and *Julius Caesar,* Shakespeare makes conclusions easier to draw because his point of view is narrower. There are counterweights to these conclusions, of course, such as our recognition that Brutus is a great and sensitive man, despite his error in conspiring against Caesar. But the audience knows what to think. At the end of the tragic sequence, however, in *Antony* and *Coriolanus,* such certainty is rarely possible.

31 The latest expression of this bias, fresh from the press, is Kenneth Muir's Oxford edition of *Troilus and Cressida* (Oxford: Clarendon Press, 1982): "That there is an element of satire in *Troilus and Cressida* can hardly be disputed; but it is difficult to see any resemblance between the play and the comical satires of Jonson (such as *Poetaster* and *Cynthia's Revels*) or those of Dekker and Marston" (p. 20).

32 Characters, situations, and even a play or two from Shakespeare's early years have from time to time been called satiric: Bottom and Dogberry, for instance, and even Falstaff have been considered satiric targets; Mercutio's cynical viewpoint has caused him to be thought of as a kind of satirist; and *Love's Labor's Lost* has been read as a specific assault on Raleigh and the "school of night" or as a general satiric attack on court manners. But in order to include these under the rubric of "satire," we must stretch the term so far that it becomes virtually meaningless.

33 For a measured discussion of Shakespeare's "complex appreciation of the theory of satire" in *As You Like It,* see David Bevington, "Shakespeare and Jonson on Satire," in *Shakespeare 1971,* ed. Clifford Leech and J. M. R. Margeson (Toronto: University of Toronto Press, 1972), pp. 121 ff.

34 Ibid., p. 118.

35 Again Bevington makes the point succinctly: "The plot against Malvolio displays fully the characteristics of Jonsonian satire: an exposure plot manipulated by witty persons against a socially ambitious hypocrite who prepares his own trap, is laughed at scornfully by the audience, and is subjected to a ridiculing form of punishment befitting the nature of his offense." Ibid., p. 120.

36 The play seems to contain a safety device: Viola's clothing is in the hands of the sea captain, Orsino will not marry her until he sees her in her "woman's weeds," and the sea captain is imprisoned at the suit of Malvolio. Thus, the marriage depends on the mollification of the steward, who must be entreated to a peace if the promised happiness is to come to pass. In other words, Shakespeare may be implying that Malvolio is not as intractable as he has seemed.

37 M. M. Mahood discusses these important parallels in her edition of *Twelfth Night* (Harmondsworth: Penguin, 1968), p. 14.

38   Jonas A. Barish has explored the Jonsonian origins of Parolles: "His career forms
      the main satiric strand in the plot. Parolles is constructed after the model of
      certain comic characters in Ben Jonson, as an impostor, or poseur, whose mis-
      sion it is to indulge his affectations for a time, impose them on others, and then,
      in a climactic scene, be stripped of them and revealed for what he is." Introduc-
      tion to *All's Well* in *The Complete Pelican Shakespeare*, p. 367. Barish goes on to
      show, however, that Shakespeare's stripping of Parolles does not destroy him, as
      Jonson's would have.

39   Ibid., p. 367.

40   Hamlet may be referring to his satiric kinsman when he guarantees Rosencrantz
      that "the humorous man shall end his part in peace" (II.ii.321). See W. J.
      Lawrence, *Shakespeare's Workshop* (Boston: Houghton Mifflin, 1928), p. 101.
      Harold Jenkins, in his recent Arden edition, doubts this (*Hamlet* [London:
      Methuen, 1982], p. 470), as do Herford and Simpson, 9:481.

41   I am aware that many have thought otherwise, most famously T. S. Eliot and F.
      R. Leavis. They and their epigones come near to regarding Othello as an object
      of satire, a foolish victim of his own pride and self-deception. See "Shakespeare
      and the Stoicism of Seneca," in *Selected Essays of T. S. Eliot* (New York: Har-
      court Brace, 1950), pp. 110–11; Leavis's "Diabolic Intellect and the Noble
      Moor: A Note on Othello," *Scrutiny* 6 (1937): 259–83; and Robert B. Heilman,
      Magic in the Web: Wit and Witchcraft in Othello (Lexington: University of
      Kentucky Press, 1956), esp. pp. 137–68.

42   See Russ McDonald, "Othello, Thorello, and the Problem of the Foolish Hero,"
      SQ 30 (1979): 51–67.

43   Kenneth Palmer comments on this dual perspective, suggesting that "while (for
      one part of the mind) there is something to be said for Thersites' opinion, yet
      sanity lies much closer to the judicious, dispassionate utterances of Ulysses."
      Introduction to the Arden edition of *Troilus* (London: Methuen, 1982), p. 61.
      Also see Kernan, *The Cankered Muse*, p. 196.

44   Robert Kimbrough makes this point convincingly in *Shakespeare's "Troilus and
      Cressida" and Its Setting* (Cambridge: Harvard University Press, 1964), p. 13.

45   Palmer argues that "what Shakespeare is doing seems to be designed for an
      audience that was familiar with Chaucer, and which appreciated the shift in tone
      and the partial degradation of characters (especially the greater triviality and
      vulgar fussiness of Pandarus)." Introduction to *Troilus and Cressida*, p. 24.
      Elizabeth Freund wittily refers to this strategy as "Shakespeare's deconstruction
      of myths": see " 'Ariachne's Broken Woof': The Rhetoric of Citation in *Troilus
      and Cressida*," in *Shakespeare and the Question of Theory*, ed. Patricia Parker
      and Geoffrey Hartmann (London: Methuen, 1985), p. 32.

46 O. J. Campbell, *Comicall Satyre and Shakespeare's "Troilus and Cressida"* (San Marino, Calif.: Huntington Library, 1938). R. A. Foakes nicely states the difficulty with Campbell's work: "In this book, and in *Shakespeare's Satire* (1943), the critical argument is presented tendentiously and without much sensitivity, but both books are important because their author was among the first to relate Shakespeare's problem comedies to the growth of satire in the period." Foakes, *Shakespeare: The Dark Comedies to the Last Plays*, p. 31n.

47 In Chambers's words, "a disillusioned Shakespeare turns back upon his own former ideals and the world's ancient ideals of heroism and romance, and questions them." E. K. Chambers, *Shakespeare: A Survey* (London, 1925), p. 193, quoted in Campbell, *Comicall Satyre*, p. 188.

48 See Susan Snyder's discussion of the way that, at this time especially, "traditional comic structures and assumptions operate in several ways to shape tragedy." *The Comic Matrix of Shakespeare's Tragedies* (Princeton: Princeton University Press, 1979), p. 4.

49 Cyrus Hoy, *The Hyacinth Room* (London: Chatto and Windus, 1964), pp. 21–22.

50 In this passage Jonson begins to acknowledge what is implicit in the term "comical satire" and what later critics have thoroughly documented, that his experimental form is a combination of various influences and traditions: Old Comedy, the pseudo-Ciceronian theory of comedy, the native comic tradition, and the various forms (Horatian, Menippean, Juvenalian) of Latin satire. See Jackson, *Vision and Judgment*, p. 39.

51 Kernan, *The Cankered Muse*, p. 34.

52 See Snyder, *The Comic Matrix of Shakespeare's Tragedies*, pp. 91–136.

53 Joseph G. Price, *The Unfortunate Comedy* (Toronto: University of Toronto Press, 1968), p. 133.

54 J. M. Nosworthy, in his edition of *Measure for Measure* (Harmondsworth: Penguin, 1969), pp. 10–11.

55 Algernon C. Swinburne, *A Study of Shakespeare* (London: Chatto and Windus, 1895), p. 200.

56 Whether one chooses "late comedies" or "tragicomedies" or "dark comedies" or "problem comedies," these plays unquestionably represent a special comic style, an original response to experience shaped by a growing consciousness of tragic possibility. If we bear in mind the difficulties of terminology, we may find some help in A. P. Rossiter's assertion that these plays result from Shakespeare's having arrived at "a *tragi-comic view of man*." Since Rossiter wrote these words, students of Shakespeare and Renaissance drama have become much more circumspect about the term *tragicomedy*, and I do not propose to apply it strictly to

these plays. But surely Rossiter is correct in describing them as examples of "a kind of drama in which the contemplation of man is on the one hand held back from the 'admiration' and 'commiseration' (as Sidney put it) of tragedy; and on the other, denied the wholehearted (or heart-whole) enjoyment of human irrationality and the human sentiment of comedy." *Angel with Horns,* pp. 116–17. It is this ambivalent attitude towards his material that yields Shakespeare's complex combination of tragic and comic forms and tones.

57 "A scurvy politician," Angelo "hotly lusts to use [Isabella] in that kind / For which" he has condemned her brother (*Lear,* IV.vi.160–61). In the comedy, "Thieves for their robbery have authority, / When judges steal themselves" (*Measure,* II.ii.176–77); in the tragedy, we wonder "which is the justice, which is the thief?" (*Lear,* IV.vi.151–52). In both, "Robes and furred gowns hide all" (*Lear,* IV.vi.163).

58 Arthur C. Kirsch, *Jacobean Dramatic Perspectives* (Charlottesville: University of Virginia Press, 1972), p. 55.

59 Frye, *The Myth of Deliverance,* p. 63.

60 Palmer, *Troilus,* p. 83.

61 "Most of the play deals with inaction. . . . In such a dramatic situation—and it is what makes up nine parts of *Troilus*—men wait, and while they wait, they question, argue and play. And it is the forms of those questions, and that play, which gives to *Troilus* its peculiar dramatic idiom." Ibid., pp. 40–41.

62 Barbara Mowat's discussion of "representational" and "presentational" dramatic styles as they relate to the romances is helpful in identifying and appreciating the style of *Troilus:* "Dramatists who wish to call attention to the theatrical medium, who create 'presentational' dramas in which the thrust is toward the 'presenting' of a stage world rather than the 'representing' of an illusively 'real' world, frequently use for their own purposes the illusion-breaking properties of obtrusive tactics, and add such tactics to their repertoire of presentational devices." *The Dramaturgy of Shakespeare's Romances* (Athens: University of Georgia Press, 1976), p. 36.

63 "Few plays contrive such a degree of symmetry, and stylization, or use more often such merely formal devices as 'passing over the stage'; few have employed so much the brief 'character', on the Theophrastan model. No other play seems to find its persons so isolated that they must be continually writing letters or sending messengers or ambassadors to one another." Palmer, *Troilus,* p. 41.

64 Arnold Stein argues that this is "a drama that specializes in reserve. . . . Our feelings are not engaged but deliberately kept at a distance." "*Troilus and Cressida:* The Disjunctive Imagination," *ELH* 36 (1969): 162, 166.

65   Palmer, *Troilus*, p. 41. This emphasis on judgment in *Troilus* has made Shakespeare, for once, liable to the charges habitually leveled against Jonson, that his work suffers from emotional coldness.

66   See the very detailed and persuasive essay by John J. Enck, "The Peace of the Poetomachia," *PMLA* 77 (1962): esp. 391 ff. "As in *Every Man out of His Humour*, the discontinuity of *Troilus and Cressida* corresponds thematically to the characters' inherent natures. . . . As in *Every Man out of His Humour*, each Greek or Trojan sets up a single goal, or attitude, which hypnotizes him more persistently than Shakespeare elsewhere tolerated" (p. 391).

67   See Anne Barton's Introduction to the play in the Riverside edition: "Argumentative and intensely verbal, almost self-consciously intellectual, *Troilus and Cressida* moves toward a position of profound skepticism. The play which contains, in Ulysses' speech on order, Shakespeare's most elaborate presentation of the medieval great chain of being, finishes by portraying a chaos which can no longer be remedied by traditional means." Introduction to *Troilus and Cressida*, ed. G. B. Evans (Boston: Houghton Mifflin, 1974), p. 447.

68   Peter Alexander, "Troilus and Cressida," *TLS* 64 (1965): 220.

69   Beaurline points out that "the dramatic problem was how to bring about a comic reconciliation in keeping with his severe disapproval of the greater part of mankind." *Jonson and Elizabethan Comedy*, p. 110. Although he describes well the mixture of disgust and hope in the comical satires, I cannot agree with the conclusion that Jonson was seeking to emulate Lyly and Shakespeare in the creation of "comic wonder" with the ending of these plays.

70   Jackson, Introduction to *Every Man In*, p. 20.

71   Barish, *Ben Jonson and the Language of Prose Comedy*, p. 129.

72   See Richard P. Wheeler, *Shakespeare's Development and the Problem Comedies* (Berkeley and Los Angeles: University of California Press, 1981), p. vii: "In the actions of single plays, but also in the transitions from one play to another, from one genre to another, and from one phase of Shakespeare's development to another, movements of extraordinary complexity radiate from simple, rhythmically recurring oppositions: attraction and repulsion, union and separation, trust and autonomy, love and authority. The troubled comic resolutions of *All's Well* and *Measure for Measure* dramatize polarized extremes grounded in such oppositions."

73   Thomas Dekker, *Dramatic Works,* ed. Fredson Bowers, 4 vols. (Cambridge: Cambridge University Press, 1953), 1:310.

74   As Cyrus Hoy puts it, the play "combines a decent (not extravagant) respect for Jonson's poetic skills, a willingness to indulge certain personal peculiarities of

his in respect of these, and the decisive announcement that enough is enough, and that Dekker the dramatist and that segment of public opinion which he represents will no longer tolerate Jonson's egregious behavior." Introduction to *Satiromastix*, p. 194.

75   Quoted in Herford and Simpson, 1:30.

76   See W. W. Greg, *The Shakespeare First Folio: Its Bibliographical and Textual History* (Oxford: Clarendon Press, 1955), p. 340, for a full discussion of the historical evidence. Palmer also treats the matter in his Introduction to *Troilus*, pp. 21–22.

CHAPTER 4: DREAMERS

1   Just as the chronological limits of the transitional phases discussed in the previous chapter are not exact, neither are the boundaries of the mature stages. Jonson's period of artistic maturity is easy to discern: *Volpone* (1605) is his first indisputable masterpiece, and *Bartholomew Fair* (1614) is arguably his last. Yet, during these years Jonson also gave us that gigantic problem *Catiline,* which is not treated here. For Shakespeare, I am studying the period from about 1601 to 1609, that is, from *Hamlet* to *Coriolanus*. Two plays I have used already to illustrate Shakespeare's progress from comedy to tragedy, *Hamlet* and *Othello,* are also treated here as instances of Shakespeare's mature, tragic style. To consider them in both contexts does not seem to me inappropriate.

2   Although this kind of thinking had fallen into disrepute for some years, the new historicists have revived it and given it a social emphasis, stressing the ways that literary texts not only reflect but actually contribute to the political and philosophical life of the period. See, in addition to the work of Jonathan Goldberg, Stephen Greenblatt's *Renaissance Self-Fashioning,* and essays by Louis Adrian Montrose, Leah S. Marcus, and Leonard Tennenhouse.

Jonathan Dollimore's work addresses many of the issues and texts considered in this chapter, but his fierce materialist bias impels him to deny the ideological and emotional tensions that animate such plays as *King Lear* and *Antony and Cleopatra*. See *Radical Tragedy: Religion, Ideology, and Power in the Drama of Shakespeare and His Contemporaries* (Chicago: University of Chicago Press, 1984), especially part 3, "Man Decentered," which contains readings of *Lear, Antony,* and *Coriolanus*. Even more myopic is Terry Eagleton's *William Shakespeare* (London: Methuen, 1986).

Roland M. Frye has examined the abuses that have attended efforts to Christianize and de-Christianize Shakespeare. See *Shakespeare and Christian Doc-*

trine (Princeton: Princeton University Press, 1963). An attempt to read Jonson in specifically Christian terms (to me unconvincing) is Robert E. Knoll's *Ben Jonson's Plays.*

3   The most pointed and familiar literary statement of this uncertainty is Donne's "The First Anniversary," *The Poems of John Donne,* ed. Herbert J. C. Grierson, 2 vols. (Oxford: Oxford University Press, 1912), 1:237.

4   See Douglas Bush, *English Literature in the Earlier Seventeenth Century* (Oxford: Clarendon Press, 1945), p. 4: "Much Jacobean melancholy, like that of our own day, was the fashionable exploitation of what in some men was authentic, and while young intellectuals were nourishing one another's disillusionment, many happy extraverts were singing the madrigals and ballets of Thomas Morley and his fellows. . . . Altogether, one could make out a strong argument for the Elizabethan age as one of pessimistic gloom and the earlier seventeenth century as one of optimistic recovery."

5   Richard H. Popkin, *The History of Skepticism from Erasmus to Spinoza,* rev. ed. (Berkeley and Los Angeles: University of California Press, 1979), p. 42.

6   Herschel Baker, *The Wars of Truth: Studies in the Decay of Christian Humanism in the Earlier Seventeenth Century* (Cambridge: Harvard University Press, 1952), pp. 354–55.

7   On the other hand, it is worth remembering that Shakespeare was reading Montaigne, and reading him closely, by 1600. For a strong statement of Montaigne's possible influence on the plays of this period, see Robert Ellrodt, "Self-Consciousness in Montaigne and Shakespeare," *SS* 28 (1975): 37–50.

8   Maynard Mack, "The Jacobean Shakespeare: Some Observations on the Construction of the Tragedies," in *Jacobean Theatre,* ed. John Russell Brown and Bernard Harris, Stratford-upon-Avon Studies, 1 (London: Edward Arnold, 1960), p. 13.

9   Moody Prior, commenting on *King Lear,* reminds us that "the impression of magnitude in this play is one of the commonplaces of criticism" and points out that references to forces of nature "give to the actions and sentiments not only a grandeur in scale but endow the specific events with the widest possible kind of generality." *The Language of Tragedy* (Bloomington: University of Indiana Press, rpt. 1966), p. 79. This emphasis on size applies as well to most of Shakespeare's other tragedies.

10   Puttenham, *The Arte of English Poesie,* pp. 191–92.

11   Madeleine Doran, "The Idea of Excellence in Shakespeare," *SQ* 27 (1976): 135. She argues that "we must make ourselves sensitive to Elizabethan responses to hyperbole, which were more varied than ours have come to be," and goes on to

217

quote Henry Peacham in *The Garden of Eloquence* (1577): "When a saying doth surmounte and reach above the truth, the use whereof, is very frequent in augmenting, diminishing, praysing and dispraysing of persons and things" (p. 135n).

12   As Mack points out, the Shakespearean idiom "depends for its vindication—for the redemption of its paper promises into gold—upon the hero, and any who stand, heroically, where he does." "The Jacobean Shakespeare," p. 14. See also J. Leeds Barroll's suggestive remarks on the circularity of heroism, "the insistence on one's greatness simply because one is great," a point that applies seriously to the Shakespearean hero and ironically to Jonson's heroic buffoons. Barroll, *Artificial Persons: The Formation of Character in the Tragedies of Shakespeare* (Columbia: University of South Carolina Press, 1974), esp. ch. 8; the passage cited is on p. 204.

13   Harriet Hawkins, *Poetic Freedom and Poetic Truth* (Oxford: Clarendon Press, 1976), p. 109.

14   See Nicholas Brooke, "Marlowe as Provocative Agent in Shakespeare's Early Plays," *SS* 14 (1961): 34–44, and M. C. Bradbrook, "Shakespeare's Recollections of Marlowe," *Shakespeare's Styles: Essay in Honour of Kenneth Muir*, ed. Philip Edwards, Inga-Stina Ewbank, and G. K. Hunter (Cambridge: Cambridge University Press, 1980), pp. 191–204. Also see Maurice Charney, "Shakespeare—and the Others," *SQ* 30 (1979): 328–29.

15   Madeleine Doran, *Shakespeare's Dramatic Language* (Madison: University of Wisconsin Press, 1976), p. 155.

16   Alvin Kernan identifies the complexity of our response to these fantasies: "We glimpse, even as we laugh, something of the Renaissance's sudden perception that the human mind through art and science really could change the world, that suffering and death need not forever be the lot of man, that things need not always be the way they are." Introduction to *The Alchemist* (New Haven: Yale University Press, 1974), p. 8.

17   On this point, see Jackson, *Vision and Judgment*, pp. 114 ff., and G. R. Hibbard, "Ben Jonson and Human Nature," in *A Celebration of Ben Jonson*, ed. William Blissett, Julian Patrick, and R. W. Van Fossen (Toronto: University of Toronto Press, 1973), pp. 64 ff.

18   Alvin Kernan, Introduction to *Volpone* (New Haven: Yale University Press, 1962), pp. 13–14. See also Leggatt, *Ben Jonson*, esp. ch. 1, "False Creations," pp. 1–44.

19   Doran puts it this way: "In the great tragedies, the most excellent characters are

not only threatened but destroyed in the clash between an ideal world and the world of contingency." Doran, "The Idea of Excellence," p. 145.

20 Bernard McElroy, *Shakespeare's Mature Tragedies* (Princeton: Princeton University Press, 1973), pp. 3, 27.

21 Alfred Harbage summarizes the affinities of the Shakespearean heroes in just the terms I am attempting to describe: "If we ask what qualities his heroes come nearest to sharing in common, we must answer their *unworldliness*, their incapacity for compromise." He goes on to identify the nature of their tragic dilemma when he describes them as "imperfect ones with dreams of perfection, mortals with immortal longings in them." See his Foreword to the section on the tragedies in *The Complete Pelican Shakespeare*, p. 821.

22 See Stephen Booth, *"King Lear," "Macbeth," Indefinition, and Tragedy* (New Haven: Yale University Press, 1983), p. 54: "Western culture is genetically incapable of producing an audience not conditioned to identify itself with the youngest of three sisters and to recognize transparent vehicles of wickedness in elder sisters pleasing to their parent."

23 Arthur Sewell, for example, remarks that "there is a sense, indeed, in which Othello is imagined as without original sin." *Character and Society in Shakespeare* (Oxford: Oxford University Press, 1951), p. 94.

24 See Brents Stirling, *Unity in Shakespearean Tragedy: The Interplay of Theme and Character* (New York: Columbia University Press, 1956), p. 54: "As the impersonal member of a conspiracy motivated largely by personal ends [Brutus seeks] in a complex way to resolve his contradiction by depersonalizing, ritualizing the means."

25 G. K. Hunter, "The Last Tragic Heroes," in *Later Shakespeare*, ed. John Russell Brown and Bernard Harris, Stratford-upon-Avon Studies, 8 (London: Edward Arnold, 1966), p. 15.

26 McElroy, *Shakespeare's Mature Tragedies*, p. 28.

27 Maynard Mack, "Engagement and Detachment in Shakespeare's Plays," in *Essays on Shakespeare and Elizabethan Drama*, ed. Richard Hosley (Columbia: University of Missouri Press, 1962), p. 289. See also Kimbrough, *Shakespeare's "Troilus and Cressida,"* where Troilus is described in similar terms as "a lesser Hamlet figure. . . . Troilus discovers that his simple, abstract philosophy cannot deal with complicated reality" (p. 179).

28 See Jonas A. Barish's satisfying discussion of how the follies of the Would-bes recapitulate the actions of the main plot: "After a patronizing recital of 'instructions' to Peregrine on the methods of deportment in Venice, [Sir Pol] confides

suddenly that his money-making projects need only the assistance of one trusty henchman in order to be put into instant execution. Evidently he is hinting that Peregrine undertake that assignment and thus play Mosca to his Volpone." "The Double Plot in *Volpone*," in *Ben Jonson: A Collection of Critical Essays*, p. 100.

29 Mack, "Engagement and Detachment," p. 286.

30 Ibid., pp. 286–87.

31 G. R. Hibbard, "Ben Jonson and Human Nature," p. 76, writes instructively on the idea of obsession throughout Jonson's plays.

32 Charles Frey, *Shakespeare's Vast Romance: A Study of "The Winter's Tale"* (Columbia: University of Missouri Press, 1980), p. 82.

33 See Susan Snyder, *The Comic Matrix of Shakespeare's Tragedies*, pp. 56–90.

34 Shakespeare's triumph in representing the glories of Egypt is demonstrated by the terms of the critical conflict surrounding the work. Is it "a tragedy of lyrical inspiration, justifying love by presenting it as triumphant over death, or is it rather a remorseless exposure of human frailties, a presentation of spiritual possibilities dissipated through a senseless surrender to passion?" D. A. Traversi, *An Approach to Shakespeare*, rev. ed., 2 vols. (New York: Anchor Books, 1969), 2:212.

35 Kernan, Introduction to *Volpone*, p. 25. Kernan also writes that in Sir Epicure's speeches Jonson achieves "density" on a " 'heroic' level," creating "raw life full of potential. . . . The phrases and passages in which Jonson describes [the "raw life"], even when it is being misused by a Volpone or Sir Epicure, are never merely grotesque, but pulsing, vital, and thoroughly exciting." *The Cankered Muse*, p. 170.

36 R. V. Holdsworth, review of Parfitt's *Ben Jonson*, *RES* 30 (1979): 208.

37 Gabriele Bernhard Jackson offers a helpful metaphor here: "The road of normality from which Bobadill and Volpone have diverged is lost to view, and well lost, behind the picturesque territory in which they have arrived." Introduction to *Every Man In*, p. 20.

38 See Robert Ornstein, "Shakespearian and Jonsonian Comedy," *SS* 22 (1969): 43: "In deliberately rejecting the earlier romantic mode of comedy, Jonson, I suspect, denied something of his own genius. . . . Contemptuous as he was of romantic fabling, Jonson had, moreover, an instinct for romantic multiplicity which, though severely disciplined in *Volpone* and *The Alchemist*, burst forth in the noisy carnivals of *Epicoene* and *Bartholomew Fair*."

39 Hawkins, *Poetic Freedom and Poetic Truth*, pp. 109–10.

40 See Robert B. Heilman, "The Criminal as Tragic Hero," *SS* 19 (1966): 21.

41 See L. C. Knights, "Shakespeare's Tragedies: With Some Reflections on the

Nature of Tradition," in *Further Explorations* (Palo Alto: Stanford University Press, 1965), pp. 21–22.

42 Again, the finest discussion of this central topic is Hibbard's "Ben Jonson and Human Nature," which offers a useful extension and modification of the view of L. C. Knights in *Drama and Society in the Age of Jonson* (New York: Norton rpt., 1968), pp. 207–11.

43 Richard Harter Fogle, "Romanticism Reconsidered," *SR* 82 (1974): 383.

44 It might be argued that *The Alchemist*, concerned as it is with a mystical pseudo-science that is compatible with a romantic view of nature, is the most fruitful ground for studying Jonson's doubts about the romantic viewpoint. I choose to discuss *Volpone* here because it seems to me that the romantic connections of the earlier text are less obvious but no less important, and less has been said about them.

I have benefited from a forthcoming essay by David M. Bergeron, " 'Lend me your dwarf': The Romance of *Volpone*." Bergeron's and my conclusions are quite similar, and I mention only the most significant examples; his study is more detailed.

45 See Barish, "The Double Plot in *Volpone*," p. 94, and Bergeron, " 'Lend me your dwarf.' "

46 John Creaser, Introduction to *Volpone* (London: Hodder and Stoughton, 1978), p. 56.

47 Leo Salingar, "Romance in *King Lear*," *English* 27 (1978): 20.

48 McElroy, *Shakespeare's Mature Tragedies*, p. 201.

49 Howard Felperin, *Shakespearean Romance* (Princeton: Princeton University Press, 1972), p. 62.

50 Felperin indicates the Jonsonian connections of Shakespeare's Rome: "When Samuel Johnson praised Shakespeare for representing 'the real state of sublunary nature,' he might have had the Rome of this play in mind, for Rome corresponds to the world as Bacon and Jonson conceive of it in everyday consciousness: a hard, unyielding, brazen reality." Ibid., pp. 135–36.

51 For the most comprehensive discussion of this contrapuntal effect, see Norman Rabkin, *Shakespeare and the Common Understanding* (New York: Macmillan, 1967), pp. 22 ff., as well as *Shakespeare and the Problem of Meaning*.

52 Jonathan Dollimore writes passionately about this one side of the issue, especially in his attacks on Antony and Coriolanus; see *Radical Tragedy*, pp. 204–30.

53 Mack, "The Jacobean Shakespeare," p. 34.

54 Aldous Huxley, "Ben Jonson," *London Mercury* 1 (1919): 187.

55   Algernon C. Swinburne, *A Study of Ben Jonson,* ed. with an introduction by Howard B. Norland (Lincoln: University of Nebraska Press, 1969), p. 35.

56   This ambivalent view of the imagination and the force of illusion is consistent with Jonson's mixed attitude toward the theater itself. See Jonas A. Barish, "Jonson and the Loathed Stage," in *A Celebration of Ben Jonson,* p. 52.

57   Hiram Haydn, *The Counter-Renaissance* (New York: Grove Press rpt., 1960), p. 10.

58   Leggatt, *Ben Jonson: His Vision and His Art,* p. 27. Leggatt makes a similar point about *Catiline:* "Jonson allows Catiline's last moments an apocalyptic grandeur denied to Sejanus. As in the ending of *The Dunciad,* the world is uncreated, and meaning itself—'the name of things'— blotted out. Not quite, of course: Catiline dies, and Rome goes on. But Catiline, freed from his shabby followers and reduced to the essential destructiveness with which he began, is allowed to be surprisingly impressive. Jonson shows that, for all its absurdity, the idea of false creation can—if only for a moment—capture the imagination" (p. 8). Even Herford and Simpson, who never fail to stress Jonson's didactic bent, speak to this point in writing of *The Masque of Queenes:* they describe "the feasts of poetry Jonson had, four years before, extorted from the foulness of Volpone, and was about to elicit from the corruption of Mammon" (2:279).

59   Harriet Hawkins shows that in the epilogue to *Volpone,* "the immoral character, having been punished by his creator's own laws, steps forward, as the chief of Jonson's works, and rightly requests the reward of applause for having so splendidly entertained us with his immoral doings. And of course the audience extends the applause for Volpone to Jonson himself, who, through his glittering grotesque sinners, has shown us 'things like truth' about certain ways of the world, and thus deserves thanks for a black and gold comedy which is so much more than a piece of moralistic propaganda implying an inevitable triumph of virtue over vice." *Poetic Freedom and Poetic Truth,* pp. 111–12.

60   *The Collected Works of Bernard Shaw,* 30 vols. (New York: Wm. H. Wise, 1930), 10:xxxiii.

61   See Stephen Orgel, "Shakespeare and the Kinds of Drama," *Critical Inquiry* 6 (1979): 118.

62   I wish to avoid giving the impression that "McDonald's view makes Shakespeare as great a cynic about human beings and their feelings as Jonson"; so Michael Manheim described the argument of an earlier version of this chapter in his review in *Comparative Drama* 17 (1983): 192. I consider neither Shakespeare nor Jonson to have been cynics.

CHAPTER 5: IDEAL REALMS

1   There are exceptions to this practice, of course. Stephen Orgel has always advocated that we "read and judge the masques as we read the rest of Jonson's poetry and drama." *The Jonsonian Masque* (New York: Columbia University Press rpt., 1981), p. 109. And Alexander Leggatt's recent *Ben Jonson: His Vision and His Art* seeks to treat the masques, plays, and poems on equal terms.

The masques in isolation have inspired a good deal of careful scholarship and helpful criticism, the tradition for which was established early in this century by such works as Paul Reyher's *Les Masques anglais* (Paris: Hachette, 1909), Enid Welsford's *The Court Masque* (Cambridge: Cambridge University Press, 1927), and Allardyce Nicoll's *Stuart Masques and the Renaissance Stage* (London: Harrap, 1937). As with virtually all other matters, Herford and Simpson's Oxford edition contains a wealth of information and insight, particularly volumes 2 and 9; the texts from which I quote are found in volume 7. Sir E. K. Chambers's *The Elizabethan Stage*, vols. 1 and 4, is also helpful. In considering particular masques, D. J. Gordon sets a very high standard of inquiry: see "The Imagery of Ben Jonson's *The Masque of Blacknesse* and *The Masque of Beautie*," *JWCI* 6 (1943): 122–41; "*Hymenaei*: Ben Jonson's Masque of Union," *JWCI* 8 (1945): 107–45; "Poet and Architect: The Intellectual Setting of the Quarrel between Ben Jonson and Inigo Jones," *JWCI* 12 (1949): 152–78. These are also available in the collection of Gordon's essays, *The Renaissance Imagination*, ed. Stephen Orgel (Berkeley and Los Angeles: University of California Press, 1975).

More recent work includes several books and chapters of books: Jonas A. Barish's "Painting, Carpentry, and Prose," in *Ben Jonson and the Language of Prose Comedy*, which is especially valuable on the contribution of the antimasque; W. Todd Furniss, "Ben Jonson's Masques," in *Three Studies in the Renaissance* (New Haven: Yale University Press, 1958); John C. Meagher, *Method and Meaning in Jonson's Masques* (Notre Dame: University of Notre Dame Press, 1966); Stephen Orgel and Roy Strong, *Inigo Jones: The Theatre of the Stuart Court*, 2 vols. (London: Sotheby Parke Bernet, 1973); and Orgel's *The Illusion of Power* (Berkeley and Los Angeles: University of California Press, 1975), an especially useful study on the theory and political implications of courtly entertainments. Jonathan Goldberg's "The Theater of Conscience" goes farther in placing the masques in their immediate social and political contexts: see *James I and the Politics of Literature*, pp. 113–63.

Some indispensable articles include Ernest William Talbert's "The Interpretation of Jonson's Courtly Spectacles," *PMLA* 61 (1946): 454–73; Dolora Cunningham's "The Jonsonian Masque as a Literary Form," *ELH* 22 (1955): 108–24; and M. C. Bradbrook, "Social Change and the Evolution of Ben Jonson's Court Masques," *SLitI* 6 (1973): 101–38.

2   Herford and Simpson, 2:261.

3   Although there may be some overlap, *Antony and Cleopatra* and *Coriolanus* seem to precede *Pericles* and the rest of the romances. Recent studies indicate that, contrary to orthodox ideas about dating, *The Winter's Tale* may precede rather than follow *Cymbeline*. If this is the case, then our notions about Shakespeare's growing command of his new form will have to be significantly revised. See *The Oxford Shakespeare*, ed. Stanley Wells and Gary Taylor (Oxford: Clarendon Press, 1986).

A stimulating discussion of Shakespeare's passage from tragedy to romance, although often it shows its age, is E. M. W. Tillyard's *Shakespeare's Last Plays* (London: Chatto and Windus, 1938).

4   Northrop Frye contributes a typically well-informed and persuasive account of the resemblances between Jonson's masques and Shakespeare's romances in "Romance and Masque," in *Shakespeare's Romances Reconsidered*, ed. Carol McGinnis Kay and Henry E. Jacobs (Lincoln: University of Nebraska Press, 1978), pp. 11–39; as usual, his focus is mostly on structure. Also useful is Jean Jacquot's "The Last Plays and the Masque," *Shakespeare 1971*, pp. 156–73: Jacquot's position on influence is fairly cautious, but he begins by affirming that "there was a constant exchange of influence between both spheres" (p. 156), and he presents an admirable summary of specific parallels (p. 164).

5   Coleridge's description is quoted in A. R. Humphrey's edition of *Henry VIII* (Harmondsworth: Penguin, 1971), p. 17. Also see the excellent article by John D. Cox, "*Henry VIII* and the Masque," *ELH* 45 (1978): 390–409, an argument which addresses many of the issues that I consider in other plays.

6   Harley Granville-Barker, *Prefaces to Shakespeare*, 2 vols. (Princeton: Princeton University Press, 1946), 1:467.

7   Although some doubt Shakespeare's authorship of this section, J. M. Nosworthy argues convincingly that it is genuine. See his Introduction to the Arden edition of *Cymbeline* (London: Methuen, 1955), pp. xxxii–xxxvii.

8   Philip Brockbank, "*The Tempest:* Conventions of Art and Empire," in Brown and Harris, *Later Shakespeare*, p. 200.

9   Bullough, *Narrative and Dramatic Sources*, 8:261–64.

10   Welsford, *The Court Masque*, p. 336.

11   Gary Schmidgall, *Shakespeare and the Courtly Aesthetic* (Berkeley and Los Angeles: University of California Press, 1981).

12   Gerald Eades Bentley, "Shakespeare and the Blackfriars Theatre," *SS* 1 (1948): 49.

13   See Wickham's "Masque and Anti-masque in *The Tempest*," *E&S* 28 (1975): 1–14, and "Romance and Emblem: A Study in the Dramatic Structure of *The Winter's Tale*," in *Elizabethan Theatre III*, ed. David Galloway (Hamden, Conn.: Archon, 1973), pp. 82–99. The limitations of Yates's *Shakespeare's Last Plays: A New Approach* (London: Routledge and Kegan Paul, 1975), are well known.

14   Schmidgall, *Shakespeare and the Courtly Aesthetic*, p. 46.

15   See J. A. Lavin, "Shakespeare and the Second Blackfriars," in Galloway, *Elizabethan Theatre III*, pp. 66–81.

16   Barbara Mowat, Review of Schmidgall's *Shakespeare and the Courtly Aesthetic*, *RenQ* 35 (1982): 329–32.

17   Frank Kermode, Introduction to the Arden edition of *The Tempest* (London: Methuen, 1954), p. lxxiv.

18   Arthur C. Kirsch, "*Cymbeline* and Coterie Dramaturgy," rpt. in *Shakespeare's Later Comedies*, ed. D. J. Palmer (Harmondsworth: Penguin, 1971), p. 264.

19   Ibid., p. 284.

20   John Bender, "Affinities between Jacobean Masques and Plays," *RORD* 17 (1974): 11.

21   Allardyce Nicoll, "Shakespeare and the Court Masque," rpt. in Palmer, *Shakespeare's Later Comedies*, pp. 160–74.

22   Orgel, *The Jonsonian Masque*, p. 35.

23   Ibid., p. 137.

24   Barish, *Ben Jonson and the Language of Prose Comedy*, pp. 249–51.

25   See Nosworthy's edition of *Cymbeline* for an excellent treatment of the play's experimental nature, esp. pp. xlviii–lxi.

26   Daniel Seltzer, "The Staging of the Last Plays," in Brown and Harris, *Later Shakespeare*, p. 163.

27   See J. H. P. Pafford's Introduction to the Arden edition of *The Winter's Tale* (London: Methuen, 1963), pp. liv–lv: "If the play is to be divided it is better to give it three parts—the first period at Leontes' Court, the second in Bohemia, and the third at Leontes' Court again."

28   Francis Berry writes intelligently on the way that Leontes' Experience qualifies the Innocence of the Bohemian festival in "Word and Picture in the Final Plays," in Brown and Harris, *Later Shakespeare*, esp. pp. 92–95.

29   Ernest Schanzer offers a useful summary of the play's organization: "Shakespeare has divided the play into a predominantly destructive half and a predominantly creative and restorative half; into a winter half, concentrating on the desolation that Leontes spreads at his court, and a spring and summer half, concentrating on the values represented by the mutual love of Florizel and Perdita and the reunions at the finale." "The Structural Pattern of *The Winter's Tale*," *Review of English Literature* 5, no. 2 (1964): 74. Schanzer goes on to describe in convincing detail the interconnections between the two parts.

30   Northrop Frye's discussion is helpful: see "Romance and Masque," p. 30.

31   Ernest Gilman, " 'All Eyes': Prospero's Inverted Masque," *RenQ* 33 (1980): 221.

32   R. A. Foakes, Introduction to the Arden *Henry VIII* (London: Methuen, 1957), p. xlii.

33   As Stephen Orgel describes this habit, "the drama resembled the other visual arts in the Renaissance: every painting—even a portrait—had its moral or allegorical meaning; every emblem had its motto; the architectural orders had their significances; even nature, God's great artifact, could be conceived as a book." *The Illusion of Power*, p. 24. Also see Brockbank, "*The Tempest:* Conventions of Art and Empire," for a specific discussion of the tendency in the Renaissance to allegorize storms.

34   Orgel, *The Jonsonian Masque*, p. 88.

35   Orgel, *The Illusion of Power*, p. 40.

36   Tillyard draws this conclusion and supports it with a suggestive discussion of a similar transition from "realism to symbol" in the career of D. H. Lawrence. *Shakespeare's Last Plays*, p. 36.

37   Stanley Wells, "Shakespeare and Romance," in Brown and Harris, *Later Shakespeare*, p. 75; see also Wells's "Shakespeare without Sources" in *Shakespearian Comedy*, ed. John Russell Brown and Bernard Harris, Stratford-upon-Avon Studies, 14 (London: Edward Arnold, 1972), pp. 58–74.

38   On Imogen, see Emrys Jones, "Stuart *Cymbeline*," reprinted in Palmer, *Shakespeare's Later Comedies*, p. 262.

39   Tillyard remarked on this point about a half-century ago: "The part of Perdita is usually taken by some pretty little fool or pert suburban charmer." *Shakespeare's Last Plays*, pp. 42–43.

40   See the first chapter, "Golden-Tongued Romance," in Felperin's *Shakespearean Romance*, pp. 3–54.

41   Wells, "Shakespeare and Romance," p. 74.

42   Jones, "Stuart *Cymbeline*," p. 252.

43   Patrick Crutwell, *The Shakespearean Moment* (London: Chatto and Windus, 1954), p. 102.

44   Ibid.

45   See J. M. Nosworthy, "Music and Its Function in Shakespeare's Romances," *SS* 11 (1958): pp. 64–65, and Seltzer, "The Staging of the Last Plays," p. 157.

46   Orgel, *The Jonsonian Masque*, p. 149.

47   Alan Brissenden, *Shakespeare and the Dance* (London: Macmillan, 1981), p. 17.

48   Ibid., pp. 94–95.

49   Ibid., pp. 76 and 96.

50   Derek Traversi, *Shakespeare: The Last Phase* (London: Hollis and Carter, 1954), p. 18. See also Wells, "Shakespeare and Romance," for the supporting idea that in the romances the love scenes "are suffused by a passion that is real in a poetic, not an everyday, sense" (p. 67).

51   Frye, *Anatomy of Criticism*, p. 151.

52   Although some of the romances were performed at Whitehall and Blackfriars, Daniel Seltzer is surely correct in concluding that "some stage structures, some painted scenes, and some costuming at Blackfriars resembled some of these elements in the Court masques; but . . . parallels with the decor in performances of Shakespeare's plays are necessarily open to question." "The Staging of the Last Plays," p. 129.

53   John C. Meagher has a useful chapter on Jonson's extensive use of light symbolism in *Method and Meaning in Jonson's Masques*, pp. 107–24.

54   Exceptions include *A Midsummer Night's Dream*, where, paradoxically, the happy mortal ending is a function of the squabbling of the gods, and *As You Like It*, where Hymen's contribution seems more benedictory than efficient.

55   For the rest of these names, see Reason's speech (lines 280–96) and Jonson's elaborate etymological and explanatory note to it in the margin.

56   On this point see D. J. Gordon's "*Hymenaei:* Jonson's Masque of Union," pp. 107–45.

57   Meagher, *Method and Meaning in Jonson's Masques*, p. 48.

58   For an excellent analysis of this tradition, see William A. McClung, *The Country House in English Renaissance Poetry* (Berkeley and Los Angeles: University of California Press, 1977), pp. 7 and 118–22.

59   Those who have written most helpfully on the Neoplatonism of the masques include Meagher, *Method and Meaning in Jonson's Masques*, pp. 42–44 and 126–29, and Gordon in the essays in *The Renaissance Imagination*.

60   Orgel, *The Illusion of Power*, p. 70.

61 Felperin, *Shakespearean Romance*, p. 169n. Felperin points out that Shakespeare may have been responding to the prohibition against the use of "God" or "Christ" in the Act of Abuses (1606), but that this stricture was not always heeded. He also urges a moderate approach toward the problem of Christian allegory in Shakespeare's texts: "The needed corrective to naive allegorization now having been provided, we can all relax a bit and feel free to discuss [the plays'] Christian elements as they arise—which is neither all the time nor not at all" (p. 67).

62 Inga-Stina Ewbank, "The Triumph of Time in *The Winter's Tale*," in Palmer, *Shakespeare's Later Comedies*, pp. 313–31, comments wisely and instructively on these suspensions of the rules.

63 Felperin, *Shakespearean Romance*, p. 63.

64 Wells, "Shakespeare and Romance," p. 76.

65 Ibid., p. 75.

66 Alexander Leggatt describes the moment of clarification as follows: "Jonson's stage directions emphasize the suddenness of the transformation. The evil of the hags is not only dark and disordered, as we might expect: it is so evanescent it hardly seems real; one blast of Fame's trumpet can disperse it, and the transformation is so complete that when the hags are gone we wonder if we ever saw them. . . .

"In moments like these the vision revealed by the dispersal of the antimasque is presented as the true one, the antimasque as false. It follows that the audience is not only seeing something different, but seeing more clearly." Leggatt, *Ben Jonson: His Vision and His Art*, p. 161. Joseph Loewenstein, in his *Responsive Readings: Versions of Echo in Pastoral, Epic, and the Jonsonian Masque* (New Haven: Yale University Press, 1984), pp. 94–95, offers some stimulating remarks about the visual perspective and "the education of the eye."

67 Orgel, *The Jonsonian Masque*, p. 74.

68 Tillyard, *Shakespeare's Last Plays*, p. 80.

69 Anne Barton summarizes this point in commenting on the revels speech: "The reality of life beyond the confines of the island, and also of life outside the doors of the theatre, is here equated with the transitory experience of the play-within-the-play. It is no more solid than, no different from, that tissue of illusion which has just vanished so completely, dissolved into nothingness at the bidding of Prospero." Introduction to the New Penguin edition of *The Tempest* (Harmondsworth, 1968), p. 49. Joan Hartwig's astute summary of this method in *Cymbeline* is relevant: "Perspectives multiply bewilderingly for those who participate in life's action, but a controller of these perspectives always reminds

the actor that the control is operative even when the power of reason cannot decipher its purpose. In the case of the play's audience, it is the playwright. But the powers of divinity and creativity mingle in the analogy, and the world into which the audience moves from the theater is a world which seems infused by complexities and controlling powers like those in the play they have just watched." *Shakespeare's Tragicomic Vision* (Baton Rouge: Louisiana State University Press, 1972), p. 103.

70   Stephen Orgel, Introduction to *The Complete Masques* (New Haven: Yale University Press, 1970), pp. 13–14.

71   Ewbank, "The Triumph of Time," p. 321.

72   See Foakes, Introduction to *Henry VIII*, p. lxiii.

73   Leggatt, *Ben Jonson: His Vision and His Art*, p. 261.

74   "All the masques can do, Jonson seems to say, is to offer a moment in which a vision of an ideal becomes a poetic and dramatic experience—becomes, in other words, a reality." Orgel, *The Jonsonian Masque*, p. 185.

75   Righter, *Shakespeare and the Idea of the Play*, p. 183; see also her Introduction to *The Tempest*, pp. 44–51.

Index

231